JOURNEY TO THE FOUR DIRECTIONS

BOOK ONE OF

JOURNEY

TEACHINGS OF THE

TO THE FOUR

FEATHERED SERPENT

DIRECTIONS

〜〜〜〜〜〜〜〜

JIM BERENHOLTZ

FOREWORD BY

RICHARD ERDOES

BEAR & COMPANY
PUBLISHING
SANTA FE, NEW MEXICO

LIBRARY OF CONGRESS CATALOGING-IN-PUBLICATION DATA
Berenholtz, Jim, 1957-
     Journey to the four directions / by Jim Berenholtz.
          p.   c. — (Teachings of the feathered serpent ; bk. 1)
     ISBN 1-879181-06-1
          1. Indians of North America—Religion and mythology.
2. Shamanism—North America. 3. Shamans—United States—
Biography. 4. Berenholtz, Jim, 1957-   —Religion.
5. Berenholtz, Jim. 1957-   —Journeys—North America.
6. North America—Description and travel. I. Title. II. Series:
Berenholtz, Jim, 1957-   Teachings of the feathered serpent :
bk. 1.
BF1622.U6B47   1993 bk.1
299'.7'092—dc20
[B]   93-229
                                                                    CIP

Text & illustration copyright © 1993 by Jim Berenholtz

Bear & Company, Inc.
Santa Fe, NM 87504-2860
Cover & interior illustration: Jim Berenholtz
Cover & interior design: Angela Werneke
Author photo: Susan Swanezy
Editing: Brandt Morgan
Typography: Andresen Graphic Services
Printed in the United States of America by R.R. Donnelley

1 3 5 7 9 8 6 4 2

*To all my teachers—
first and foremost,
the Earth.*

C O N T E N T S

I L L U S T R A T I O N S

PART ONE: Powhatan-Renape Nation Tribal Symbol
PART TWO: Kokopelli Keeps Walking

COLOR PLATES

ACKNOWLEDGMENTS

First I would like to thank my literary agent, Michael Bass, for having the courage and foresight to take me on as an unpublished writer. His support and counsel through the entire process of creating this book, as well as finding a good home for it, have been invaluable in bringing *Journey to the Four Directions* to fruition.

I also want to express my deep gratitude to Barbara Hand Clow of Bear & Company. Like Michael, Barbara was instrumental in giving shape to this book—and in inspiring the larger trilogy project. I thank her, too, for recognizing the value of my work and for having the vision to take me in when other publishers would not dare.

The birthing of this book has been a long and challenging labor in many ways. There were days when I was down to my last bag of rice and didn't know how I would come up with next month's rent. My deepest thanks again to Michael, to my dear friends Mary and Eric Lloyd Wright and Bob Wempner, and especially to my parents, Marjorie and Harry Berenholtz, for assisting in times of need.

Thanks also to my other friends who, over these last few years, have given me a meal or a place to stay when I had none. Thank you all for letting me know that I am not alone and for helping me to pursue my dreams in life.

There are other fellow dreamers whom I also wish to mention for the special forms of assistance they have provided during the process of creating this book. Thanks to Lonnie Corey for finding me an agent. Thanks to Ron Anastasia and Uschi Gerard for helping me to learn word processing. Thanks to them both and to Mauna Lia for their expert typing skills when I was on deadline and my one-finger technique just wouldn't do. Thanks to my brother Joe Baruday for backing me up with credit when I needed to get my own word processor. Thanks to Mari Red Moon, Sundae Merrick, Johanna Brown, and John Sanger for their brilliant psychic and astrological counseling relative to the book.

Thanks to Wave, Marjorie Saint Clair, Bob Wempner, David Sonnenschein, Jude Lev, Sheryl Lee, Mazatl Galindo, and Mary Wright for being the first to read the unedited manuscript and provide me with valuable insights. And an extra big thanks to my wonderful editor, Brandt Morgan, who allayed all my fears that an editor is necessarily a butcher. It has been a pleasure to work with someone who not only respects me and understands my material, but who has taught me to be a better writer in the process. Thanks as well to Barbara Doern Drew and Hanna Fields for their great skill and devotion as we worked together on the final edits and to fellow visionary artist Angela Werneke for her outstanding design work.

A special thanks to Doug Self and Guy Fisher of Huelo Point Flower Farm on the island of Maui. The first chapter of this book was written in their spectacular home looking out across the North Pacific. Almost two years later, the last chapter was written there as well.

As I moved into the contract-negotiating phase for the book, my Greek friends at Agence Unique were extremely generous with their telephone and fax machines. My sincere appreciation goes out to them, particularly to Antigone Deliou and Themis Papacharalambous. Similarly, thanks to Ronit Small and Gabrielle Riera at Kampo Cultural Center in New York City, Anna Penido and David Sonnenschein at Dreamvision Productions in Rio de Janeiro, and Andrea Siedel of DanceArts Foundation in Miami.

It is one of the curious ironies of this book that the contract for it was finally signed at Andrea's former house in Homestead, Florida, and mailed from the nearby post office. Neither that house nor the post office exist anymore. They were destroyed by Hurricane Andrew a couple of months after my brief visit to Florida. Such extreme elemental phenomena are the very sort Native American prophecies warn will increase dramatically if we humans do not correct our relationship with the Earth. As this book is much concerned with these prophecies, I cannot help but wonder at the synchronicity of committing it to publication from a place so suddenly and surprisingly caught in the whirlwind of prophetic change.

I have saved my teachers for last, because to each of you goes the greatest thanks I can offer—without you this book would not exist. Your wisdom and beingness were the inspiration for its creation. May these pages honor your names and your ancestral lineages. For those whose names I have changed, know that I do this out of respect for your privacy. The honor and gratitude I extend to you is no less great.

Particularly to "El Maestro," my thanks for the tremendous gift of your teachings. More than anyone besides myself, it is you who lives in the pages of this book. Thank you for showing me the Smoking Mirror.

I also wish to give special thanks to those treasured teachers who are part of this book but who are no longer with us: Adrian Chavez, Phillip Deere, Mad Bear Anderson, and Kai Yutah Clouds, who was tortured to death for defending the rights of the Maya in Guatemala. From his death I learned to cry again. My thanks as well to the teachers who have inspired me but who died before I could know them.

Finally, these acknowledgments would be incomplete without the mention of my enlightened roommate, Tlahuizkalpantekuhtli, affectionately known as "Kalpan." Though he has no arms or legs, he has taught me more about movement than any being I have ever known. As it is movement that lives at the center of the Four Directions, so Kalpan guides me toward the birthing of this and my next two books. The three form a trilogy entitled *Teachings of the Feathered Serpent*. Kalpan, appropriately, is a snake— and a special one at that.

F O R E W O R D

Jim Berenholtz's *Journey to the Four Directions* is an extraordinary account of a never-ending quest that seems to have no beginning and no end. Jim is at the same time a protester, dreamer, wanderer, and visionary, a stranger winding his way through a land of magic, delving into the meaning of ancient prophecies. He is also a fine artist with a unique style of his own and a musician whose music echoes the sounds of nature.

Like a hummingbird, flitting from flower to flower to extract the nectar, Jim wanders from buffalo to jaguar to plumed serpent—from Mohawk country in upstate New York to Harney Peak, seat of the thunderbirds, in South Dakota; on to the canyons of the American Southwest, home of Kokopelli, the humpbacked flute player; and to Palenque, the abode of the quetzal-plumed Lord Kukulkan. Wherever he goes, Jim gathers new insights. His journeys into the past are always a pathway to the future, a flight from the conventional religions of properly dressed, tie-wearing churchgoers into the realm of shamans, *brujos,* and medicine men.

I was enchanted reading *Journey to the Four Directions.* I first met Jim in 1972 on the Mohawk reservation. At the time we both donated some of our talents to *Akwesasne Notes,* the marvelous Pan-Indian newspaper founded by Rarihokwats, a close mutual friend. I was nearing sixty, while Jim was not yet twenty years old. We both struggled in the same cause, walking the same road, occasionally with the same friends, but at different points in time, which colored our perceptions. While we both lost ourselves in the beauty and profundity of the *Popol Vuh,* the sacred book of the Maya, my more advanced age also forced me into the awareness of the quivering, steaming heart torn from the victim's breast during the rituals of human sacrifice.

Jim found his different reality—different from that of the typical white American—within the eerie, twisted spires of the South Dakota Badlands. I found mine inside the fifteen-thousand-year-old painted caves of the Dordogne in southwestern France. We both found refuge in nature—Jim out of the womb of a decaying New York, I out of cities filled with medieval churches and baroque palaces.

My journey now nears its end, while Jim's is yet in its beginning stages. With all our achievements, I feel that we are both still sorcerer's apprentices. We cannot help it; we are fated to penetrate, with much trembling, what for a white person of Eurocentric background is still a limitless terra incognita. We have been allowed to lift a tiny corner of the veil that covers much of what perhaps should remain hidden. Being half my age, Jim will go on exploring the partially unexplorable vastness, to the profit of us all. He has done much of it already—with delicacy, humility, and much intuition. He is an incomparable searcher and interpreter, and we kindred souls look eagerly forward to works that will follow.

Years ago, doing photographic studies of Mayan sites, I ventured into one of the smaller temples of Palenque. Inside, I came face to face with a young, cross-legged, long-haired man, American by his looks. His eyes were closed, his face wrapped in a dream, lost in the raptured trance of meditation. Feeling like an unwanted intruder, I tried to leave discreetly, unobtrusively, and unnoticed, but suddenly coming out of his reverie, the young meditator stopped me, saying: "Stay, man! You are giving me good vibes." He was not Jim Berenholtz, but he easily could have been. *Journey to the Four Directions* is a book to treasure.

Richard Erdoes
Santa Fe, New Mexico
February 1993

Richard Erdoes is the coauthor of Gift of Power, Lakota Woman, American Indian Myths and Legends, *and* Lame Deer, Seeker of Visions, *and the author of* Crying for a Dream: The World Through Native American Eyes. *He has pursued the protection of indigenous people in North America throughout his life.*

The life of a human being is a journey through time and space—a journey through which we grow and evolve, consciously and unconsciously, toward the fulfillment of our destiny. For each one of us, the journey is unique, yet ultimately through it we all have the opportunity to experience spiritual transformation. In this way we see divinity. In this way we see ourselves. Whatever our path, there is a power in knowing that the outer journey can become a path to inner realization, so that with each new place we visit, with each new experience, we are touching some previously untouched part of our own being.

Journey to the Four Directions is based on a true story. It was born out of the recognition that the ancient native cultures of the Americas are still alive and that their teachings speak with utmost relevance to the dilemmas that plague modern society. Beyond this, it arose out of a passionate need to experience an intimate connection with the natural world, to embrace bird and tree and rock, and absorb something of their knowing.

In my quest of discovery, I have traveled from the green forests of the Eastern Woodlands to the red-rock canyons of the American Southwest, from the snow-covered volcanoes of the Pacific Northwest to the steamy jungles of Central America. I have traveled as a human being must circle the Medicine Wheel of life in order to become whole and arrive at the center of his or her existence. My guides have been the living teachers of many native nations, but only to a point.

The greatest teachings have come when I have had to encounter alone the indigenous sources of knowledge—the plant, animal, mineral, elemental, and spirit presences of desert and ocean, cliff dwelling and pyramid. In this way of direct experience, the ancient native symbols of spiritual transformation have taken on a new and expanded meaning for me, at once awesome and wonderful. Though the journey has been a deeply personal one, in these pages I have undertaken to fully communicate it because I understand that its implications are universal.

Before you embark on this journey with me, I would like to provide you with some information that you may find helpful along the way. First I want to clarify that not every detail of the story is written exactly as it happened in my life. The sequence of experiences has occasionally been changed, and at other times I have combined two or more experiences into single events. The same is true with adapting real people into characters. This has been done both to be concise and because the archetypes of personality and experience were more important to me than a literal or linear chronicle.

Where the journey traverses the realms of visions and dreams, these have occurred as written in the vast majority of cases. But there have also been times when, in the process of writing and reliving my original experiences, a new dimension was revealed. As these dimensions became parts of my reality, some of them also became part of the story.

Finally, following are some important points on pronunciation and spelling. You will likely come across many Native American words that are unfamiliar. Vowels in these words are generally pronounced the same as in Spanish. For example, *i* sounds like *ee* and *e* sounds like *a*. The letter *x*, used in many Nahuatl and Mayan words, is pronounced either as *sh* or *s*, depending on which vowels precede or follow it. To allay any questions, a phonetic pronunciation guide is provided at the back of the book. As my native teachers have taught me, it is important to "sound" a word correctly in order to receive its full meaning.

For this same reason, I have chosen to use the letter *k* instead of *c* or *qu* wherever these letters would usually appear in a Nahuatl or Mayan word to indicate a *k* sound. For example, the name Quetzalcoatl is spelled Ketzalkoatl. This is now the accepted and preferred manner of spelling among the indigenous Nahuatl and Maya with whom I trained in México. On my most recent visit there in 1991, I was fortunate to attend the opening day of classes at the new Universidad Nahuatl, where the preferred *k* spelling was in full use. Thus, partly out of respect for this movement to reaffirm indigenous identity, I have reformed my spelling as they have.

The most obvious exception to this rule is the spelling of Mexico City. Since this is a modern locale, in contrast to ancient México-Tenochtitlan, it is spelled in a way that reflects its proper context. On the other hand, Palenque, the magnificent Mayan ceremonial center, retains its common spelling because it is not the center's original Mayan name. Palenque is a Spanish word meaning "palisade."

My apologies to those anthropologists and historians who may find such spellings disconcerting. But just as we adjusted to the Chinese changing the Westernized spelling of Peking to Beijing a few years back, I trust that we will adjust to similar reformations in the Americas. In any case, there is no truly correct way to spell Native American words with a European script, since originally native languages were notated quite differently, if at all.

All that I have written in this book I have done with the utmost respect for the indigenous traditions of the land in which I was born. It is my prayer that this book may do honor to those traditions, and contribute to the much-needed healing between our peoples. The past cannot be changed, but after five hundred years of ecocide and genocide, surely it is time to dream anew. For the sake of our future generations, may we dream well.

October 12, 1992

JOURNEY

TEACHINGS OF THE

TO THE FOUR

FEATHERED SERPENT

DIRECTIONS

P R O L O G U E

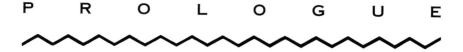

We are the people of many lands and cultures. In an ancient time and a sacred place, we gather to fulfill a prophecy. In our dreams we have remembered this prophecy and awakened to it.

As the luminescent orb of the sun lifts above the horizon, a young boy in white cotton garments raises a conch shell and sounds it to the Four Directions. At the same time, a young girl in white offers burning herbs in a ceramic vessel. The smoke rises in spirals through the branches of a great tree at the center of the gathering. The tree is laden with enormous flowers blooming in red, yellow, blue, and white. Multitudes of butterflies and hummingbirds drink the nectar of these flowers, weaving a rainbow of iridescent color around the Great Flowering Tree.

Not one of us is absent from this sunrise celebration. Flowers open, birds sing, and we rejoice in the splendor of the new day. Silently facing the light, each of us gives thanks to the Creator for the gift of life. We open ourselves to receive the sun, to feel the kindling of the inner fire that guides us on our sacred journey.

The conch shell sounds for the fifth and last time, calling us all to the center. There we form a circle around the Great Flowering Tree. Eight elders—four women and four men—sit around a large drum by the roots of the tree, and together they begin to mark a slow, steady beat. The rhythm is like that of our hearts, and on the drum is painted the design of the Earth's body. Our hearts soon beat as one to this planetary drum. Then our feet join the pulse, and our circle begins to move.

We are people of the sun. We are people of the Earth. Our dance reflects the movements woven in the heavens, which provide the choreography for our earthly lives. We love the Earth. It is our joy to be part of it. Thus have we painted our bodies with the patterns of our animal relatives. Thus do we wear masks recalling the faces of our closest allies. Yet we also still remember that we are of the stars. They, too, are painted on our bodies and shine through our eyes.

Our dance grows in power as the sun climbs higher. We spiral in toward the trunk of the Great Flowering Tree, wrapping ourselves around it like the body of a giant serpent. When we can get no closer, we open again, spiraling out into our original circle. Over and over the spiraling dance repeats itself, expanding and contracting like an endless flow of breath.

At last the sun reaches its zenith. Then the drum stops beating and all outward movements cease. Gradually the sky begins to darken. Flowers close, butterflies pause, birds go silent. It is as if day has turned to night. In a single motion, we all look up to see the dark moon covering the face of the sun. Only a thin outer ring of light is visible against the deepening sky, which is now full of stars.

A strong-legged woman with a jaguar-painted body steps into the center of the circle. She is joined by two men who stand on either side of her. One is part eagle, the other part snake. The three speak in alternating phrases as all eyes and ears turn to focus on them.

"Each of you has been called here to play your part in the fulfillment of an ancient prophecy. The heavens signal that we are about to enter a period of darkness. Today we stand here as one family, but soon we will forget our oneness. Brother will turn against brother, tribe against tribe, nation against nation. Hate will replace love, and war will be the way. Out of fear we will become intolerant of all those who are different from us. Even our plant and animal relatives will become strangers. They will be cast out of their homes, and we will forget how to communicate with them. The very Earth herself will be treated as though despised—brutalized for personal gain, and in some places rendered lifeless."

All of us listen with rapt attention as the three continue. "At this moment the sun and moon are merged in primordial union. When they part, we too shall part. We shall divide into four groups, and we shall follow the path of the lightning to each of the Four Directions of the Earth.

"We shall not see each other again for thousands of years. As our spirits travel from lifetime to lifetime, as our children descend from generation to generation, we will become part of a larger society based on the myth of separation. In this society we will be taught to see ourselves as separate from the Earth and nature. We will even learn to see ourselves as separate from our Creator and each other. We will nearly forget all that we know and hold dear.

"But we will not forget completely, because at this moment of union between the sun and the moon, a seed is being planted in each of us. This seed is an awareness, and by it we will finally remember everything we have forgotten.

"Eventually we will seek out other human beings with similar memories. In this way we will begin to heal our pain. Like magnets, we will be drawn back to each other. Like a web, our network will be woven together again and will grow broader and stronger. At last our remembering will lead us back to the sacred center where this journey began, by the roots of the Great Flowering Tree."

With these final words, lightning strikes to each of the Four Directions, and the sky explodes with thunder, though there is not a cloud to be seen. Slowly the sun and moon part, and light returns to Earth. We gaze at one another one last time, eyes meeting in a moment that seems like an eternity. Then our circle unwinds into four arcing lines, and our feet begin to move toward the lightning that illuminates our separate paths against a cloudless sky.

CIRCLING
PART ONE
THE WHEEL

the keeper of the woods

I AM NOT ALONE

As far back as I can remember, I wanted to be in nature. When I was a child, that was not always easy, since I grew up in New York City. Almost everything was under concrete. But on the outskirts of the city, where I lived with my parents and my brother, there were still a few forests and swamps left to explore. Though a far cry from wilderness, they were nevertheless vast realms in the eyes of a little boy.

Even an area the size of a few square blocks was a huge territory for me. I got to know every path and tree, and the best places to find frogs in the daytime and fireflies at night. I would discover which kinds of butterflies liked to visit the shaded areas of the woods and which preferred the open fields. I learned quickly that each living thing had its favorite place. I became acquainted with all their habits by quietly observing them, and this brought me great satisfaction.

Sometimes when I was in the woods, I would hear other children coming down the trail and I would quickly hide from them. I loved to watch them go by without even noticing I was there. It reinforced my feeling that I was part of the living forest. This special relationship with nature was very private and personal, and I couldn't share it with most people. Though some friends occasionally went with me into the woods, they at least also knew they were there to be with nature instead of just passing through it.

Regardless of my great love for nature, there was no denying that I was still a city boy, and there were certainly many things about it that I liked. There were fascinating objects to look at in the shops and museums, as well as interesting foods from all over the world. Most exciting was the incredible diversity of music, dance, theater, movies, and other forms of entertainment from every imaginable culture. The city was a great place to arouse my youthful curiosity. There was always something new to admire or learn about.

But in other ways I didn't like the city. It was crowded and dirty and gray. And it was missing the most important part: the animals and trees. All the impressive creations of people, whatever form they took, could not begin to match the simple joy I experienced when I entered the woods. There, without anything else, I felt completely at home.

Why this was true couldn't be easily explained, except that I was sure I was born with this sensibility. And curiously, when I was in the heart of the city looking at all its buildings, streets, bridges, traffic, factories, and power plants, I didn't just see those things as they were; I also saw the green forests and native villages that had been buried beneath them. When I looked at the sky that was hazy with pollution, I also saw the sky as it had appeared long ago, in beautiful shades of blue. When I looked at the rivers, I didn't just see them filling up with the city's wastes; I saw them flowing clearly as they once had, with many kinds of fish. And when I looked at the masses of people swarming through the city's streets, I also saw the Indians and the different species of animals that had once walked this same ground together.

The memory of these things grew so strong with me that I couldn't look at anything in the city without seeing what lay beneath it. And the more I saw what was underneath, the more I felt like *that* was what was real—that everything above it was only an illusion or, at best, a short-lived phenomenon that would soon pass.

Often when we drove across the bridge from Queens to Manhattan, I would actually see the city crumbling before my eyes and disintegrating back into the earth. After some time, plants and trees would begin growing again, the rivers would clear up, birds would return to the skies, and the native people would return to the land. Whenever I watched this amazing scenario unfold, I always felt good afterward. It was comforting to me. Of course I knew that no one else would understand, so I kept these impressions to myself.

Yet at the same time that nature was returning to the city in my visions of the distant future, the city was steadily overtaking nature in the present moment. With each passing year, the forested spots I had frequented when

I was three or four began to disappear. First the fences would go up, cutting across paths I had once taken to reach my favorite places. Not that I let this stop me. Climbing over and crawling under fences quickly became two of my greatest talents.

But then came the land-movers and the big machines that pulled down the trees. This got me worried. Late one spring, after an absence of many months, I returned to the site of my favorite swamp to find it gone. I couldn't believe it. The place I had spent all my summers catching frogs and watching dragonflies dart across the water had completely vanished. In its place was a tennis court. And the nearby grove of huge oak, maple, and sycamore trees that had been the best spot to watch for butterflies had been replaced— by a parking lot. Even the hillside behind it had been flattened. Now, in place of woods stood a twenty-five-story luxury apartment complex.

Such changes were a source of great sadness for me as a child. I felt personally wounded by them, alienated from the very society in which I was being raised. Although I was very young, I was already aware that I was being drawn into a way of life that was destroying me, my family, and the entire Earth.

Clearly the gray stuff pouring out of smokestacks, cars, and buses was filling the very air I was breathing. I smelled it and felt it inside me. I knew my food and water were being similarly poisoned, and it made me angry. Why should I be a victim of such a system? On the other hand, I knew that someday, somehow, things would turn around. My visions from the bridge gave me hope.

Meanwhile, another source of personal grief began to reach me through the television set: the Vietnam War. By the time I was seven, the war was well under way. Every night I would watch the terrible scenes of death and destruction on the news, and all through my body a voice would be screaming, "WHY?!" Young as I was, I could see right through the calculated explanations of the politicians. Behind their clever rhetoric was a cruel reality that hurt me deeply.

I did not need to live in Vietnam to be a casualty of the war—I lived it right at home. When I saw the bombs falling on the village fields and tropical forests, I felt as if bombs were exploding inside me. The sight of every bleeding body was like a cut into my own heart. I wanted to reach out to these people of Vietnam and tell them that even though they were being attacked by American troops, there were Americans who loved them and who desperately wanted the killing to stop. I wanted to reach right through the TV screen and gather those people into the safety of my arms.

My empathy for the Vietnamese people grew steadily, in part because they reminded me of the native people I saw in my visions beneath the streets of New York City. I knew these were not unrelated conditions. The force that I saw victimizing the Vietnamese was the same force that had destroyed the ancient Native Americans and that was now polluting the skies and destroying the woods near my home. Somehow I had to find a way to oppose it before it destroyed everything.

People are pushing against my body from all directions as we scream, "OUT NOW! OUT NOW! OUT NOW!" The place is Bryant Park, in the center of New York City. The time is 1968. The occasion is the first moratorium against the Vietnam War. I am eleven years old. My friend Michael and I have skipped school for the day, and my mother is beside herself. She is terrified that I am going to get clubbed or caught in a riot.

Last night, I stayed overnight at Michael's house. My mother called repeatedly, insisting that I not go, but there was nothing she could do to stop me. Finally, out of desperation, she decided to go with me. I told her that if she wanted to come, she would have to carry a peace sign, too.

Thus has my mother reluctantly become a political activist, if only for a day. But while we demonstrators repeatedly scream, "OUT NOW! OUT NOW! OUT NOW!" she pleads from behind me, "Jimmy, be careful . . . be careful . . . be careful!" providing an odd counterpoint to the rising frenzy of our chant.

I, however, am tired of being careful. Writing my congressmen and the president to say that I want them to stop waging war on Vietnam has been too meek. Working as a volunteer in the McCarthy campaign has been too tame. I want to do something strong, something dramatic. Finally, in Bryant Park, I feel that I am *doing* something, by putting my body and my voice out on the streets along with millions of other like-minded people across the country.

For the next five years, I protested the war at every opportunity. The height of that experience came on May 11, 1970, when I joined masses of people converging on Washington, D.C., to express outrage over the U.S.

invasion of Cambodia and the subsequent murder of protesting students at Kent State University in Ohio.

I am standing on the steps of the U.S. Capitol, listening to Dick Gregory deliver a brilliant and impassioned speech against the war. Suddenly I hear explosions like gunshots in the distance. I turn to look. Riot police with helmets and raised guns are running toward us through clouds of thick white smoke. It seems like an eerie dream.

I'm afraid the police are going to start shooting, but there is no escape from the middle of the crowd. My heart is racing. All I can think of are the recent killings at Kent State. I feel a stinging in my throat and realize we are in the middle of the smoke cloud. Everyone around me is coughing. We have been teargassed.

Soon I find out that the "gunshots" were actually exploding firecrackers set off in a garbage can at the bottom of the hill. Everyone around me is saying it was the work of agents provocateurs who gave the police an excuse to attack. All I know is that by the time I board the train home to New York City that night, my throat feels like a raging inferno . . . .

I've been in bed for a week, running fevers ranging from 103 to 105. I've never been so sick in my life. I've told my parents I want to sue the United States government. Meanwhile, the war in Southeast Asia rises to its highest pitch yet. I cannot believe that a country that supposedly stands for freedom and the sanctity of life is so heinously violating those very principles.

During this period of growing activism against the war, the budding environmental movement also began to seep into the national consciousness. Like many other lovers of nature, I felt a great affinity with this movement. My ecological concerns quickly expanded far beyond the forests of my childhood and became a planetary passion.

In the peace marches, I began to carry placards informing people that more than sixty species of animals had gone extinct in Vietnam over the course of the decade. The environmental impact of war was not high on the agenda of antiwar concerns in those days, but to me it was clear that war against humanity and war against nature were inseparable.

I felt it no accident that the first Earth Day, on April 22, 1970, marking the official birth of the environmental movement, came during the same period as the U.S. invasion of Cambodia and the greatest upsurge of anti-war activity. Even if most people were not conscious of the connection, voices across the land were beginning to demand a redirection of our violent relationship to life.

During this awakening, I was compelled to look within and examine the many ways in which I myself fostered violence against other living things. I saw how I had confused my love for nature with my desire to possess it. No longer could I bring myself to catch butterflies and squeeze their heads to add them to my beautiful collection. No longer could I catch frogs or buy exotic fish and lizards to keep in tiny tanks. No longer could I stand to watch my pets bang their heads against their glass enclosures. I wanted to liberate everything.

So it was that I came to join the Animal Liberation Front and other groups dedicated to the eradication of "species-ism," the belief that human beings are superior to other life forms. Once a week, we would meet to discuss how we perpetuated species-ism in our personal lives, even to the point of killing cockroaches and other household "pests." We came to see that there were alternatives to our habitual patterns, and we began to apply them. We also encouraged others to do the same.

Most notably, we took our process into the streets, where we staged some outrageous forms of guerilla theater. One Easter Sunday, for example, we all dressed up as exotic animals, built mock cages around ourselves, and paraded through the Central Park Zoo screaming, cackling, hooting, and howling to be free. On another occasion, we enacted a massive symbolic clubbing of fellow members dressed as baby seals, right in front of models wearing sealskin coats at New York's annual furrier convention on Seventh Avenue. From demonstrating in front of the fanciest department stores to storming the roughest and toughest rodeos, we were relentless in our campaign to shock people out of their complacent participation in cruelty to animals.

Yet as my involvement in the antiwar, environmental, and animal rights movements grew, I again came to feel that it was not enough. Always protesting what I didn't like was getting old; I wanted something more. The solution to the world's ills wasn't just a matter of not killing or exploiting people. It wasn't just a question of equal rights or being kind to animals or wise use of resources. Some essential element was still missing—something I felt in my very bones.

In fact, I had always known this essential element. It had been a part of my consciousness since my boyhood days in the woods. It was the recognition that every living thing has a soul and that we are all made of the same shimmering, pulsating, primal essence called life. It was the recognition that to be alone in nature was not to be alone at all, but rather to be in the company of my closest family, an infinitely diverse gathering of relations who each had something to teach me. Somewhere, I knew, there had to be other people who understood that nature was spiritual as well as material and who embodied this realization in every aspect of their being. In my dreams I began to meet these people.

Dancing shadows rise and fall against the skin wall of our tipi. In the warm glow of the fire, I see the faces of my parents, who sit on either side of me. These are not the same parents that I know when I am awake, yet they are familiar and very comforting to me.

A voice at the door flap reveals the presence of my mother's sister, who is invited to enter. Soon many more relatives arrive, and the tipi magically expands to include them all. My family members speak in gentle, compassionate voices with long spaces of silence. Never in my waking life have I felt such a profound spiritual presence, such togetherness among people, or such ease and grace of expression. . . .

It is now much later, and I am leaving the tipi with my uncle to visit another tipi for men only. Outside, crickets sing and leaves rustle in the wind. I feel at home and completely safe in the embrace of the forest.

As my uncle and I walk along the path, we pass many tipis glowing golden like cones of light against the blackness of the night. Soon we arrive at the other lodge and enter it. Men of all ages are painting each other's bodies with geometric designs in black, white, and various shades of brown. They are preparing for a special midsummer ceremony.

One of the oldest men calls me over and begins to paint my body. Then I see my older brother, who smiles sweetly at me as our eyes meet. He looks strong and clear, the very essence of manhood. He comes up to me with a feather and ties it in my hair.

Suddenly I hear the drums beating, and the men begin to exit the lodge. As we walk toward the center of the forest clearing, I can see that the circle of tipis is enormous. In the middle of these a great fire is burning, its flames leaping wildly into the air. Many groups of men and women, each wearing their own unique colors and patterns, are coming from all directions now, merging with each other and moving toward the center.

As the drums beat louder, the people move into a series of concentric circles around the fire. I hear a voice crying out in song, and everyone joins in unison, singing a melody that begins in a very high pitch and descends slowly, as if to the Earth itself. At the same moment, the circles begin to turn, and I feel as if I am rising into the air.

We all dance as one body. We dance the whole night long. We dance until the forest begins to sing back to us with the melodies of birds and animals. We dance until it seems as though the whole world is singing with us and the forest is glowing with the same golden light that shines from the center of the clearing. . . .

Now the sky is getting lighter, turning blue. It is the most beautiful blue I've ever seen, and still the stars are shining above us. I know that the sun will be coming soon from the east. I can feel it. Just before sunrise, I awaken.

This dream recurred many times during my early years. I always found myself in the same place in the forest, and I always awoke just before sunrise. But it wasn't until my early teens that the meaning of the dream became clear. At the height of my alienation from modern society, the original Americans were calling to me.

Since I didn't know where to find Native American people in New York City, I began to make frequent visits to the library. I read everything I could find on their culture, history, and spiritual traditions. The words of these people spoke clearly to me, like an echo of my innate understanding. Never had I heard natural wisdom expressed with such poetic eloquence.

Brothers, the spring has come.
The Earth has received the embrace of the sun,
and soon we shall see the children of that love.
All seeds are awake, and all animals.
From this Great Power, we too have our lives.
Therefore, we concede to our fellow creatures,
the same rights as ourselves
to live on this land.

These words of Sitting Bull touched me far more deeply than anything I had ever read in an environmental or animal rights publication. They reached me because they had roots in a sacred world. I could feel that this great leader not only spoke but lived the expression of the Earth's spirit. When I read another quote of his, "Healthy feet can feel the very heart of Mother Earth," I knew he was speaking of a state that he had actually experienced.

I became intently absorbed by the story of Sitting Bull's life and the history surrounding it. He and his people, the Lakota, were the last to have struggled for their freedom before they were finally and tragically crushed by the United States government in the great Indian Wars of the late nineteenth century.

I found this history strikingly reminiscent of what I saw happening in Vietnam every night on TV. Foreign invaders had been decimating native people for nearly five hundred years. The relentless march of Manifest Destiny had not ended at the Pacific Ocean; now it was pushing through Asia. I saw the My Lai massacre as a twentieth-century version of the Wounded Knee massacre, another mass murder of innocent human beings.

Despite the awesome momentum of the powers of destruction, I had the distinct feeling that their days were numbered. I was inwardly convinced that a new way of being was coming to Earth, a way that had begun in the sixties. It was a great affirmation to discover that Native American people had foreseen this change.

In the last year of Sitting Bull's life, a prophetic movement had been born, and it had swept rapidly across the entire North American Indian world. It was known as the Ghost Dance. The founder of this dance was a Paiute Indian named Wovoka. In the late 1880s, he had a vision on the shores of Pyramid Lake in Nevada. In this vision he was taken to a beautiful land of green grass and flowing rivers where buffalo roamed in great numbers and the Earth was full of animals and birds. Here he also saw all the native people who had been killed in the Indian Wars since the arrival of the first Europeans. They had come back, and they were living happily again, following the ancient ways of their ancestors.

Wovoka was shown that before this world could come into being, the Indian people would first have to reunite and reclaim their spirit. He was given songs and the steps of a sacred dance to teach them—steps by which they, too, would be able to journey into another dimension and see the world that he had seen. He was instructed to tell his people that they must lay aside all the material things that had been brought to them by the white man, even their guns. They were to dance only in their native clothes, painted with special symbols like the Morning Star, and they were to be completely peaceful in all ways. Then, through the power of their dancing, prayers, and songs, they would bring on the new world.

Wovoka said that a great wave of water would come from the west and wash over the land. The Earth would roll up, taking inside of it all the bad and unclean things that had been introduced during the last centuries. But the people who danced the Ghost Dance would not be destroyed, for they would go to the highest mountain. There, as the world went through a great change, they would be lifted into a cloud. And when it was over, the cloud would set them down upon a new Earth, where they would live in peace forever. Wovoka said this would all come to pass in the next springtime.

Because this vision was revealed when the Indian people were in their darkest despair, it caught on like wildfire. Forcibly confined to reservations, hungry (and in many cases starving), denied even the basic right to express their culture or spirit—out of these conditions a new sense of hope was born. Now Native Americans could journey to the spiritual world and see their loved ones who had been killed in battle or by new and strange diseases. Once again they could follow the teeming herds of buffalo, which on Earth now numbered less than a thousand. And so they danced, awaiting the new world, certain that it would arrive in the spring of 1891.

The springtime of their visions never arrived. On December 15, 1890, Sitting Bull, the living symbol of Indian resistance for the American public, was assassinated as part of a United States government conspiracy to stop the Ghost Dance. Exactly two weeks later, over three hundred Lakota, mostly women and children, were shot down by the Seventh Cavalry as they danced the Ghost Dance in the snow. The place was Wounded Knee, South Dakota. A blizzard came, burying the dead and bringing with it a harsh and bitter winter. The Ghost Dance was over.

So goes the history, and in most books about the subject this is the final chapter. But I saw it differently, for with the passing of every winter, spring must come again. Perhaps the "next springtime" of Wovoka's vision was not literally the following year, but a much larger cycle of time. Perhaps the native people he saw returning were not just people of Indian blood, but people of all races who listened to the callings of the Earth. Perhaps my generation would be the one to fulfill the Ghost Dance prophecy. Already I could see signs of this truth. Already the flowers of a new springtime were beginning to open their petals to the growing light.

As I read and thought about Wovoka and the Ghost Dance, I reasoned that perhaps my visions from the bridge were not so unusual after all. The world that I saw under the concrete was not just the world of the past but the world of the future. As if to confirm this reasoning, a new dream came into my life; and like the other, it occurred again and again.

I am at an American military base somewhere on the coast of Southeast Asia. The base is very busy, with soldiers and merchants moving fast in every direction. All about is constant noise, crowding, and a general sense of confusion.

Suddenly I hear a great roaring sound. I turn to see many bombers flying low across the ocean toward the base. I cry out to warn the people, but no one hears me. I shout and wave my arms, but no one sees me. Everyone is completely absorbed in their own affairs. I run for shelter beneath a wooden shack that sits on stilts on the beach. Bombs are dropping all around me and everything is bursting into flames. I know I will have to get out of here if I want to survive.

With all the energy I can muster, I make a rapid sprint across the beach toward the jungle. I don't look back; I just keep running, tearing through vines and thick undergrowth, covered with blood and sweat. I come upon a trail and keep on running. When night falls, I am still running. I run for days; I can't stop. . . .

At last the jungle growth opens up, and I see a vast, desolate landscape of bomb craters and houses that have been burned to the ground. Everything is charred and smoking. In some spots, fires still burn. I stand at the edge of the jungle breathing heavily, my heart pounding. It seems there is not a person left alive. Overcome with grief, I fall to my knees. My body stretches over the naked earth, heaving in waves of despair. My hands clench the rock and soil. My feet kick up dust. . . .

I lift myself up and begin to walk again, searching the charred remains in the hope of finding another living person. The destruction seems to continue forever, but something inside tells me to keep walking.

Just as I am about to collapse again, I reach the top of a hill. There, stretching before me, is a landscape of strange rock formations that appear to be unscathed by the bombing. In the distance are mountains that look almost green, but it is hard to tell because thick gray clouds still block the sunlight. Before long I see a trail, and I know I must follow it.

As I reach the rock formations, I am amazed to discover that they are the ruins of some ancient civilization. All the stones have been carved with intricate designs and mysterious symbols. Ferns and mosses grow out of their cracks, and a rust-colored lichen covers much of their gray surface.

Where the trail gradually climbs and the land begins to rise once more, the carved stones become even bigger and more intricate. In a strange way I feel as though they are absorbing my sorrow. For the first time in days, I can truly breathe again. As I fill my lungs, a brilliant beam of sunlight breaks through the clouds and shines precisely down upon a high, distant point. I can see now that the trail is leading to this point, and all the carved stones seem to be focusing energy in its direction.

Nearing the high point, I realize that the top is actually a temple: a conical pyramid built of concentric rings of stone, each progressively smaller than the next. The sunlight is still beaming down on it like a laser. I am so strongly attracted to it that I feel like I am being pulled by a magnet.

Then I hear voices—rich, resonant voices chanting in deep tones that seem to rise from the Earth. They are coming from near the temple, yet there is no one in sight. I hurry on, so excited I'm almost crying. Suddenly, without warning, a procession appears. I stop, transfixed by a scene so remarkable that I cannot believe it is real.

Men and women of seemingly every race, all clad in radiant yellow and orange robes, are slowly walking up an ancient stairway that emerges from a huge cavern in the Earth. The entire way is lined with massive, exquisitely carved stones. The people walk in pairs, carrying flaming torches made of gold. Looking directly ahead, they chant in perfect unison. As they reach the Earth's surface, they break into two processional lines and follow the curving pathways that lead toward the temple. They converge again to pass through a single door into the temple. The light that shines from this door is almost blinding.

I join the end of the procession. As we enter the temple, we split apart again, moving in opposite directions through a circular corridor surrounding the interior. This corridor is filled with the blinding light. Gradually my eyes adjust to it, and I'm able to see again as we enter the inner chamber together.

In the very center of the chamber is the source of the light. It is form-less and far more brilliant than that in the corridor, yet I can look directly at it without squinting. Strangely, it also seems to emit a sort of music that whirls in spirals. Combined with the group's chanting, the resulting har-monies have a uniquely spherical quality.

Everyone gathers around the light, spreading their arms to welcome its healing rays. The feeling of love in this space is beyond anything I have ever experienced. As I join the others around the light, I know I am one with it. No longer am I alone. I am one with the source of all life.

THE CENTER OF
THE UNIVERSE

N O R T H

The dreams of ancient people moving in a circle around a luminous center continued to come to me in endless variations. My fascination with Wovoka's sacred vision continued to be my primary source of inspiration. Consequently, I began to work obsessively on a musical epic about the story of the Ghost Dance. Neither my family nor friends seemed to understand why this held such profound meaning for me. They assured me that Indian culture was a thing of the past and that I ought to be spending my time on more relevant pursuits.

Nevertheless, I persisted. As I developed my invisible connection to a distant people of a previous time, I felt increasingly disconnected from the society in which I had been raised. Yet while I no longer felt inwardly alone, "Indians" were still an abstraction to me. In terms of tangible human beings who could substantiate my perspective, I remained outwardly as alone as ever.

Then one summer night in 1971, those circumstances began to shift. I happened to be up late and was feeling restless. I decided to switch on the television for some mindless distraction. What I got was anything but mindless. There in front of me, on the electronic color screen, sat an old, heavy-set, white-haired man talking about the "Sacred Hoop of the Nation." He was being interviewed by talk-show host Dick Cavett, and his words were setting off alarms inside me.

The man was John Neihardt, and though it was only a television image, he was the first flesh-and-blood human I had ever seen who knew the Indian way from intimate experience. He expressed with great eloquence the same sacred principles I intuitively understood and cherished.

Interestingly, the words Neihardt spoke were not originally his own, but those of a Lakota holy man named Black Elk. Neihardt had first met Black Elk during the summer of 1930, while doing research on the Pine Ridge Reservation in South Dakota for an epic poem about the Ghost Dance. He was led to Black Elk because of the holy man's direct involvement in this movement, but he soon discovered that what Black Elk had to share went far beyond the Ghost Dance.

The result was *Black Elk Speaks,* a book that was destined to become a classic. And it was from this book that Neihardt was reading when I turned on the TV. Tearfully he recited the holy man's last prayer atop Harney Peak:

> Grandfather, Great Spirit, once more behold me on Earth and lean to hear my feeble voice. . . . You have set the powers of the four quarters to cross each other. The good road and the road of difficulties you have made to cross; and where they cross the place is holy. To the center of the world you have taken me and showed the goodness and the beauty and the strangeness of the greening Earth . . . At the center of this Sacred Hoop you have said that I should make the tree to bloom.
>
> With tears running, O Great Spirit, Great Spirit, my Grandfather— with running tears I must say now that the tree has never bloomed. A pitiful old man, you see me here, and I have fallen away and have done nothing. . . .
>
> Again, and maybe the last time on this Earth, I recall the great vision you sent me. It may be that some little root of the Sacred Tree still lives. Nourish it then, that it may leaf and bloom and fill with singing birds. Hear me, not for myself, but for my people; I am old. Hear me that they may once more go back into the Sacred Hoop and find the good red road, the shielding tree.

I could see it: a tree growing at the center of the universe, its roots drawing strength from the Four Directions, the four unique powers that make the world whole. I could see it, and I could feel it. Never before had a cosmology resonated so strongly within me. The roots of that Sacred Tree were in my own heart. Nor had they died; they had only gone dormant for a period, as in the passing of a winter. And if the feeling in my heart was any indication, then spring was surely close at hand. Once again, the tree would flower and fill with singing birds.

I thought of the ghost dancers who would take a sacred cottonwood tree and paint it red. In their tradition, red was the color of life. And I remembered how they would hang eagle feathers on that tree so that their prayers could fly to the Great Spirit to be heard. It was clear to me that Black Elk's vision of renewal and Wovoka's vision of the next springtime were one and the same.

As I imagined the ghost dancers circling around that tree, singing for its life, each cell in my body became a ghost dancer circling around my heart to nourish the root that still lived. My heart told me that there were many others who still held this dream, and that some of them had been carrying it for a long time. It also told me that others would soon be awakening to its reality.

When I finally found *Black Elk Speaks* and read it, it confirmed what I already sensed. Black Elk had participated in the Ghost Dance because he recognized how close it was to the vision he had received as a young boy. Though he had not witnessed the fulfillment of this vision in his own lifetime, he nevertheless remained faithful that it would come.

For myself, I realized that in order to participate in this fulfillment, it would no longer be enough to read or listen to great words, or to write or speak or sing them. I needed to taste, touch, and smell the words. I needed to find them written in places where nature was still untouched. I had to go out from the comfortable world where I had been raised in order to find the world where I would genuinely be most at home.

Around this time, I heard about a group called Wilderness Bound, which led Western backpacking and mountain-climbing expeditions for teenagers. I had never been farther west than Pennsylvania, and I had always traveled with my parents. Though we had visited many beautiful places, all these trips had been tame compared to what I needed now. To appreciate nature from the window of a car or bus was an unbearable frustration for me. I was desperate for freedom and adventure, and Wilderness Bound seemed like the answer to my prayers.

But to my mother, the prospect of my being an antiwar protester was nothing compared to the thought of my taking off into the wilderness. She was terrified. She did all she could to make me stay. Nonetheless, I was fifteen now, and there was no controlling me.

On June 30, 1972, I kissed my parents good-bye and boarded the train at New York's Grand Central Station. Hours later, I arrived upstate to join eleven other teenagers and three young guides. The next morning, we left together in a van and began traveling toward the place of the setting sun.

I am in ecstasy—Wilderness Bound has opened up a new world for me. I've never slept outside under the stars before. Never have I known my roof to be the sky, nor my walls to be the encircling horizon. Indeed, sensing the difference between the soft, sweet earth and the hardness of a floor is like coming home.

Nature is far more alive and vibrant in the mountains than I could ever have imagined. The sky is so big that I can see the rain coming for miles before it arrives. The wildflowers that answer this rain are of every imaginable color hidden within the light of the sun. My body feels different, too, as though all life is breathing through me. Even time flows without boundaries. Only when we come down the trail onto the paved road do I have the slightest desire to define how long we have been gone or what might come next. . . .

After our first week in the Colorado wilderness, we drive into a little town at the entrance to Rocky Mountain National Park. There, a flyer with a drawing of a tipi catches my eye. It speaks of the return of the Indian way of harmony with the Earth and of the many people who are gathering to support that way. I read on to discover that over the past few days, something called the "World Family Healing Gathering" has been held very close to where we were camped. I know now with certainty that it is no accident I have come here at this time.

Next to the flyer someone has posted a poem written by a Nez Perce Indian named Smohalla, who at the turn of the century led a prophetic movement known as the Dreamer Religion. His words echo the very thoughts that have been gestating inside me during this past week in the wilderness:

> My young men shall never work.
> Men who work cannot dream,
> and wisdom comes to us in dreams.

You ask me to plow the ground.
Shall I take a knife and tear my mother's breast?
Then when I die, she will not take me to her bosom to rest.

You ask me to dig for stones.
Shall I dig under her skin for bones?
Then when I die, I cannot enter her body to be born again.

You ask me to cut grass and make hay and sell it,
and be rich like white men.
But how dare I cut off my mother's hair?

All the dead men will come to life again.
We must wait in the house of our father,
and be ready to meet him in the body of our mother.

Smohalla speaks about people living in a way that is consistent with their understanding of the world. He speaks about people not engaging in activities that harm the Earth, because for him the Earth is sacred. Wovoka spoke in similar terms. He said that if the Indians wanted to hasten the Earth's renewal through the Ghost Dance, then they would have to forsake all the material things that had been introduced to them since the coming of the white man. Only then could the ancestral ways genuinely re-embody themselves through the people still living . . . .

I consider these things. I consider how much pain I have felt about living in contradiction. Somehow, here in the West, where so much land is still unspoiled, the contradictions hit me more dramatically. It becomes impossible for me to hide from them any longer as I continue traveling with the group.

Like Smohalla, I see my mother's body being ripped apart. I see her being strip-mined for coal and uranium to fuel my society. Like Smohalla, I see her hair being ripped out. I climb her mountains only to look down upon clear-cut forests that have given their trees for products that I consume. Unlike Smohalla, I see many other things being done to the Earth— things far worse than he saw in his day. And all this to support a lifestyle in which I am participating.

I can't bear these contradictions any longer. Somehow, I know, I must begin to make a real, tangible change in the way I live, or all my words and ideals will be for naught. How far I can take that change in a year's time, or five, or ten, I don't know. I only know that I must begin . . . .

My journey with Wilderness Bound has conjured up a strange and passionate mix of bliss and grief in me. The farther west we go, the deeper I feel compelled to gaze into the mirror of my life—to reflect on the Earth not merely as my mother but as my lover, and in so doing to truly dedicate my life to her. After a week of hiking in the High Sierra wilderness of California, I sit by a lake and write these words:

> Earth within me,
> Earth without,
> O soothe my aching soul.
> Drink of my tears,
> and know that I cry for you
> who heals my spirit.
> O make me whole again.
>
> Embrace me now as I embrace
> life only you can give.
> I touch the Earth.
> It makes me soar
> to feel you pulse and live.
>
> Our Mother belongs to no one man.
> She can't be fenced away.
> For life cannot be bought or sold,
> regardless what you pay.

When I think back now to the summer of 1972, I can see that many things were laying a foundation for my future and foreshadowing events to come. I remember sitting in a field of yellow flowers on California's Mount Tamalpais one afternoon with my hands raised to the sun. Its warmth penetrated me in a way I had never felt before, as if I were energized and illuminated from within. Though I did not realize it then, this was my first mystical experience with the sun. In later years, making that solar connection would become a central part of my spiritual practice.

Farther up the coast of northern California, and again in the Olympic Peninsula of Washington State, I recall my first conscious, primordial experiences. Early one evening before sunset, as I ran barefoot through the temperate rain forest, leaping over rocks and roots with boundless energy, I suddenly had the feeling that I was a big cat, like a jaguar. The feeling lasted only a matter of seconds, but in those moments the outer observer vanished. I was completely present and one with everything around me. Nothing had ever felt so positively good or right or real to me.

In the Olympic coastal rain forests and beaches, I tried to recreate this experience, but I was unable to *make* it happen. What I received instead was a broader sense of the eternity all around me. I felt as if I were living in both the present and in prehistory. I sensed the presence of my human counterparts of twenty thousand years ago filling the misty atmosphere of these shores. They were so close at times that I felt as if I were seeing the world through their eyes.

The words of Chief Seattle, reputedly spoken at a treaty signing in 1855, seemed especially prophetic to me:

> When the last red man has perished, and the memory of my people is a myth among the white men, these shores will swarm with the invisible dead of my tribe. And when your children's children think themselves alone in the field, the shop, the store, or in the silence of the pathless woods, they will not be alone. At night, when the streets of your cities and villages are silent and you think them deserted, they will throng with the returning hosts that once filled them and still love this beautiful land. The white man will never be alone . . . . Let him be just and deal kindly with my people, for the dead are not powerless. Dead, I say? There is no death, only a change of worlds.

In those same days, I contemplated the giant fir and spruce trees that had fallen and were rotting on the forest floor. Even before they had fully decomposed, new trees were growing from their trunks. I saw how the ancestors did indeed live through the bodies of the generations that followed. And what was true for trees surely had application to the human realm, I thought. In spite of all our ridiculous attempts to separate things, there was only one life flowing in an eternal cycle through many forms, the past forever dwelling in the present, the present forever becoming the future.

This interpenetration of time frames was revealed to me at the base of Mount Saint Helens in a way that I would not understand until many years later. In 1972 the mountain was still a near-perfect cone. We had climbed to its summit, then descended to its base to spend the night on the forest floor. There, beneath the full moon, I awoke in the middle of the night to see the trees all around me glowing a bright orange, as if they were burning. I did not consciously imagine then that in eight years this same forest would be incinerated by a dramatic volcanic eruption. But in my subconscious mind, the future was already present.

On the morning of August 17, our Wilderness Bound journey culminated in a climb to the summit of the Grand Teton in Wyoming. What a thrill it was to be higher than I had ever been before. Yet little did I know then the significance of that moment. In exactly another fifteen years, I would greet the dawn of a New Sun from Egypt's Great Pyramid—my own "peak experience" at the moment of Harmonic Convergence.

Regardless, the ascent of the Grand Teton was momentous for me right then and there. I knew that the Tetons had traditionally been a sacred gathering grounds for the Lakota Nation, whose spiritual guidance I felt most strongly at that time in my life. On my return to the city, that guidance would at last become personified.

When I got off the train at Grand Central Station, a mere two months after kissing my parents good-bye, my poor mother didn't even recognize me. My hair had grown considerably longer, my face was weather-beaten, and my clothes were ragged. In my right hand, I carried a tall stick painted with black, white, red, and yellow stripes, with a feather tied to the top. My mother had surrendered to her son's inevitable journey into the wilderness, but never did she suspect that he would come back with the wilderness inside him.

Slowly, uneasily, my parents adjusted. Where before they had just had to put up with my unconventional ideas, now they had to deal with actual consequences. There were all kinds of things I wouldn't do, wouldn't eat, wouldn't wear, or wouldn't use. We gave each other a hard time over that next year.

Meanwhile, one of the few people I did know who understood and appreciated my unconventionality came to me with a surprise. This friend's name was Lisa, and she told me of a woman she had met who lived only a couple of miles away—a woman who, she said, just happened to be the grandniece of Sitting Bull.

I was astounded, but it was true. Her name was Yellow Robe, and she lived in an apartment building. Lisa had spoken to her about the musical I was writing, whose central character was her great-uncle. She was naturally intrigued, so a meeting was arranged.

Yellow Robe was a very elegant and beautiful woman in her sixties. Her straight, silver hair was pulled taut around her head and woven neatly at the top. Her aquiline nose and high cheekbones revealed the strength of her heritage, and in her eyes I could see the gleam of her famous ancestor. Amazingly, this woman was the first Native American I came to know personally.

We talked for many hours about Yellow Robe's great-uncle and why I felt so drawn to the history of her people. Finally she asked me to wait a moment and left the room. When she returned, she was holding a beautiful beaded bag of arm's length. She said, "I want you to see this. This bag held the pipe of Sitting Bull."

I felt extremely honored to be so close to something that obviously held deep spiritual meaning to Yellow Robe and her family. Yet at the same time, the pipe bag was a part of *her* tradition, and I felt strangely uncomfortable around it. Growing up in the polluted air of New York City, I had never smoked anything before. I knew that my lungs were already stressed, and I didn't want to make matters worse. I believed that the human body was a sacred vessel for spirit. It was hard for me to imagine that doing something "unhealthy" could also be spiritual. How could I politely explain my dilemma to Yellow Robe?

I decided to broach the subject by asking her why the pipe was so sacred to the Lakota. Admittedly, it was a blunt question, but Yellow Robe was very patient with me. She understood that I was new to her world and its ways.

"We have just met, Jim," she began. "Normally to discuss this matter we would have to know each other far better and have some time to develop a relationship of trust. I hesitated to even show you this bag, but I felt your sincerity. I thought it would be good for you to sense the spirit of my great-uncle through something that belonged to him. Clearly you are an eager young man, and I suspect at times that eagerness may get you into trouble. Just the same, you have a good heart, so I will tell you something of what I know."

Yellow Robe went on to tell me about the legend of Ta Tunka Wian Ska, or White Buffalo Calf Woman. Long ago, she said, this woman appeared to the Lakota people clad in a white buckskin dress. But this was no ordinary woman, for she carried with her a gift that had the power to unite heaven and Earth. That gift was the Sacred Pipe, which was to become the Lakota way of communing with the Great Mystery.

"You have never smoked a pipe before," Yellow Robe continued, "and I sense your concern for your lungs. No living thing should have to spend its first years breathing in a city, so you might think about this: Our people always grew where the air was fresh and sweet. Simply to breathe was a form of nourishment for our bodies." As she said this, she placed her large, gentle hands upon her heart.

Yellow Robe explained that today most people smoke tobacco in an addictive way, doing great harm to their already debilitated health. However, for the Lakota, tobacco and other herbs used in the pipe were considered a sacred medicine, to be smoked only on special occasions.

"You have said you wish to know our tradition more closely," she continued. "Maybe you are thinking that this cannot happen unless you smoke the pipe. But I see clearly that the pipe is not for you at this time, and that is good.

"You have been given a special gift, and it is your music. Through your flute you will learn to speak with the Great Spirit and everything that lives. The flute that you have brought with you today is much like our praying flute. The song that rises from it is like the smoke that rises from the Sacred Pipe. It carries your prayers. It unites heaven and Earth, spirit and matter. It brings you to the center of your being."

"But how can I know the center of my being here in the city?" I asked. "There are so many distractions and so much stress."

Yellow Robe thought for a moment, then looked straight at me with her kind and knowing eyes. "The way of the Pipe teaches us that no matter where we are, we stand at the center of the universe. This sacred place is everywhere present at all times. Yet it is also true that certain places hold special power for certain people. For many who live in this city of New York, it is absolutely the center of the universe. In their minds, the whole world revolves around it. When they are here, they feel anchored, connected. When they leave, all they can think about is coming back.

"Your orientation is different. You feel your center most when you are closest to the Earth. And there is not one, but many, many places you will go in your life that will fill you with this sense of being at the center, until finally you are able to feel it wherever you are. For now, consider this: You have read Black Elk, so you know that for the Lakota our spiritual center is the Paha Sapa, the Black Hills. The highest spot there is called Harney Peak. It is a power center. Go there. Take your flute with you, and you will find what you are seeking. It will only be a first step, but you must begin."

After my initial meeting with Yellow Robe, I did not see her again for many months. Winter came; then in late February of 1973, the explosive news about Wounded Knee hit the television screen. The American Indian Movement (AIM) was staging an armed encampment on the site of the tragic massacre of 1890. They were demanding an end to the Bureau of Indian Affairs' control of the surrounding Pine Ridge Reservation. They were protesting the ongoing harassment and persecution of traditional native people. They were calling for international recognition of the independent Oglala Lakota Nation and for the honoring of treaties broken by the United States.

But in spite of the encampment's political intentions, its basis was spiritual. Members of many Native American nations and all races were present in support of the Lakota people. They were holding purification lodges, praying with the Sacred Pipe, speaking about the fulfillment of prophecies . . . they were even doing the Ghost Dance again.

The Sacred Hoop of the Nation was coming back together. That is what the leadership was saying at Wounded Knee. I was thrilled. I felt connected now, part of a movement with many others, both Indian and non-Indian, who shared the same dream. All I wanted was to go out to South Dakota and be with them.

I called Yellow Robe to see what she thought of the encampment, expecting her to be at least as enthusiastic as I. Instead, she was mainly concerned for the safety of her relatives. The confrontation at Wounded Knee was turning into the largest armed conflict on U.S. soil since the Civil War. Police, military, and FBI agents were surrounding the encampment with guns, tanks, and helicopters. Tensions on the reservation were extremely high, increasing the likelihood that anybody might get shot at any time for any reason.

As Yellow Robe spoke, I could see her side of the situation. She was a woman of peace. Regardless of who was "right," she felt it was better to go about resolving problems in a peaceful way. Yet I also understood the extreme desperation that had driven AIM members to take a warrior stance.

I felt torn between my own commitment to nonviolence and wanting to support them. It was hard for me to see the pipe and the gun in the same circle.

Had it not been for high school obligations and a lack of money, I probably would have left for South Dakota. But practicalities won out. So I did what I could do to support the people of Wounded Knee through local protest actions. It was also about that time that I began wearing pigeon feathers in my increasingly long hair. There weren't any eagles in New York City.

Eagles of another sort, however, did come to New York one day. On March 25, spiritual leaders of the Lakota and many other Indian nations, along with renowned Indian authors, singers, and activists, converged on the enormous and ornate Cathedral of Saint John the Divine for an "Indian Mass." They were joined by the largest turnout of native peoples I had ever seen, along with thousands of others of varied ethnic backgrounds. It was a true gathering of the tribes.

What I most remember that day was an act of healing. A priest walked down the aisle with frankincense burning, asking that the abuses of the white man against native peoples be ended. He prayed for all the buffalo that had been killed by the white man. He prayed for the cleansing of these sins from our collective past. Finally he prayed for forgiveness for the unjust imposition of Christianity upon Indian people. I was astounded to hear all this in a church. It was obviously another sign that the tide was beginning to turn.

Support actions for Wounded Knee continued throughout the spring. Finally, on May 8, members of AIM laid down their weapons, effectively bringing the seventy-day occupation to a close. They did so following U.S. government assurances that their grievances would be thoroughly investigated and real solutions found.

Not surprisingly, once the government had the Indians' weapons, they proceeded to criminally prosecute the AIM activists. The rationale seemed to be that if they couldn't get away with killing Indians, at least they could put them in jail. Meanwhile, violence and property destruction against traditional people on the reservation actually increased after the surrender. The tribal chairman's "goon squad" did what it pleased, while U.S. officials turned the other way. In some cases, the FBI even participated in this campaign of harassment.

These things were not surprising. AIM had little reason to trust the United States, given its previous record. If possible, they would have continued the occupation. But toward the end, they were running out of food, medicine, and other essential supplies due to a government blockade. Starvation loomed. Only a century earlier, it had been official U.S. policy to exterminate the buffalo and thus starve the Plains Indians into submission or death. Unbelievably, in the 1970s, the government was still carrying on the same policy and getting away with it.

Of course, not all Americans agreed with U.S. policy. An important difference between the 1870s and the 1970s was that now there was widespread, active support for the native cause by non-Indians. I personally had collected hundreds of pounds of food and clothing from fellow students at my high school to send to the encampment. Many others across the country had done the same. Of those most closely involved, more than five hundred people were arrested for attempting to transport much-needed food and supplies to the Indians. Some were caught driving carloads or truckloads of food to Wounded Knee. Others actually risked their own lives, moving through blockades at night, sometimes crawling on their hands and knees in order to avoid being seen and shot. At dawn on April 17, three single-engine planes successfully parachuted almost a ton of food into Wounded Knee. Those responsible for the airlift were also caught and arrested.

However disappointing the outcome of the occupation, there is no question that the drama of the event drew world attention. In doing so, it sparked a major resurgence of Native American spirituality and political awareness that has continued to grow over the years. From the very place where the Indian Wars ended, it seemed a most appropriate transformation that there, too, should begin a rebirth of the Indian spirit.

Precisely for that reason, I still felt I had to go to Wounded Knee. Nor had I forgotten what Yellow Robe had told me about Harney Peak. These places called to me. Yellow Robe agreed it would be good for me to go to Pine Ridge also, to see for myself what life was like on the reservation. But she counseled me to wait. It was not yet safe. With my long hair and hippie attire, I would be easily singled out as an AIM sympathizer.

Finally, in the early summer of 1974, Yellow Robe and I decided that the time had arrived for my journey. "Pay careful attention to everything you see on the reservation," she told me. "Some of your cherished beliefs may be shattered. Try to look past the obvious to that which lies beneath. And don't forget to take your flute with you. You will need it on Harney Peak."

With three hundred dollars in my pocket and a backpack slung over my shoulder, I climbed into a Volkswagen bug with two high school classmates I barely knew. They were headed to the West Coast and had agreed to stop in South Dakota on the way.

The ride out was terrible. My classmates were smoking and eating junk food almost constantly. Rick and I got along nominally, but Peter despised me. By the time we crossed the Mississippi, he was brandishing a large knife and threatening to kill me every few hours. I figured he was just joking, but I wasn't absolutely sure.

We arrived in the Badlands just before sunset. Around us stretched a bizarre and weathered landscape, like I imagine an old person's skin might look through a microscope. Small groups of pronghorn antelope grazed through the sparse dry grass, their ochre coloring made brilliant by the sun's dying rays. We went to the campground to pitch our tent before the light disappeared.

Later that evening, I hiked alone to the edge of some eroded cliffs facing Pine Ridge. Here in these Badlands, so named because of the difficulty white men experienced in traversing their rugged contours, the Lakota chief Big Foot and his band of ghost dancers had found refuge. They had hidden here for days before they were discovered by the Seventh Cavalry and forced to continue walking south toward a creek called Wounded Knee. I wondered if that was why, when the Lakota say a person is "going south," they mean he or she is going to die.

As I sat on the cliffs, gazing into the darkness, I heard a distant but steady drumbeat. I could also make out a faint chorus of human voices. My curiosity led me slowly and carefully down the steep switchback trail. When I reached the bottom, the sound was a bit stronger. I stepped over clumps of sagebrush, moving toward the sound and what now appeared to be the glow of a small fire.

At last I reached the clearing. The sound was full now, and I could see that many people were dancing in a circle around the fire. I stayed where I was, not wanting to disturb them. But then one of the dancers noticed me and motioned me to join them. As I stepped forward, the circle opened to include me. We moved slowly and steadily, stepping first with our left feet, then with our right. The drummers were sitting together in their own smaller circle.

The dance continued nonstop, and eventually I got tired. I felt like I should be getting back, but I didn't know how to excuse myself. I didn't want to break the energy by speaking, so I just stepped out and backed away, my eyes meeting and thanking the one who had welcomed me.

In the morning I broke camp with Peter and Rick, and we continued on to Wounded Knee. I didn't say anything about the previous night's experience; it didn't feel right to share it. Besides, I knew that they had no interest in the Lakota or Wounded Knee. They were going there only because they had promised.

When we arrived in the little hamlet (just a few scattered homes and a trading post), a big sign pointed toward the site of the mass-burial graveyard. Peter and Rick told me to go ahead but not to be too long. I thought how ironic it was that after all the time I had waited to come to Wounded Knee, now I had to rush.

As I walked past the plastic flowers, the simple wooden crosses painted white, the gravestones with names like Flying Hawk and Hard to Kill, I began to realize that I didn't know what to do here. I wanted to pray, but I didn't know how. There seemed to be a wall between myself and the past, keeping me from feeling anything—perhaps because the present was so strangely unreal.

I surrendered to my dilemma by simply focusing my thoughts on the spirits of the people who were buried at Wounded Knee. Silently I told them that their dance was not dead—that I and many others were with them. Then I walked back to the car.

"OK, let's go," I said. "I'm done." But in my heart I knew there was much, much more to do.

We drove on toward Pine Ridge. Except for an occasional tree, the land was barren. Burned-out car wrecks littered the roadside, along with beer and soda cans. This was not the Indian country I had pictured. In the town of Pine Ridge I found a supermarket and tract homes. Teenagers stood listlessly on street corners. Wind blew dust around the streets. It was like Anywhere, U.S.A., but more depressing. There seemed to be an unbearable weight hanging over the place.

Then I remembered that Yellow Robe had told me to look beyond the obvious. What could she have meant? I wondered. I decided to call her relative, a nontraditional, tribal government official. As soon as I mentioned Yellow Robe, he told me to come over.

Again Peter and Rick reminded me not to be too long as we pulled up to the official's home. He came to the door, a man of medium build with very short, black hair and thick glasses. We talked on his doorstep for half an hour at most.

I asked him what he thought about the Wounded Knee occupation. "We've got a lot of problems around here," he said. "You can see for yourself. But the AIM people made a lot of trouble, stirred things up. Now it's worse than before."

"Well, what can be done then?" I asked. But he had no answer. I could see he was as downtrodden as the kids on the corners.

"Just be careful," he said. "I mean you and your friends with your long hair. You shouldn't go around here alone. People will associate you with the wrong types. It's probably best if you leave soon."

I decided he was right. There was no reason for me to stay any longer, especially since Peter and Rick were so obviously ready to leave. Besides, I still had to get to the Black Hills.

It was late afternoon as we headed west to Deadwood in the center of the Black Hills. I kept thinking about the Indians I had been dancing with the night before. How odd it was that they were just out in the middle of nowhere, dancing. Yet I had felt very good with them. Driving around the reservation, on the other hand, had just left me feeling disturbed. I hadn't liked seeing what had become of a culture I so admired. At the same time, I knew that I had no right to judge it—that the Lakota were people like all of us, struggling in their own unique way to deal with the contradictions of late twentieth-century life.

Finally the Black Hills came into view, their rounded contours silhouetted against the horizon. Big cumulus clouds gathered in a cluster above them. The land became gradually greener, with more trees. Before long we could see herds of buffalo. In contrast to the desolation of Pine Ridge, the Black Hills seemed abundant and fertile, an oasis for all living things.

The next day we visited Mount Rushmore. I really wasn't interested in going there, but this time it was Rick and Peter's turn to insist. I had to agree with them: it was impressive. But to me there was something terribly perverse about carving the faces of a conquering race into the most sacred place of those who had been conquered. It was like desecrating a temple.

We camped on a beautiful, grassy field by the shores of Sylvan Lake that night—the same lake where Sitting Bull had received a song from an eagle: "My father has given me this nation. In protecting them I have a hard time." In a hundred years, I thought, the reality of that song had not changed much.

In the morning, we began our hike up the trail to Harney Peak. It was a beautiful, clear day, with lots of blue sky and sunshine. Birds hopped about and sang from the branches above us. Peter and Rick were in a hurry to get to the top and dashed ahead. I took my time, enjoying every step. As the trail climbed higher, views of spectacular rock formations opened up through the trees. Before long, I could see the summit to my left—only 7,200 feet above sea level, but the highest point east of the Rockies.

A few hundred feet below the summit, I found Rick and Peter waiting for me at a cabin. They were tired but happy. At last, nature seemed to be getting through to them, calming down their hard-core city vibes. We left our things in the cabin and hiked together the last stretch to the top. Nearing it, we saw a wonderful sight: four mountain goats—a mother and three babies—stepped lightly about the rocky precipice, occasionally standing so still as to appear like statues. Their fluffy white bodies with little black eyes and delicate horns seemed the perfect complement to the rugged, slate-gray stone surfaces of their natural home.

Just below the summit, I found a spot that felt like the right place to sit and be still. Rick and Peter went off exploring, which was fine with me. I only wanted to be left alone.

I am here—finally. Here at the center of the universe, at the place where Black Elk was taken by the spirits in his great vision—where he came to make his final prayer to the Great Spirit. I look around. It is late afternoon, and the sky is still blue. Yet strangely, to each of the four cardinal directions, I can see little groups of dark clouds forming in the distance.

From where I sit, I feel like I am in the center of a great wheel or hoop. I take out my wooden flute and begin to play a melody I've composed for a Ghost Dance song. I close my eyes and let the song carry me. I merge with the music and the rock. . . .

I feel the wind on my face and open my eyes. The clouds are much closer now, and much darker, but still distinctly positioned to the Four Directions. Never before have I seen a storm congeal in this way. It appears that a great rain is imminent.

I continue to play my flute, this time with eyes wide open. I play to the four winds, letting them become the very wind that blows through me and animates my flute. The storm increases in intensity. Lightning flashes all around me. The wind swoops in spiraling currents, and thunder crackles— north, east, south, now west. The atmosphere is buzzing with electricity. The wind roars and howls. What little air I am able to blow through my flute is nothing compared to the gushes that sweep through it from the storm, playing it all on their own.

Suddenly the lightning flashes from all four directions at once. I jump to my feet, startled, and as I do so the rain begins to fall. But this is not like any rainstorm I have experienced before, because the rain is falling up! It appears that the storm clouds are actually below the peak, yet the winds are so strong that they carry the rain upward. The rain flies hard against my face, compelling me to look straight above. There I see an eagle circling directly over Harney Peak.

I clutch my flute close and rush toward the summit. The rain seems to be pushing me there, the eagle calling me. When I reach the top, I find Rick and Peter huddled against the rocks, trying hopelessly to stay dry.

As the lightning flashes again, I look at my friends and begin to laugh. Their hair is standing on end, sticking out in all directions. They are laughing, too: my hair is doing the same! "Come on," Rick says. "Let's get down from here or we're gonna get fried."

As we ran down the peak, I felt utterly exhilarated. We slept that night in the cabin, our wet clothes spread out to dry, doing our best to stay warm. The storm continued through the middle of the night, then finally died down. I slept deeply and awakened before sunrise.

I went out of the cabin and stood at the mountain's edge, facing east. All was absolutely still, as though the storm had never happened. Above me the sky was clear. Then, as the sky slowly lightened, all the stars began to fade. I looked east again to see that one star still shone brightly. I looked deeply into it, and it filled me with tranquillity.

It was then that I realized I was looking at Venus, the Morning Star.

Though I had read of it in countless songs and prayers, never before had I actually seen it. I was overcome with joy. What better place to first see the Morning Star than from the center of the universe?

Now looking east, the sky growing ever lighter, the Morning Star slowly fading, I could see that the entire prairie below Harney Peak was covered by a thick layer of blue clouds stretching to the horizon. Soon a brilliant glow filled the sky. As the rim of the sun peeked over the clouds, its rays spread out like a million fingers to touch the waiting earth. It was then that I remembered my favorite song of Black Elk, then that I knew I was seeing what he saw, perhaps from this very spot:

> See where the sacred sun is walking.
> In the blue robe of morning he is walking.
> With his power greenward walking.
> Hey-o-ha, hey-o-ha, hey-o-ha, hey-o-ha!

THE WHITE ROOTS
OF PEACE

E A S T

With my experience on Harney Peak, a new dimension entered my life—the dimension of the miraculous. No longer were miracles merely the stuff of myth. No longer were they limited to people of other times and cultures. Miracles were accessible and real. They were the unseen side of everyday reality. Yet most people, I knew, had become so divorced from the whole of existence that they could accept only an extremely limited reality.

I concluded that one of the reasons I had been born into modern society was to challenge such limitations by serving as a bridge between conventional and alternate realities. That, after all, was the role of the artist. With this realization, I was ready for what is often referred to as "higher education."

Upon my return to the East, I began my freshman year at Amherst College in Massachusetts. I soon discovered that the college's (and the town's) namesake was a famed soldier of the British Crown: Lord Jeffrey Amherst.

Lord Jeffrey had been the British commander in chief in North America during the French and Indian Wars that preceded the American Revolution. In 1763 he was faced with a difficult situation in the western region of Pennsylvania. British troop morale was low, and the Indian allies of the

French were putting up an increasingly militant resistance to foreign encroachment on their lands.

For this reason, Amherst began to calculate an alternative plan to the more commonly known tactics of war. In a letter to Colonel Henry Bouquet, the ranking officer for the Pennsylvanian western frontier, Amherst wrote, "Could it not be contrived to send the small pox among those disaffected tribes of Indians? We must, on this occasion, use every stratagem in our power to reduce them."

As the Europeans knew well, smallpox was a disease to which Native Americans had no natural resistance. It had already decimated hundreds of thousands, if not millions, of them since the beginning of the European invasion of America.

Following a favorable response from Bouquet, Amherst sent a follow-up letter, writing, "You will do well to try to inoculate the Indians, by means of blankets, as well as to try every other method that can serve to extirpate this execrable race." By the spring of 1764, smallpox was rapidly spreading among the Delawares, Mingoes, and Shawanoes.

Given this knowledge of Lord Jeffrey Amherst as one of the earliest proponents of biological warfare, there was only one thing I could do: start a campaign to change the name of the town and the college. No sooner did I begin than I found that such a campaign already existed. Unfortunately, its members numbered a mere handful. We got nowhere except to raise consciousness a bit. Traditions were not wont to die so easily in this small New England community. Outrageous as it seemed to me to honor a man who was clearly a murderous racist, to those who had been here longer the name Amherst was synonymous with cherished ideals. For the time being, I gave up the campaign.

Around this time, however, I began to learn about atrocities similar to those experienced by native North Americans that were currently taking place in the jungles of South America. Amazonian Indians were dying from a host of diseases introduced by advancing settlements of outsiders. Their lands were being forcibly stolen. Tribes were being hunted down and intentionally eliminated.

I realized, too, that the Trans-Amazonian Highway being built across South America was a twentieth-century version of the Transcontinental Railroad laid across North America a century before. The opening of such transportation corridors always brought mass destruction of the natural world. Especially affected were the living things that native people depended upon for their survival. Before, it was the buffalo; now it was the trees.

Again, I was outraged that such overt genocide and ecocide could be tolerated—even promoted—by the society in which I lived. Thus, I was excited to learn that a Massachusetts-based alternative magazine called *East West Journal* was planning to publish a special issue, called "North/ South," around such concerns. I felt called to contribute something and so produced a drawing of the South American continent being formed out of the bodies of its indigenous inhabitants. (See figure 7.)

The drawing was published, and as a result I was introduced to the editors of the "North/South" issue. Their names were Red Moon and Blue Sun. Red and Blue, as I soon became accustomed to calling them, were an amazing couple. Both in their late thirties, they had literally traveled the world and familiarized themselves with many of its ancient mysteries. Their house near Boston was like a museum of magical artifacts, an outer reflection of their inner world. Rare masks from Papua New Guinea hung above turn-of-the-century Hopi kachina dolls encircling a basket of corn on the floor. Tibetan ritual objects made from human bones were laid upon intricate and colorful Andean weavings draped over a massive ironwood table from West Africa. Everywhere the eyes turned were reminders of ancient spiritual power.

As man and woman, as well as by name and more, Blue and Red were natural reflections of polarity. Though not Native American, from an early age both had been deeply involved with indigenous culture. He (Blue Sun) had been born in the misty forests of the Pacific Northwest Coast, passing his youth beside one of the last great carvers of giant totem poles. She (Red Moon) had been born in the rugged deserts of the American Southwest, adopted by an old Hopi woman who had carefully instructed her in the secret knowledge. Both Blue and Red shared a strong mystical link to the native cultures of Peru, where they had lived for many years together. There, they had adopted as their personal emblem the ancient Inca symbol of a crescent moon beneath a solar disc.

Upon returning to North America, the eclectic interests of Blue and Red had synthesized into a new foundation they called the Fourth World, one of whose primary purposes was to create greater awareness of native prophecies. I soon learned that the prophecies of Black Elk and the Ghost Dance were only the tip of the iceberg. There was a vast tradition of prophecy throughout the Americas, much of it pointing to great transformations in our times. Many spoke of the coming of redeemers, such as Viracocha among the Inca and Pahana among the Hopi—great ones who would bring back harmony and balance to an ailing world. Blue and Red believed that the redeemer was a collective force and that this was what had drawn the three of us together.

Red especially seemed to have a kind of psychic ability to see things that lay in my personal path of destiny. Without my telling her, she already knew that I had been to visit the Lakota and that I had not made my hoped-for connection with the people on the reservation. She told me that it was not yet time—that I first had to come to know the native people of my own region. From that, she said, everything else would follow.

So it was that Red advised me to gain experience living among the native peoples of the Eastern Woodlands. I explained to her that, much as I wanted to, I had no connections to begin such a process.

"But I do," she said with a generous smile. "From the moment we met, I could see that a certain man was in your path of destiny and that he would become a great teacher for you. He is a Mohawk, and he lives in upstate New York, near the Canadian border. His name is Rarihokwats."

A few weeks later I arrived at the door of Rarihokwats's cabin, deep in the forests of the Adirondack Mountains. I was greeted by a robust, middle-aged woman and taken into a room where many people were busily working on various tasks. What Red Moon had not told me was that this was also the headquarters of *Akwesasne Notes,* the Pan-Indian newspaper that had done so much to inform people during the Wounded Knee occupation. Then I realized why Rarihokwats's name was so familiar: since he was the editor of the paper, I had seen his name in print many times before.

An even bigger surprise came when Rarihokwats entered the cabin and introduced himself. He didn't look at all like I had expected. With his fair skin and green eyes, he was clearly as much a white man as I. Yet his nationality was considered to be Mohawk. I later discovered why. Many years before, after founding *Akwesasne Notes,* he had been adopted into the Mohawk Nation. The Council of Chiefs had given him his name, which translated as "He Who Digs up Buried Information." He could not have received a more fitting designation.

In the first days of my visit, I was astounded by the steady stamina and devotion of this man. The volume of articles that flowed from him was endless, covering everything from the violation of native fishing rights in Washington State to genocidal campaigns against the Ache Indians in Paraguay. Whatever was happening to threaten the existence of native peoples in the Americas, Rarihokwats seemed to know about it. And if he knew about it, he was exposing it. In balance, he also had a vast knowledge of indigenous history and culture, and he could speak for days on the spiritual precepts that guide the lives of native peoples. The man was a living library.

Yet even though he knew a great deal, Rarihokwats was not one for idle chatter. When he was sharing information, his hands were at least as busy as his brain. Whether it was picking strawberries, braiding sweetgrass, or slicing potatoes for the soup, he was always doing something to contribute to the collective needs while he talked. What made Rarihokwats a teacher for me was not so much what he wrote or said; it was what I was able to learn by simply observing him.

But what most impressed me was Rarihokwats's serenity. Perhaps it was due to the years he had passed alone in the rugged and isolated Canadian wilderness, traveling only by foot and canoe. However he had achieved it, he was as serene as the vast forests surrounding his cabin, as clear as the shimmering atmosphere. He belonged there. This was what made him native; the color of his skin was irrelevant.

One day toward the end of my stay, while Rarihokwats and I were out hiking in the woods, I asked him if he could share with me something about the Mohawk tradition.

"Good," he said. "I've been waiting for you to ask me, and so we can begin. At this time, you are most familiar with the traditions of the Lakota, who were among the greatest warriors and mystics of North America. The Iroquois—or as it is said in the Mohawk language, the Haudenosaunee [of whom the Mohawk are but one nation]—are known among native people as the great orators and statesmen of this continent. The Haudenosaunee excel in the arts of governing and peace. How it came to be this way is a very wonderful story. Let us sit here by this tree so you can learn the roots of this land where you were born and raised."

And so Rarihokwats told me about the Five Nations of the Haudenosaunee. Long before the coming of the white man, he said, there was a period of much warring among the Five Nations. Thus the Great Spirit determined to send a messenger who would teach them "New Mind," or how to live with one another in peace.

This messenger, destined to become known as the Peacemaker, was born in a Huron village near Taiendaneka on the north shore of Lake Ontario. When he had grown up, he surprised his family by carving a canoe out of white stone. Nobody believed it would float. But one day he got in the canoe, bid his family farewell, and paddled south across the lake.

When the Peacemaker arrived on the southern shores of Lake Ontario, a group of curious hunters approached him. He told them, "I come to bring the good news of peace and power to your people. I come from the west and go toward the sunrise." The hunters quickly realized that this was no ordinary man, and they took his words to heart.

Soon the Peacemaker was traveling from village to village, sharing his peace plan with the people. It was based on the concept of the longhouse, a place where many families live together peacefully under one roof. He explained how this same model could be used to create a family of nations, each centered around its own council fire yet all living peacefully as one community.

The Peacemaker found that everyone genuinely wanted to live in peace, if only they could trust that others would do the same. Because he was so clear and strong, he was able to inspire people with that missing sense of trust. Everywhere he went, the people embraced the New Mind.

But the Peacemaker's task was not without challenges. Deep in the forest, there lived a monstrous man who was known to eat human beings. He terrorized the villages, and everyone was in constant fear of him. The Peacemaker saw that there could be no real peace in the land until this one they called Hayonwantha had embraced the New Mind. So he went to Hayonwantha. By combining cleverness with compassion, he managed to transform the monster into his greatest ally.

The Peacemaker told Hayonwantha he would return. Then he continued traveling toward the sunrise. At last he came to the lands of the Mohawk, who were the strongest warriors of all. The Mohawk leaders were not ready to trust him, so they proposed a test. He was to climb out on the limb of a tree hanging over a high cliff beside a waterfall. They would cut the tree from its roots, and if the Peacemaker survived, then they would embrace the New Mind.

The Peacemaker accepted their test, falling with the tree into the chasm. When he returned to the village alive and whole, the Mohawk leaders realized they were dealing with a man of extraordinary power, and they became the first nation to commit to the Great Peace.

Soon the Peacemaker had won over all Five Nations of the Haudenosaunee, traveling among them with his new friend and ally, Hayonwantha. Now only one obstacle remained. In the lands of the Onondaga, at the center of the Haudenosaunee Nations, there was an evil sorcerer named Atotarho, whose body was as twisted as his mind and whose tangled hair was filled with snakes.

The Peacemaker and Hayonwantha assembled the chiefs of the Five Nations by the shores of Lake Onondaga. Asking them to wait, the two paddled across the lake to confront the sorcerer.

Atotarho was full of denial and resistance, and he had no interest in the good news of the Peacemaker. Nevertheless, the Peacemaker spoke. He told Atotarho that the chiefs of the Five Nations had agreed to come together as the "People of the Longhouse," to live in peace as a family of nations. In the very place where they now stood, he told Atotarho, the chiefs would soon assemble. There the Great Tree of Peace would be planted, and all nations would be invited to take shelter beneath its branches.

Atotarho did not see why he should care about such a thing. Then the Peacemaker told him that he was to become chief of all the chiefs and to tend the council fire that never dies at the center of the Longhouse of Nations. Still, Atotarho did not believe him. How could such a thing come to pass?

So the Peacemaker told Atotarho to wait and see. Swiftly he departed with Hayonwantha and returned to the chiefs. Then together as one body, they paddled back across the lake. The sorcerer tried to stop them with his magic, but to no avail. When they arrived, the Peacemaker explained that the combined strength of all the chiefs could not be resisted, but that if Atotarho would commit to the New Mind, his voice would become the voice of all the chiefs.

By this diplomacy, Atotarho was won over. Hayonwantha combed the snakes out of his hair, and the Peacemaker removed the seven crooks from his twisted body. Then the Peacemaker placed deer antlers on the heads of all the chiefs as a symbol of their authority and their commitment to the Great Peace. To the Mohawk he gave the responsibility of guarding the Eastern Door, to the Seneca the guardianship of the Western Door, and to the Onondaga the title of Firekeepers at the center of the Longhouse of Nations.

The peoples of the Haudenosaunee were called together around an enormous pine tree, which they uprooted at the Peacemaker's instruction. Then he invited all the warriors to place their weapons in the cavern of the tree's roots, to be buried forever. As the men did so, they embraced one another, thus reaffirming the brotherhood they had forgotten. Finally the Haudenosaunee replanted the beautiful white pine, to be called the Great Tree of Peace, and filled the hole with earth again.

The chiefs circled the tree, grasping each other's hands tightly. This represented unity, which became the most highly prized principle. "If the tree should fall, " said the Peacemaker, "you chiefs will hold hands in unity so tightly that the tree will not hit the ground, and thus it can be raised upright once again." This meant that if the people should quarrel, the chiefs would remain united until the problems could be settled.

The shining white roots of the Great Tree of Peace spread to the Four Directions. The Peacemaker said they would continue to grow beneath the forest floor until they had extended across the entire Earth. And he told the Haudenosaunee, "If any person or nation desires to trace these roots to their source and obey the law of the Great Peace, they will be welcome to take shelter beneath this tree."

As the Peacemaker spoke, a beautiful white eagle alighted in the uppermost branches of the tree. This eagle, he told the people, would serve to watch over them and to warn them of any danger that might threaten the Great Peace. But if the peace was weakened from within, he added, then the descendants of the Haudenosaunee would find him among them once more.

"Call my name in the forest," he told them, "and I will return." Then the Peacemaker covered his body with bark and disappeared into the earth.

Just as Rarihokwats finished speaking, a branch creaked in the forest, as if to sound the concluding note.

"It's amazing that so few people know this story," I said, "particularly when this area now called New York State is once again home to a United Nations."

"Yes," Rarihokwats agreed. "As you can see, the Peacemaker established the first United Nations here a long time ago. Because that energy was already planted, it was able to regenerate in a new form. But there is more to this story."

Rarihokwats explained that the writers of the U.S. Constitution had studied the Haudenosaunee way of governing and that it had inspired them to set up a union of semisovereign states with a system of checks and balances. But, he added, they had left out some of the most important things. For example, among the Haudenosaunee, in order to maintain the balance of power necessary for peace, only women have the authorization to choose chiefs and declare war. And the Haudenosaunee would never consider majority rule to be democratic; all decisions have to be made by consensus. "The teaching of the Peacemaker was to deliberate until everyone agrees," said Rarihokwats.

But most important, he emphasized, is that government and daily life are inseparable from spiritual life. "It is because the Haudenosaunee respect the sacredness of all things and always consider how their decisions will affect future generations that this society has the power to endure," Rarihokwats stated. "For native people, the otters and the turtles, the eagles and the crickets, the rivers and the forests all have a voice that must be included in every decision. This spiritual consciousness is missing from the United States government, and now it is the responsibility of the people to bring it back."

It was good to be at the little community of Akwesasne, not only to experience the wisdom of Rarihokwats but to see so many native sisters and brothers actively reclaiming their spiritual roots. Not that there weren't problems, just as there were at Pine Ridge. But at Pine Ridge I had not witnessed the indigenous renaissance in process. Though I had known it was there, I had needed to see it firsthand. I was grateful to the people of Akwesasne for giving me that opportunity.

To make the circle complete, I wanted to give something back to the Akwesasne people, so I did a drawing of the North American continent formed from the bodies of its indigenous inhabitants. It was a perfect complement to the South American drawing I had done previously, so I joined the two by representing the Isthmus of Panama as a rainbow. This new hemispheric image was published in the next issue of *Akwesasne Notes*. (See figure 7.)

A couple of months later, while I was on college break visiting my family in New York City, I received a phone call from a man named Nemattanew. He identified himself as a chief of the Powhatan Confederacy. I couldn't imagine what he wanted or how he had gotten my number. Then he explained that he had seen my drawing of the Americas in *Akwesasne Notes* and that he wanted me to design a tribal symbol for his community. I was dumbfounded.

The next day, Nemattanew was at my door. He was a large man who wore a big-brimmed hat with a beaded band. He greeted me by the name I had used to sign my drawing: "Keeper of the Woods." I invited him to sit in my room. I told him how pleased I was to meet him, but that honestly I didn't know anything about the Powhatan people.

"That's why I'm here," he said. "Today you can start to learn."

Nemattanew explained that when the Europeans arrived on this continent, the Powhatan people inhabited the tidewater area of what is now called Virginia. They formed more than a hundred different villages comprising thirty-two nations. These nations were united into a confederacy similar to that of the Haudenosaunee, and like them the Powhatan lived in longhouses made of wood and bark.

"We lived on the land, but we understood that it did not belong to us," said Nemattanew. "We were part of it. We were great hunters and gatherers, fishermen and farmers. We spoke our own language and held ceremonies to commemorate the seasons."

Nemattanew went on to explain that the name *Powhatan* means "spiritual power" or "the desire to have sacred knowledge." He said that the first English settlements in America were on Powhatan land and that the treaty of 1646 was the first ever made between a European and a Native American government.

Of course, the treaty was not kept by the British, and through a combination of guns and disease, the Powhatans were nearly destroyed. Only a strong, determined few escaped the genocide. But Nemattanew said that cultural genocide had taken an even greater toll on the Powhatans than their physical struggle for survival. Losing their land base, their link to the natural world slowly eroded, and with it their traditional lifestyle.

As Nemattanew spoke, I felt overwhelmed. Before me was a survivor of all the atrocities I had been learning about since my exposure to the Amherst history. He was a survivor of not one or two, but of *four centuries* of genocidal campaigns, plus the Industrial Revolution and the usurpation of his land by major urban centers. In spite of this, his spirits were high, his determination unshakable. He had risen above it all—even above anger and resentment.

I told Nemattanew that because I had been born on the eastern shores of North America, I could imagine no greater honor than to contribute in some tangible way to the renewal of a tradition that had also been born on these shores. I knew that we had come together to help heal the past and bring beauty to the future.

"Keeper of the Woods," he said, "I like the way you talk. Know that we are also honored to receive your gift. If you can help us with this tribal symbol, your contribution will be great."

As Nemattanew proceeded to describe the elements he wanted in the symbol, I recognized many affinities between his cosmology and that of the Haudenosaunee. I told him that although much of this was new to me, I would do my best to create a vision on paper that reflected the essence of his culture. But, inside, I doubted that I could do it. Had it not been for Nemattanew's total confidence in my ability, I would not have accepted the task.

Before he left, Nemattanew asked me where my name, Keeper of the Woods, had come from. I answered that my father had recently told me it was the translation of our last name, Berenholtz.

"It's a very good name," he said. "You should ask your father what more he knows. Every human being needs to know their roots in order to be strong. As our great leader Wahunsonakok said many centuries ago, 'One must learn how to live, not just how to make a living. But how to find a path of beauty in this life? We *begin* by knowing who we are.'"

On my way back to college at Amherst, I decided on an impulse to visit Blue and Red in Boston. I arrived to discover that Red had already moved to Taos, New Mexico, and that Blue was preparing to join her.

"We need to talk," Blue said, placing some cushions on the floor. "I've been thinking about the theater piece you're writing on the Ghost Dance prophecy. There's a very old Lakota medicine man who adopted me as his grandson some years ago. His name is John Fire Lame Deer, and he's one of the last surviving Indians with direct experience of the Ghost Dance. He knows the steps and the songs and all the deeper meanings. I think you should meet him."

"Of course," I said enthusiastically, "but how?"

"Grandfather is coming to stay with us in Taos next summer. If you can come out for awhile, then it's all set."

I told him I would try to arrange it.

Then Blue said, "I've got something I want to give you." From his pocket he pulled a small black object about the size of a grape and handed it to me. "Have you ever seen anything like this?"

"No," I said. "What is it? It has the feeling of something that's been formed naturally, yet it looks like it's been carved."

"Precisely," Blue answered. "Actually, it's a crystal, and it's been carved by the forces of nature."

Most surprising to me was the shape of the crystal. It was a perfect cross—not a Christian cross, where one stem is longer than the others, but a four-directional Native American cross with all its stems of equal length.

Blue continued: "Our new home in Taos overlooks the mountain where these crystals come from. It's one of only six locations in the world where they can be found. Place the crystal between your palms and tell me what you feel."

I did as he instructed. Almost immediately I began to feel a pulse that moved in spiraling waves through both my palms. Soon it was very intense, and my hands were getting extremely warm. I explained the sensation to Blue.

"That's great," he said. "Not everybody can feel it right away."

Just then the phone rang. Blue excused himself and went into the other room to take the call. I continued holding the black cross between my palms. It was almost as though my hands were being held together magnetically. I had no desire to release them. I was filled with a sense of well-being.

When Blue came back, he seemed upset. "That was Red Moon," he said. "She had bad news. Grandfather has just gone into the hospital. Apparently he's very ill, and the doctors say he might not live. I need to go to my room and do a prayer ceremony for the rest of the night. Will you be OK out here? You're welcome to sleep on the couch."

"No problem," I said, and asked Blue if there was anything I could do. "Just pray," he said, as he left for his room.

Sitting comfortably on the couch, I hold my hands together in prayer position with the crystal between them. I close my eyes and concentrate all my energy through the crystal, sending it toward a Lakota medicine man I've never even met. Still, for the first time, I can feel the strength of my prayer....

Suddenly I am awakened from a deep sleep by a low, mumbling voice. I hear it for only a few moments, my eyes still closed. Then I feel hands— not so much fingers, but definitely the force of two hands holding and gently massaging my feet. As the hands move slowly up my legs, I am afraid to open my eyes. Even though the touch feels friendly, I am afraid to look. These hands are not human, not like anything I have experienced before.

The hands move slowly up my body to my head, then they leave. The whole process takes about five minutes. Uneasily I open my eyes. No sound, no movement, no sign of any presence. I turn on the light. There is no one in the room but myself.

In the morning, Blue told me that he received another call from Red Moon in the middle of the night and that for the moment, at least, Grandfather was holding steady. I told him about my experience with the hands and asked whether he could explain it.

"It's not for me to explain," he said, "but I don't think it's bad. Do you feel any different?"

"Actually, I feel great," I answered, "as if I've been made whole."

"Just let it be," said Blue. "Don't try to define it. I'll only say it appears that a door has been opened for you, and I'm happy."

Later that morning I returned to Amherst. The trees in the Berkshire Mountains reflected all the vibrant colors of autumn. I was so high on life that the thought of school seemed almost irrelevant. Over the next few weeks, I somehow managed to fulfill my class requirements, but my mind and spirit were elsewhere.

Whenever possible, I worked on the tribal symbol for Nemattanew. It came to me a little at a time, like puzzle pieces. First came the central image: the Sacred Tree in front of a longhouse. Together these formed the vertical and horizontal axes of a cross. Then I saw the four animals that Nemattanew told me about. These were the bear, the turtle, the human being, and the eagle. They were moving in a circle around the cross. Soon the drawing began to take on a life of its own. (See part one illustration.)

One night in my dormitory room, about a week after I had visited Blue, I decided to take out the black cross crystal again. I was a little nervous, not knowing what to expect. I closed my eyes and meditated with the crystal between my hands, just as before. Soon I fell asleep.

Like the first time, I was awakened by a sound in the middle of the night. But this time it was very different. It was not one, but many voices. And the voices were not mumbling—they were singing. The sound was at once awesome and wonderful. The voices seemed to weave together in a spherical shape that moved around the room—like a chorus of angels from another world, like the sound from the temple of my recurring dream.

Then the hands came again—not two this time, but an indefinable number. As before, they started at my feet and moved slowly and gently up my body. I was surrounded by inexplicable touch and sound. I was not afraid; even so, I didn't open my eyes until it had stopped. Then once again, silence and stillness.

The next night, I had another unusual experience. It was late, and I was walking home across campus under a clear sky with a full moon. As I neared the dorm, for no apparent reason I stopped to look up. In the sky was a thin cloud in the precise form of a cross within a circle. I couldn't believe my eyes. Then, as I watched, it moved toward the full moon . . . until the moon was exactly in the center of the cross.

At that moment I was struck by a massive realization. The crystal that Blue had given me was shaped like a cross. The tribal symbol I was doing for Nemattanew was a cross within a circle. From Rarihokwats I had learned of the Great Tree of Peace, which grew in the center of a circle of people with its roots to the Four Directions. Black Elk's Sacred Hoop contained two roads, and he had said that the place where they crossed was holy. Now I was looking at that place, and I could feel its holiness.

Suddenly I felt like I was on Harney Peak, at the center of the universe.

Yellow Robe had been right. This center was everywhere that I could feel it within myself. I realized that the cross within the circle was not only a spiritual symbol of the Western Hemisphere; it was also my personal symbol, and it would guide me throughout my life.

In the weeks that followed, I continued to have many synchronistic experiences. It seemed all I had to do was think of someone and I'd meet them or they'd call. If I was preoccupied with an issue, events would occur in rapid-fire order to define and clarify it. I began to learn that synchronicity was the universe's way of letting me know if I was on track. It was like the voice of the Great Spirit made manifest.

My explorations with the black cross crystal also continued to deepen. Whenever I meditated with it, which was always just before sleep, the hands would come to me in the night and massage me. They were like the hands of an invisible friend.

Then one night I felt one of the hands stroking my own hand, which was lying palm up on the bed. I had the sudden thought that if I grabbed the invisible hand, maybe I would find out who or what it was. So I did. But when I grabbed, the hand slipped away, leaving my palm empty. The hands never came back after that, no matter how much I meditated with the crystal. Maybe they were telling me that if I tried to grasp and hold onto something spiritual, I would lose it. I needed to let it move freely through my life; I needed to trust.

Thus did the drawings continue to flow through me, as my art became increasingly known and requested by different native groups. I never knew exactly how they would turn out. My joy came in the process of letting them reveal themselves. The only essentials were the initial vision or spark of inspiration . . . and trust.

I was intrigued by Michelangelo's concept of sculpting. He believed that the finished sculpture was already one of God's creations preexisting within the unhewn stone. His job was simply to remove the excess stone. Similarly, the native sculptor asks the raw wood or rock, "What is it that you wish for me to help you show?" I strove to approach my art in the same way. And in like fashion, my art became a parable for my life.

When I returned to visit Akwesasne in the autumn, Rarihokwats asked me to do the cover for the newspaper. He told me he wanted it to be something that expressed the strength of indigenous America.

I kept thinking about the words of Manitonguat, a Wampanoag Indian I had first met at Akwesasne. He explained to me that for his people, as well as for the Haudenosaunee and most natives of the Eastern Woodlands, the Earth was symbolized by a turtle. More specifically, most native people referred to North America as "Turtle Island." In Haudenosaunee legends, it was a giant turtle that emerged from the primordial waters. In allowing all the different life forms to root and settle upon its shell, it formed the continent, the sacred Earth, called Etenoha. Throughout much of Asia and other parts of the world, it is similarly believed that the Earth is a great, turtlelike being swimming through space.

The wisdom of this analogy is that the turtle is one of the most ancient and long-lived animals in existence. If killed, its heart continues to beat. Manitonguat called this heart Mettanokit, meaning "The Sacred Heart of Mother Earth." It was in this heart that I saw the eternal strength to which Rarihokwats was referring. A wounded and broken heart still had the power to transform itself into an instrument of healing. I decided that my drawing had to be a vision of Turtle Island. (See figure 8.)

I went back to Akwesasne again in midwinter with the promised drawing. What had come through was an image of the many faces of the native nations, animal as well as human, on the back of a turtle.

I had also discovered that the shell of a turtle always grows in thirteen sections. Some indigenous traditions say this represents the different groupings of people on the continent. I saw a parallel here to the Judeo-Christian tradition of twelve tribes or twelve Apostles united in some manner by a thirteenth element. It was clear to me that the thirteenth element for indigenous America was the children, the future generations. So in the center of the turtle shell, I drew the face of a child.

It was in May of 1977 that I actually got to meet many of the different native peoples of Turtle Island. Rarihokwats had organized an eclectic touring group called "The White Roots of Peace," inspired by the ancient Haudenosaunee teachings. (The word *white* referred to the light that emanated from the roots.) The group was comprised of indigenous Guatemalans of Mayan descent, indigenous Mexicans of Aztec descent, and indigenous people of North America (both the United States and Canada) from many different native nations. There were more than fifty people in all.

The White Roots of Peace traveled to schools, community centers, and reservations across the continent, teaching and performing, so as to increase consciousness about native spiritual ways. I agreed to coordinate their presentations in the Amherst area, where I knew they would be well received. But their visit was not without surprises.

Toward the end of their stay, we threw a community potluck dinner to honor them. We had been given permission to use Amherst College's Alumni Hall and facilities to host the event. About half an hour before our guests were to arrive, one of the students working with me came running out of the kitchen with a plate in her hands. She was panic-stricken. "Jim!" she said. "Have you seen these plates? We can't serve them food on these!"

She was right. The plates were rimmed with a repeating design that depicted Lord Jeffrey Amherst on his horse. He was holding a gun, which was pointed at two feathered Indians running away through the forest.

I asked my friend to please hurry out and buy two hundred paper plates, unecological though it was. By the time the White Roots of Peace and other guests arrived, we were fortunately ready to serve them without the embarrassment of Amherst's cruel history staring them in the face.

But I didn't want to hide it, either. So after dinner I told the story about Amherst, including what we had just discovered. Then I passed a plate around for everyone to see. We all agreed that it was outrageous. The fact that people would still eat off these plates helped to reinforce a blindness that was ultimately damaging to all human society.

I later discovered that the plates in the Alumni Hall were all that survived from a dining set once used by the entire student body. In the early seventies, some students protesting racism broke into the dining hall and smashed nearly all the plates. After numerous meetings with the college administration, I finally got them to agree that even the remaining plates should be removed from use. It was a small victory. I didn't get the town or the school to change its name, but at least they budged a little. Now, just maybe, we could eat in peace.

Later that spring Nemattanew invited me to visit him and his relatives. He explained that many Powhatans had migrated north into the Delaware Valley over the past two centuries. Consequently, some of them lived in Philadelphia, while others lived across the Delaware River in Camden or more rural parts of New Jersey. Between this visit and my time with Ycllow Robe in Queens, whatever stereotyped images I had held of American Indians wearing buckskin and living in tipis had long since passed. Something far more profound and wonderful had taken their place.

The first thing Nemattanew wanted to know was what more I had found out about my name. I told him that my father said my grandparents had come from a village in Poland called Kotsk. My more distant ancestors had lived deep in the forest, where it was their responsibility to protect the animals and the trees. From this work they had gotten their name, Keepers of the Woods. I was extremely excited when I heard this, because it made me feel that there really was a connection between me and my ancestors. I saw that my work in this life was in many ways a continuation of the work they had done. I couldn't understand why my father had never told me about my name before. But when I brought up the point, he simply responded, "You never asked."

"He's right," said Nemattanew emphatically. "You can't expect your elders to tell you everything they know. You have to show them that you care."

"He told me something else, too," I said. "He told me there was another way to translate our name. *Beren* also means "bear," so *Berenholtz* could also be interpreted as "Bear of the Woods.""

"I thought so," said Nemattanew, this time with a big smile. "In fact, I suspected all along that you were bear clan."

"I am?"

"Of course you are. So am I. So is Rarihokwats. That's what connects us. In the old ways of the native people here, even if you were from different tribes or nations, being from the same clan made you like relatives, part of the same family."

"But what does it mean to be bear clan?" I asked.

"The bear is like the lord of the forest to us," answered Nemattanew. "He's the biggest and most powerful. And the bear is much like a human being. It can eat almost anything, it can stand on its hind legs, and its tail is very small. When a bear is standing, it almost looks like a big man. For these and other reasons, the bear is like the counterpart of the human being in the animal world. You showed this recognition yourself by placing bear and human opposite each other in our tribal symbol. It is this parallel relationship that made the bear an especially important animal to our medicine people. By uniting their consciousness with that of the bear, they could communicate with the rest of creation."

"Do you think my ancestors were doing that in the forests of Poland?"

"I suspect they did, Keeper of the Woods. Maybe you will have to go there yourself to find out."

For the next two weeks, I stayed at the offices of the little cultural center in rural New Jersey that Nemattanew had established for his people. It felt good to see the design I had made for them printed and being used. But this was only the beginning. In the months and years ahead, I would come to visit the Powhatan on many occasions—and eventually come to live with them. I would work closely with Nemattanew as an artist, writer, and advisor. I would help him to defend native burial rights, to strengthen toxic waste laws, and eventually to win back more than three hundred acres of land from the U.S. government for the first Indian reservation in New Jersey. These victories were relatively small; nevertheless, they were tangible and deeply significant for the Powhatan and other local native people.

As word of Nemattanew's success began to spread, he became a leader in the struggle for Native American sovereignty. This was particularly true among the Eastern Indian nations, many of whom were not federally recognized. In helping Nemattanew bring their representatives into council, I saw once again the spiritual roots of the Great Tree of Peace seeking to find expression through a sacred union. And as the Tuscarora medicine man Mad Bear had told me one evening after council, there were prophecies that such a union would be inspired in these times by a native leader of the central Atlantic coast. (See figure 1.)

Interestingly, Nemattanew came from the Rappahannock Nation of the Powhatan, whose original lands included the very area now occupied by Washington, D.C. I often wondered how the United States might be affected if it could be proven that its capital had been built on stolen land guaranteed in treaty to another nation.

But for now, the base of the Powhatan Renape Nation, as Nemattanew called his new confederation, was at the place of Rankokus, the "Land of Living Stars" in rural New Jersey. Here a new cultural center would be established, much larger than before. Plans were set in motion for the building of a traditional village, and Nemattanew sent me out to Rankokus to envison how it might look.

Nemattanew also dreamed that certain ancient but only dimly remembered music, dances, and ceremonies would return to his people, and he asked me to go to Rankokus to try to retrieve them in their "seed" forms. I struggled to accept my role in all this. I had started growing up as "a nice Jewish boy from Queens," but somewhere along the way, I had taken a few unusual turns. Now before me were some equally unusual responsibilities. I could not let my doubts get the better of me, so I sought the council of Rarihokwats. Certainly he had faced similar challenges.

Rarihokwats's answer was simple: I had no need to put any artificial limits on my reality or self-definition. This was the game of society. I only needed to be "in the moment" and respond to each moment with the truth that came from my own core.

"But Rarihokwats," I said, "how can I be true to the process of remembering ceremonies from a time and culture that are not my own?"

"As Nemattanew has reminded you, you have been given special gifts for such tasks," he said. "Now you are being asked to use them. So I will share with you a secret that may help you.

"All forms that have existed in the past continue to exist as energy in the present," Rarihokwats went on. "With knowledge, we can access this energy and translate it into form again. What is required is to contact the guardian spirit of the past form. Whether you are talking about a specific musical tradition, a dance ritual, or any sacred ceremony, all of these things have a unique guardian spirit. These spirits continue to live even after the forms die. They may be sleeping, but they are still alive.

"If you can demonstrate your sincere interest and you are ready to listen and observe, you may be able to wake them up. Then these spirits will guide you to fill in the missing details."

I took the words of Rarihokwats to heart and returned to Rankokus. I told Nemattanew I needed to be alone there. I went into the forest and sat among the trees. I listened to the songs of the birds. I began to find the teachers I was looking for by being still and quiet while in the company of nature. The results were not automatic but gradual and often subtle. I felt good because I knew that there was no middle person for my learning. I was going directly to nature, the same source that all native peoples have gone to in seeking to know the mysteries of the universe.

I am walking back down the trail from Rankokus and come upon a turtle. I watch it for a long time, which is easy because it moves so slowly. Suddenly I have a brilliant image in my mind's eye, like a glowing, green orb that is slowly turning. As I see it more clearly, the image becomes a four-headed turtle. I have the immediate feeling that it is the symbol of Rankokus, the Land of Living Stars. I *know* it in my body.

At the same time, I also know that this is a symbol of my life. The heads of the turtle are pointing to the Four Directions, forming a cross as they connect with one circular body. They are telling me that I will journey to the Four Directions of the Earth. They are telling me that I have many sacred things to do and learn in each of these directions. They are saying that in this way I will find wholeness in my life, by uniting the different directions within me. [See figure 6.]

I was certain what the turtle was showing me was true, because already my life was unfolding this way. In November of 1977, when Rarihokwats returned to Amherst on another tour, he showed me how I was naturally following a journey to the Four Directions. He revealed how my quest had begun with a journey of introspection, traveling west with the wilderness group. It had continued as I journeyed north to Harney Peak to directly encounter the wisdom of Black Elk's teachings. From there, the appearance of the Morning Star told me that I was ready to journey east and learn the principles of peacemaking, such as Rarihokwats had shared with me through the teachings of the Great Tree.

"But wait, Rarihokwats," I said, "I thought Harney Peak was supposed to be the center of the universe, yet you're telling me I went there to connect with the north. Which is true?"

"They're both true, Jim, and that is the beautifully paradoxical nature of life that you must learn to appreciate. In each direction there is a center that is *the center* for the people who live there. For the Lakota, in the north, it is Harney Peak. For the Haudenosaunee, in the east, it is where the Peacemaker planted the Great Tree.

"These truths are not contradictory, for all aspects of what we call the Medicine Wheel are actually present in each direction. Every place on Earth is in some way a microcosm of the whole universe. Without going anywhere, you can experience that entire universe if you want to. However, some of us whose lives are full of movement have the special blessing to experience the universe not just metaphorically but physically."

"Does that mean I have a trip coming up?" I said with a grin.

"I think so, younger brother."

"Where might that be?" I asked.

"Where do you feel most strongly called to go?" Rarihokwats countered.

"Guatemala. The Guatemalans with the White Roots of Peace invited me to come stay with them. I've always been drawn to that part of the world, but now it's very strong."

"You see, Jim, you already have the answer. It's time for you to journey to the south, to the land of the Maya. There you will have lessons involving your youth and innocence. You will learn about ceremony and sacred architecture. You will connect with the power of the plants. You will feel the Earth spirit in a new way, and your body will start to change."

"How do you know all these things, Rarihokwats?"

"Because it is natural law," he said. "Each direction has its properties. In the north you deal most with the mind, in the east with the spirit, in the south with the body, and in the west with the emotions. Each of these directions has an elemental force to which it is connected: fire in the east, earth in the south, water in the west, and air in the north. Because you are a creative person, your creative lessons and involvements will vary according to which direction you are in.

"In the feeling place of the west, you are most connected to your music. You haven't even begun to discover how much is really there for you. In the mind place of the north, you are busy as the writer and researcher, creating works like your show about the Ghost Dance. In the spirit place of the east, from whence come visions, you become the visual artist, the painter. Look at all the art you've been doing for the native people of the East.

"So when you go to the body place of the south, you will develop new powers and new ways to express yourself. You don't have to believe what I'm telling you. Just watch and see what happens. And always remember, you may have to go back to the same direction many times before you are able to fully receive and integrate what it has to offer you."

Rarihokwats could not have been more perceptive, as I increasingly came to appreciate in later years. In my journeys around the Medicine Wheel, there were always new levels to be touched upon in each direction. So it was not entirely surprising when, many years later, on a return visit to the East, the Seneca elder Yahwehnode honored me with a new name: Hayá Doha—"He Who Paints the Truth."

THE SACRED TWINS

SOUTH

I felt like I was in heaven looking down upon a pristine Earth. The waters glistening with early morning sunlight almost touched the radiant blue sky. Only the three massive volcanoes that embraced the far side of the lake prevented it from flooding into the abyss beyond the horizon. Never had I been anyplace where I could so clearly see the curvature of the Earth. I wanted to fly, to lift off from my airy perch and glide right down to Atitlan, the sacred lake of the Maya.

The bus began its piercing honk, letting us know that our time at this lookout was finished. As we continued, the road curved and climbed toward the village of Chichicastenango, in the heart of the Guatemalan highlands. There, brightly clad people of every imaginable color filled the streets, and the smoke of *kopal* incense wafted on the air. As we strolled through the festive marketplace, I told my friend Hilario that my first views of his country made it very hard for me to imagine that the horrors of Panzos were actually so close in time and space.

This was early July of 1978. Just a few weeks before, well over one hundred Kekchi Maya had been shot down by the Guatemalan army in the village of Panzos for protesting the forced appropriation of their traditional farmlands by developers searching for oil and nickel deposits. The pictures of dead bodies being carted away in trucks reminded me of scenes from the Holocaust, of photos from the aftermath of Wounded

Knee, of the all-too-familiar history of people who become the victims of genocide.

Hilario knew well enough the grief inherent in his country's searing contradictions. A gentle man in his late twenties, he, too, had come from a small Mayan village. Our paths had first crossed on his White Roots of Peace visit to Amherst. During that visit, I had befriended not only Hilario but many other traditional Maya from different communities. I had followed this root so that I could be with the Maya and learn the teachings of the south.

Now, with Hilario as my guide, the journey had begun. "This afternoon," he said in his broken English, "we will go to visit Don Adrian in Ketzaltenango. He asked especially to see you."

As bus changes would have it, we did not arrive until early evening, and I was concerned about our lack of promptness. But I soon realized that in Guatemala, such delays were to be expected.

Don Adrian, whom I had also met at Amherst, was a delightful old man of tremendous vitality and humor. As he was one of the most respected elders of the Quiché Maya, I was surprised to find him living in a small, rundown apartment all by himself. I had pictured him in more of a village setting or at least in the company of an appreciative community. Not so.

Perhaps that made him all the more happy to see us. He welcomed us with avid enthusiasm, almost dancing around his apartment as we entered. He stood five feet high at the most, his hair combed forward into an odd sort of tail that pointed to the center of his forehead. His eyes sparkled whenever he smiled, which was frequently. He was like a little elf, playful and good-natured. But I already knew from his visit to Amherst that behind his childlike innocence was a reservoir of great wisdom.

Don Adrian brought us some tea made with a strange herb. He said he'd picked it in the mountains not far from town. The taste was somewhat bitter but not unpleasant. He kept looking at me and grinning with his eyebrows raised high as I sipped the tea. This made me a bit nervous, so I decided to try out my fledgling Spanish, telling him how pleased I was to see him.

"O, *muy bien, muy bien!*" he said then and every other time I tried to speak in Spanish. Fortunately, Hilario was there to translate. Don Adrian told us that we had arrived at a very happy time for him, because he had recently completed work on a book that had involved a lifetime of research.

It was his translation from the original Quiché language of the Mayan Book of Time, which he called the "Pop Wuj." Hilario explained that I was probably more familiar with the name Popol Vuh, but that Don Adrian was very particular about the proper spelling and pronunciation of the ancient words.

I asked Hilario to convey to Don Adrian that I had heard of the Mayan Book of Time before, but that I knew very little about it. I would be more than happy to know anything he felt inclined to share with me. Don Adrian responded that it was very important for me to know the Book of Time because it was the sacred treasure of Siwan Tinamit.

"What's that?" I asked.

"It's the true name of the land now called Guatemala," he responded. "As you are here, you must know about these things. The Pop Wuj came to us through our ancestors and was spoken for many, many generations before it was finally written down. It is so old that it goes back even beyond our first emergence on the land of Siwan Tinamit."

The Pop Wuj, Don Adrian explained, tells the story of the creation and ordering of the universe. It reveals the divine, dual nature of reality that is present in all things. In the beginning, all was quiet and still. Floating upon the primordial waters was Lord Tepeu Gucumatz, the *Ketzal* Serpent, wrapped in precious feathers of green and blue. Then the Creator Hurakan, Heart of Heaven, spoke through Tepeu Gucumatz, sending the inspiration to make life become manifest.

"It is said that Hurakan is known by the name of One Leg—a most curious expression," said Don Adrian. "The hidden meaning of this is that Hurakan is neither male nor female, but both. Thus does the power to bring forth the magnificence of life lie within our concept of Hurakan. Only such a one could be the Creator."

I was extremely intrigued as Don Adrian explained this concept. Only the month before, Nemattanew had told me virtually the same thing: that the Powhatan understanding of the Creator was of one being who was simultaneously male and female.

Don Adrian continued, explaining that the Pop Wuj tells of the Four Creations and of many attempts to engender a perfect expression of the human form. First it was attempted through clay, then through wood, but both failed. Then in the Third Creation, the Hero Twins, Hunahpu and Xbalanke, were created through a magical insemination with saliva. They, too, expressed a duality as the earthly ambassadors of Hurakan, the force of goodness. Through many adventures, they finally overcame the cruel powers of the lords of the underworld. Then Hunahpu and Xbalanke ascended to the heavens to become the eternal givers of light, the sun and the moon.

"In the Fourth Creation," said Don Adrian, "at last the human being was made manifest in the perfected image desired by the Creator. This was done with *ixim*: corn. So were our ancestors known as the 'men and women of corn'; and so are we, their children, the 'people of corn.' From the first four men and the first four women we were born. From four, the duality of duality. So was it done with corn.

"Still today this sacred food is our body," Don Adrian continued. "We eat it, and it becomes our flesh. It grows in the four sacred colors—red for the east, yellow for the south, black for the west, and white for the north. So do we take all the powers of the Earth into us when we eat the holy corn of our mothers and fathers. Today we can see that the four races of humanity are also red, yellow, black, and white. They reflect the four colors of corn by which the first four men and women were made."

Don Adrian spoke as well of the Four Cosmic Trees that hold up the arc of the heavens. Each of these, he said, is a sacred ceiba, a silk-cotton tree called a *yaxche*, and each is colored according to its direction. He also said that the unity of the Four Directions is represented by the Mayan cross, a cross with all four "roads" of equal length. This cross lies at the base of an enormous pyramid formed by the four quarters of the sky. Where the quarters meet at the top is the House of Hurakan.

"To reach the House of Hurakan, you must climb—one step at a time," Don Adrian said. "For this reason we built our temples in the form of pyramids with steps, to reflect our vision of the universe. Thus do we call the pyramid Oâm Ja, which means 'Staircase House.' When you stand before Oâm Ja, you will see the duality of which I speak. I hope that Hilario is planning to take you soon so you can experience it for yourself."

Hilario assured Don Adrian that he intended to take me to certain pyramids, and that I would later be traveling on my own to many Mayan pyramid centers. "Good," Don Adrian responded. "When you are there, you must stand facing the center of Oâm Ja, with your spine aligned to the staircase. You will feel how the right and left sides of your body are connected to the right and left sides of the pyramid, and you will climb the staircase to the top where the two sides meet. In this way you will begin to understand things that no one can explain in words."

I was fascinated by what Don Adrian had to say; yet all the while he spoke, I found myself growing more and more tired. I had a hard time just keeping my head up. Don Adrian filled my cup with some more tea, then asked if he could see my hands. I held them out. He pressed around my palms and mumbled to himself.

"Don Adrian says that you have a very sensitive nature," Hilario told me, "and that it's important for you to get plenty of sleep while you're here in this country. He says that you can see many things, but there is a lot about yourself that you still don't know. He says you are like a bright star."

Suddenly Don Adrian pushed his left thumb strongly into the palm of my right hand, and I jerked up in my seat. It felt like an electrical shock. Then he took his right thumb and began to press it into the center of my forehead. Hilario told me to close my eyes, which I did. I felt like I was on water, floating somewhere, seeing sparks of light in the darkness of my mind.

Then I heard a high, whistling sound, so I opened my eyes again. Don Adrian was looking right at me with his elfin smile. His eyes seemed to flash for a moment, then the sound stopped. He told me he was very happy that I had come to see him and that he hoped I would return again soon.

I thanked him and said I felt wide awake now. I asked him what he had done. He didn't answer, saying only that it was important for me to get a good night's sleep. Hilario and I said good-bye and went back to our hotel room a few blocks away. I was still wide awake when I got into bed, but as soon as I put my head down on the pillow, I fell into a deep sleep.

The next morning Hilario took me to the offices of *Ixim*, a newspaper based in Ketzaltenango that defended indigenous people's rights. There we met with one of the editors named Alberto to discuss the political situation of the Maya in Guatemala. I wanted to know more about what was going on, since I was in a new country in the middle of an obviously tense situation.

"One of the things that is most difficult for us," Alberto said, "is that our people are being forced to participate in their own destruction. Many of the soldiers who shot the villagers in Panzos a few weeks ago were themselves Mayan villagers. The army just goes in and grabs young men off the street. Some of them are barely teenagers. They take away their native clothes and give them a uniform in its place. They put a gun in their hands and say, 'Here, go kill these people.' If they refuse, they risk being beaten, imprisoned, or even murdered. You can see for yourself that this is a very militarized state."

"Yes, it is true," I agreed. "When I arrived in Guatemala City, there was a soldier with a gun on almost every street corner."

"Exactly," said Alberto. "This tells us that our government is afraid of its own people. And why should that be? Because 1 percent of the population owns 80 percent of the land. But there is no way that can continue forever. Without land, we have no life. We need it to grow our corn. This is why we call our newspaper *Ixim*. It is the basis of our survival, and for us it is sacred."

"Last night Don Adrian was telling me that the Maya believe they were created from corn," I said.

"Even the word itself tells us this," responded Alberto. "*Ix* means 'womb' in Maya, and Imix is the Earth. The cycle from *Imix* to *Ix* to *ixim* is eternal, because even when we die, we go back to *Imix* and our bodies become the fertilizer for *ixim*, which will feed our children."

I was amazed that one word could signify so much. After we left the offices of *Ixim* to continue our journey toward Huehuetenango, Hilario explained more of the intricacies of the Mayan language and expressed his disappointment that it was disappearing. "The missionaries and government teachers punish us if they hear us speaking in Maya," he said. "They call it a dialect. Yet as you can see, it is very highly developed."

Hilario also expressed his sadness that elders such as Don Adrian were living apart from the people who had most to learn from them. "We have to work so hard these days to preserve the knowledge of our ancestors. I fear that these elders are dying with their great knowledge. Each time we lose one of them, it is like a light has gone out. We become as children trying to find our way through a darkness that keeps growing."

"Doesn't Don Adrian come from a village?" I asked. "Someplace where he could teach others?"

"Yes, from a very beautiful place called San Francisco el Alto. He told me last night that he wants to take you there when you come back. But as for the people who live there, it is like everywhere else in Guatemala. The fabric of our lives has been broken. Most of the men have to leave their families to work on the plantations for months at a time, and the women are left alone with lots of children. Many die of malnutrition. Those who survive grow up increasingly influenced by a foreign value system. Western music and movies and television have found their way into even the most remote villages. The young people don't want to sing the old Mayan songs anymore. Everyone is just too busy trying to survive."

I knew that Hilario was right, and yet his description was only part of the picture. In spite of its problems, there was still a great deal of happiness in Guatemala. I could see it in the faces of the people, especially the children. In Guatemala the smiles were fuller and the laughter freer than in any country I had known. Perhaps simple joys were also a survival food, a source of strength like corn.

After checking into a little hotel in Huehuetenango, Hilario said he wanted to take me to a nearby place called Zakulea before the sun set. I followed him through many narrow streets until finally we came out on an open, grassy field. There, all around us, were groupings of small pyramid and temple structures. As we walked around the site, Hilario told me that he used to come here when he was a boy, and at that time it was a very special and mysterious place. But then, he said, the United Fruit Company decided to reconstruct Zakulea. They brought in some archaeologists, who poured a layer of white cement over the temples and tried to make them look "nice" for the tourists. In doing so, they trapped the spirits of the stones inside. "Now it's not so easy to feel the power as it used to be," he said.

Again I could sense Hilario's great sadness. Deciding to wait for another time to try Don Adrian's pyramid exercise, I suggested we go back to the hotel. As we turned around and started walking, the sky cracked with thunder and a heavy rain began to fall.

The next morning before dawn, we squeezed into a funky old bus with twice as many people as there were seats. Women with chickens clutched underneath their *huipiles*, men with enormous sacks of flour strung on their backs, crying babies, and the incessant blaring of ranchero music on the radio made the ride a genuinely "human" experience. We were destined for a tiny village in the highlands called Todos Santos, home to one of the most traditional Mayan communities in Guatemala, including a number of marimba players I had befriended at Amherst.

As the sky gradually lightened, the bus climbed through the thick morning mist until we came out onto a desolate, windswept altiplano almost devoid of trees. Our passage across this eerie terrain seemed endless. Every bump in the rocky road felt like a hammer hitting my North American stomach, which was starting to succumb to the unfamiliar microorganisms of the South.

Finally, though, the road began to drop again, and we entered a lush green valley with terraced hillsides, illuminated in patches by the sun breaking through the clouds. Soon I could see clusters of homes with mud walls and thatched roofs. Streams were running everywhere, both freely and channeled through carved wooden irrigation troughs. People were scattered about, sitting by their homes or walking along the many dirt paths, all dressed in colorful cotton clothes. An atmosphere of harmonious order and tranquillity pervaded everything in view. I felt like I was entering a pre-Columbian Shangri-la.

In the center of the village, the bus stopped and let everyone out. We were immediately surrounded by an explosion of color. Scores of local men wearing bright red pants with stripes running lengthwise crowded around the bus. Nearby stood a group of men in dark red ponchos with black pants. Beyond them was an entire family wearing small straw hats with blue leather bands. Hilario pointed out that clothing design was an important way for people in the highlands to distinguish precisely which village a person was from. It struck me that birds in the forest must use similar means of color and pattern differentiation to tell each other apart. To see such organic wisdom so beautifully adapted and still functioning among human beings was a true delight.

Hilario guided me down a path that led to a house at the bottom of a hill. There he called out to announce his presence, and our friend Jacinto appeared at the door. "*Hola, hermanos,*" he said, and embraced us. "*Pásale, por favor, pásale.*"

Jacinto's home was quite dark inside, save for a shaft of light coming through a small square window. In the center of the house was a fire pit. Steam rose from a large earthen pot of boiling black coffee as Jacinto's wife, Amalia, rolled *masa* (corn dough) in her hands, forming it into tortillas. A little girl of about three, who appeared to be their daughter, was breaking sticks to feed the fire.

Soon Jacinto's neighbors were coming to the door, curious to see who his guests were. They were all welcomed in, and before long there was a big group of people waiting to shake my hand. Jacinto placed a large pot of black beans beside the coffee to warm them, and everyone sat down on small wooden stools around the fire.

As I looked around at the gleaming eyes and high cheekbones that caught the light of the fire, I was reminded of my recurring childhood dream of being in a tipi with my relatives. The same warm mood pervaded this home. The sound of people speaking in Maya was somehow comforting. That I could not understand them was unimportant; I felt at ease here among my friends. The food was rich in flavor. I could taste the Earth's sweetness, and also its wildness.

After we had finished eating, the mood in the house became very serious. Jacinto was talking, gesturing excitedly with his hands, and occasionally there were exclamations from the others. Finally Hilario turned to me and said, "Jacinto is very upset because he just found out yesterday that his brother died."

"What happened?" I asked. "Was he very old?"

"Only thirty. He had a wife and four children. Over the past two months, he'd been away from Todos Santos because he was working on the *fincas*, the plantations by the Pacific Coast where they grow cotton, sugar cane, and bananas. The conditions on the fincas are very bad for the workers, and Jacinto's brother had been protesting them for a long time. Yesterday Jacinto received news that his brother was killed in an accident on the finca. But he doesn't believe it; he thinks he was murdered."

Jacinto stopped Hilario and indicated that he wanted to talk to me directly. Hilario translated:

"Please tell the people back in the United States to stop sending all their chemicals here. We've heard that whatever has been made illegal there, they send to us. For many years now, they have been sending airplanes over the fincas, spraying DDT while the workers are down below in the fields. It's making us sick. Some people have died from it. My brother Clemente was trying to organize the workers to stop the airplanes with the DDT from taking off. Now they've killed him, too!"

Jacinto suddenly burst into tears. I told Hilario to please tell him how sorry I was, but Hilario said it was probably best if we left and came back another time.

We walked up the path toward the center of the village. When we got there, a big flatbed truck was loading up with men. I asked Hilario where they were going, and he answered sullenly, "To the fincas."

"But why?" I asked. "Why would they want to leave Todos Santos?"

Hilario explained that years ago the people used to farm many other lands but that gradually the ranchers and plantation owners took them away, causing a shortage of food. When the big plantations started up along the coast, word was spread that they needed workers and would pay well. The poor villagers had little choice.

Many men, he said, began to leave for weeks and months at a time to work on the fincas. It was very hard for the villagers, who were not well adapted to the hot, humid climate of the coast. Moreover, rent accrued for every night they slept on the hard floors of their workers' shacks, and they were charged for every meal. The companies kept records of everything they provided. Then when it came time for the workers to be paid, they showed them a bill and said, "You'll have to come back and work some more so you can get out of debt." Workers who refused to cooperate were turned over to the police.

"Under this system, nine out of ten men in Todos Santos do at least some work on the fincas each year," said Hilario. "I've seen them leaving on this truck as young as seven or eight years old. The ride takes fourteen hours, and everyone is crowded together like you see. They have to sleep standing up."

The next morning Hilario said he needed to see his family in Jakaltenango, a day's hike over the mountains. While he was gone, I stayed in Todos Santos with a friend of his named Fernando, whose family took me in as one of their own.

As a feeling of trust developed between myself and the villagers, they confided things in me that were normally not discussed with outsiders. I discovered, for instance, that many of them had had contact with Marxist guerrillas who hid out in the mountains. On occasion these guerrillas would come into the village to preach revolution and try to win converts. They played on the villagers' frustrations.

But no one I spoke to seemed to trust the guerrillas. They were perceived as one more form of outside interference interested only in using the Mayan people for their own political ends. And the guerrillas posed certain dangers, too. The villagers were afraid even to be seen talking with them, since government soldiers would periodically come through town in order to harass, beat, or even kill those who were suspect.

By the time I left Todos Santos, I no longer held my idyllic first impression, yet I had grown to love it. It was home to a peaceful people with a beautiful way of life and a will to endure the tests of time, however difficult or tragic.

I still had a few days before I needed to be back in Guatemala City to meet Hilario again, so I decided to return to Lake Atitlan. There, more than anywhere else in Guatemala, I had felt something mysterious and wondrous. It was this that compelled me to return.

My first night at the lake I stayed in Panajachel, a tourist town with an active international counterculture. The next day I looked for transport to the other side of the lake. There was none. Undaunted, I stuffed everything in my backpack and started walking down the road encircling the lake. No sooner had I put my thumb out than it began to rain . . . and rain . . . and rain. Finally a small pickup stopped. I told the two men in the cab that I was going to Santiago Atitlan, and the driver said he could take me only halfway. At that point, any ride was welcome, so I hopped in the back and off we went.

By the time we got to San Lucas Toliman, I was completely drenched. I thanked the men for the ride and started walking toward a flatbed truck that I had been told was heading for Santiago Atitlan. The truck was packed like a sardine can, full of locals on their way to the fincas. Just as I approached, it started to pull out, and all the guys began screaming for me to jump on. So I did. Everyone was laughing.

The flatbed had a frame with a tarp stretched over it to protect us from the rain, but it didn't work very well. Every time we hit a bump in the road, the accumulated water would come pouring off the tarp onto my head. That made all the guys laugh even more. The truck bounced to and fro with all of us squeezed together. Our clothes were as wet from sweat as from rain.

By the time we arrived in Santiago Atitlan, it was evening and not a thing in my pack was dry. I got a room at a small guest house by the lake and laid out all my clothes. In the morning they were still wet. The only things I could possibly wear were rubbers for my feet, rain pants, and a rain poncho. Thus peculiarly attired, I set out to make contact with the locals.

Fortunately, I had been given a couple of contacts by an anthropologist in Guatemala City, one of whom was a North American painter and musician named Miguel. I was greeted by Miguel's wife, Imelda, a beautiful Mayan woman in traditional dress. She invited me in, then went into another room to call Miguel. I could hear him speaking with her in Maya. A few minutes later, he entered wearing a traditional village costume that matched his wife's, but with a distinctly nontraditional head of curly blond hair.

When Miguel saw me in synthetic clothes, he burst out laughing. Imelda couldn't resist the temptation to join him, and I felt so ridiculous that I also began to laugh.

Finally we calmed down enough to speak. I told Miguel how I had heard of him and explained that I was very interested in learning more about Mayan music. At first he was cautious, but when he discovered that we had a mutual friend in Rarihokwats, his whole attitude changed.

He walked to the corner of the room and pulled out a huge, dark log that had been carved with intricate designs. "We call this *tunkul*," he said, "or in the Aztec language, *teponaztli*. This is the *real* Mayan marimba." Then he grabbed a stick and began to strike the tongues of wood carved into the body of the log. The instrument produced deep tones that varied slightly in pitch and resonated through my entire body.

"Are these instruments still used here?" I asked.

"Officially, no," Miguel said, "but secretly, yes." I waited for him to continue, but he only gave a hint of a smile and remained silent. His mysteriousness only heightened my curiosity.

"How did you get here, Miguel? How did you become so involved with this village?"

"We all have our destinies, I suppose," he said. "Mine is here. How I got here is really of no concern to you, is it?"

"Yes, I want to know."

Miguel hesitated and looked away, as if he were looking into a distant and perhaps painful part of his life. Then he told me he had grown up on the Santo Domingo Indian Pueblo in New Mexico, where his mother had been a schoolteacher. Though Caucasian, he was raised with the Indian children speaking Tiwa. He didn't even speak English until he was ten.

Miguel said his mother greatly admired the Indian culture and did all she could to promote it in her classes. When the officials from the Bureau of Indian Affairs told her she had to teach the regular curriculum, that made her even more determined. She worked her way into a powerful position in the state educational system and began to institute a lot of changes. Shortly after that, she was found dead.

"Everybody knew she'd been killed, but we couldn't prove it," Miguel said. "The Pueblo Indians loved her. They held a special funeral ceremony, and two big rainbows formed in the sky. The Indians said it was my mom up there. Nobody needed to prove it."

After that, Miguel said, his life was filled with turmoil. People didn't like his broken English, and he got into a lot of fights. Finally he traveled through Mexico to Guatemala, where he stayed on to help the survivors of the big earthquake that hit Chimaltenango. And there he met Imelda, who brought him back to her village. Eventually they were married and he was adopted by the village.

"So now I'm here with her raising our little baby," he said. "When I'm lucky, if she lets me, I do my painting and play music with the guys."

Imelda, who knew enough English to realize that Miguel was teasing, gave him an affectionate shove. He laughed.

Miguel said he would see about inviting me to his rehearsal that night. I said I would like that. "But why is the music so secret?" I asked.

"See that altar behind you?"

I turned around to see an almost life-sized wooden carving of a man dressed in colored robes with numerous hats piled on top of his head. Surrounding him was a wide variety of ceremonial objects.

"That's our altar to our spiritual protector, Maximón," said Miguel. "We honor him through our music. He has two wives. One of them is Mayan, the other is Spanish. Maximón symbolizes the marriage of these two worlds, and it's a happy marriage. He is also worshiped in three other places here in Guatemala, but Santiago Atitlan is his center."

Miguel explained that periodically Maximón manifests as a human being and comes to the village to deliver prophecies. He said that the last time Maximón appeared, he predicted a kind of Mayan renaissance in the last decade of this century, a return to the "Indian Magnificence."

"Meanwhile," he added, "there is a lot of repression here, and much of it comes from the church. The priests don't like the Maya worshiping Maximón; they think it's pagan. They'd rather have them worshiping statues of the saints, although they are merely stand-ins for the old gods. Anyway, Christianity is politics here, so we play our music in secret to avoid trouble."

"Actually," I said, "not many people wanted to help when I mentioned your name. A couple of them said you were a sorcerer."

Miguel laughed. "I know. Everybody here is afraid because it's such a powerful place. The Maya consider Lake Atitlan to be the navel of the world. And this particular village is known as the center of sorcery throughout Central America. One thing's for sure: a lot of people here do sorcery through animals. Sometimes the battles can get pretty fierce."

I could see that Miguel was quite serious. I didn't know how to respond.

"Look," he said, "I need to do some things. Why don't you come back here around six, and I'll let you know if it's OK for you to come to the rehearsal."

"Fine," I responded. "But before I go, have you heard of a sculptor named Andres?"

Miguel looked very displeased. "Yeah, what about him?"

"I'd like to visit him, but I don't know where he lives."

"I don't think it's a good idea for you to visit Andres," Miguel said.

"Why not?" I retorted.

"Believe me, there's nothing for you there." But before I left, he reluctantly pointed out the direction to Andres's house.

I suspected there was some friction between Miguel and Andres. All the same, I wanted to meet the sculptor. After asking a few people, I found the name of the right street. But when I got to the corner and began walking up the street, a small black dog jumped out and started barking at me. I tried to get past it, but it bared its teeth and growled as though it would attack.

I retreated to the opposite corner to wait. The dog went back to its corner and sat quietly. In the meantime, many people turned and walked up the same street without incident.

Once the dog appeared to be asleep, I crossed to make my way up to Andres's. This time the dog growled even more viciously than before. It seemed ridiculous that a stupid little dog could keep me from my business.

After another five-minute wait, I made a final attempt. It was hopeless. The dog seemed determined to keep me off that street. And strangely, when I walked past it in any other direction, it did nothing. I decided to take this as a warning to forget about Andres and go back to the guest house.

When I got to my room, I was happy to find dry clothes. I changed from my clammy raingear and at six returned to Miguel's house. Miguel informed me that the rehearsal had been canceled so that the religious brotherhood of Maximón could perform a healing ceremony for an ailing woman. However, Miguel said I could come to the ceremony as his personal guest, as long as I was completely respectful. I assured him I would be.

After the other musicians had arrived, we all walked to a remote part of the village and the site of the ceremony. Following introductions, an elder walked to the center of the room and began to chant monotonously in Maya, all the time lighting and placing white candles on the floor. After more than two hours of chanting, hundreds of candles illuminated the room. I could hardly sit still, but I kept reminding myself what a unique opportunity it was.

Finally the musicians began to play a song. Meanwhile, some other men came up and offered bottles of beer to all the musicians, including me. I tried to explain that I didn't drink, but they didn't understand.

"Take the beer!" Miguel whispered loudly in my ear. I told him I couldn't, that it was a lifestyle choice. He insisted that if I didn't drink, the people would be insulted and that it would reflect badly on him. I reiterated that I couldn't, and he became visibly angry.

Finally the elder guided a sad-looking woman into the room, and the musicians began to play another song. The chords and words were very repetitive, adding to the trancelike atmosphere in the room. The elder walked over to a large trunk behind the woman, lifted out a heavy blanket, and covered the woman completely with it, chanting all the while. After twenty minutes, he placed a second blanket over the first, still chanting. (Miguel explained that the blankets were the robes of the ancestors, some of them many hundreds of years old. "They carry healing power," he said.)

As the ceremony went on, the elder periodically placed more blankets on top of the ailing woman. I couldn't imagine how she could breathe. Occasionally the musicians switched to a new song. All this went on for hours. Meanwhile, both men and women kept offering us beers, which the musicians kept drinking and I kept refusing. To make matters worse, I kept nodding off; I was having a hard time staying awake.

Miguel continued to warn me that I was making a bad impression, and I kept telling him I was doing the best I could. Finally, when I just couldn't stay awake any longer, I whispered to Miguel that I had to go.

"Don't!" he pleaded. "You can't go till it's over!"

I told him I was sorry but I couldn't stay. I got up and quietly walked around the sides of the room toward the door. Then, well aware that everyone's eyes were on me, I opened the door and left.

Once outside, I felt much better. All I could think about was getting back to the guest house and into bed. I walked briskly down the deserted street, hoping I was taking the right turns. Occasionally a dog barked, but I just kept walking.

After a while, I realized that a couple of dogs were following me. I started walking faster. I heard other dogs barking as I passed other homes, and sometimes I saw them come out before I passed. Soon I got the feeling of more dogs nearby. I turned to see about eight of them following me. I kept walking, hoping I was getting near the guest house.

Then all the dogs started barking. I thought about running, but my better judgment told me that would be a mistake. I just kept walking at a brisk, steady pace.

When the guest house finally came into view, I glanced back to see a pack of at least twenty dogs barking and growling. They were less than a hundred feet behind and gaining fast. I dashed for the door, praying that it was unlocked. But when I got to it, my worst fear was realized.

As the dogs closed in, I started screaming and banging madly on the door. At six or seven feet, they prepared to attack. Then I heard the key in the door. When it swung open, I practically fell through as the dogs leaped up to get me. The owner, still half asleep, shut the door and looked at me in dismay. I apologized for waking him up, went straight to my room, and collapsed on the bed.

In spite of my late night, I woke up fairly early the next morning. I felt worn but anxious to get moving. I decided to take a hike out of town toward the volcano, where I figured I wouldn't have to deal with any people or dogs. As the trail climbed, I saw wonderful views of Santiago Atitlan and the entire lake. I felt relieved, back to my old self again. Then I stopped to rest under a tree.

Suddenly I got the funny feeling I was being watched. I looked up to see that the branch above me was hanging down low from the weight of a huge flock of black vultures. The tree was thick with them, and they were all staring right at me.

I jumped to my feet and started walking without looking back. Farther up the trail, I passed under another tree full of vultures. Then another fifty feet ahead, some vultures landed on the ground in front of me, flapping their enormous wings.

That's it, I thought. I've had it! I turned around and started walking back toward Santiago Atitlan. As soon as I got there, I went to my room, packed my things, and checked out as fast as I could. Within minutes, I was on a bus out of town.

On the long ride back to Guatemala City, I thought about what I had just been through. I wondered if I had made a mistake refusing to drink with the others during their ceremony. And who knows what energetic flows I might have broken by opening the door in the middle of the healing? The more I pondered, the more amazed I became at my own rigidity, already so well fixed at the young age of twenty-one. If nothing else, the dogs and vultures were certainly a mirror of my own fears of moving beyond boundaries of comfort and familiarity. I knew that unless I was willing to face them, those fears would chase me forever.

Reentering Guatemala City was a mild culture shock following my journey through the highlands. Billboards for all the big North American corporations and fast-food chains bordered the roads into town. Dealing with all the traffic and noise made me want to turn right around.

Fortunately, that was the plan. The next day, my college friend David flew into Guatemala. We rendezvoused at Hilario's house, and from there we caught a bus to the Mexican border, where we began our pilgrimage to the ancient jungle centers of the Maya. After we had descended into the tropical lowlands, our first stop was the magnificent ceremonial complex of Palenque, the place where the Mayan civilization of the Classic period reached its most refined expression.

David and I slept in hammocks at a jungle campground within a ten-minute walk of the ancient site. During the night I awoke to a primal roar that echoed through the trees—a roar that was accompanied by the sound of a million insects droning in eerie harmony. I roused David, telling him I thought I'd heard a jaguar, but he assured me it was howler monkeys.

At the first sign of light, we arose and began walking up a path beneath towering trees enshrouded in mist. The bizarre cries of a bottle bird cascaded from its hanging nest. Other species unknown to me began singing in anticipation of the sunrise.

We arrived at the entrance to the site while the guards were still asleep, so we quietly slipped past the gate. The path led to a large, thick-leaved tree, where we sat down between massive roots. At first only the bottom steps of the closest temples were visible; everything else was enshrouded in fog.

Gradually we were able to discern the silhouetted forms of the pyramids and temples. The initial impression was that of a two-dimensional world in tones varying from black to white. Then slowly the mist cleared, and one by one the structures were revealed in their full-color, three-dimensional splendor. Like an exquisite goddess gracefully removing her veils, Palenque made us wait, keeping us at every moment poised on the edge of ecstasy.

Never had I been to a place where natural and humanmade worlds appeared to be in such perfect equilibrium. Clear, sweet water flowed through a stream that divided the city into two sacred sectors. Hundreds of butterflies, nestled into cracks along the stone pathways, burst skyward like multicolored fireworks when we came near. The impeccable geometric order of the white limestone temples was balanced by the sensuous patterns of the tropical foliage. Palenque was the embodiment of harmony in every proportion and dimension, the essence of the "Indian Magnificence" that Maximón had prophesied would return.

Soon I stood before the Temple of Inscriptions, the greatest pyramid of Palenque. This was indeed Oâm Ja, the Staircase House, a microcosmic model of the universe. I did as Don Adrian had instructed and aligned my body to its center. I focused on feeling every line of my body connected to the corresponding lines of the pyramid. Then I began a slow ascent of the staircase to a temple with five entrances at the very top.

When I reached the top and entered the temple, I discovered a narrow passageway leading down into the core of the pyramid. I lit a small candle that I carried in my pack. As I descended the passageway, droplets of water slid along the ceiling and fell on my face. I walked carefully down the slippery steps until at last I came to a vaulted chamber. Within it was an enormous stone slab carved with exquisitely detailed and complex imagery. Though I did not understand the symbols, it was obvious that the slab had been the lid of a sarcophagus. I was standing inside a tomb.

Curiously, the feeling was not one of darkness but of light. I had the distinct sense that whoever had been buried here had been a highly enlightened being. I blew out my candle and sat in the silence, overcome with reverence. At last I began my ascent again, feeling my way up the steps. As I emerged into the summit temple once more, I could hear voices outside. I looked down to see that the tourists had arrived. Then I saw David at the bottom of the pyramid, waving.

I began walking down the steps to meet him, still focusing on my alignment to the pyramid, feeling the back of my spine connected to its core. In that moment I was struck with a profound realization, a knowing that virtually exploded through every cell of my body: The same harmonic proportions that existed in this structure also existed in me! The same passageways, the same steps, the same ascents and descents, even the same holy inner chamber—all were a part of my own being. I, too, was a pyramid. I, too, was a microcosm of the universe—a living, breathing model of all creation.

At the bottom of the pyramid, I asked David where he had been. He said he had gone to the three pyramid temples on the other side of the river, where he had met an old Maya. The man had told him that there used to be a beautifully carved stone panel in the middle of one of the temples, but that it had been cut out by archaeologists and taken to a museum in Mexico City. The man said the panel had borne a symbol known as the Cross of Palenque, which was actually an image of the Tree of Life that grows at the center of the universe. The tree, he said, grows through seven different heavens above the Earth, and at the top lives the Creator.

The Tree of Life symbolism was, of course, already very familiar to me, not only from various native North American traditions but from my own ancestry as a Keeper of the Woods. I told David that here at Palenque I had received a related teaching, in which I had been shown how my body was a model of the universe just like the pyramid. "Now I can see how it's also just like the tree," I said. "I think all these symbols and forms are trying to teach us how to reflect back to our own consciousness a perfected image of ourselves."

I asked David if the old man had said anything else. "Yes," he said. "He said he had dreamed that the panel with the Cross of Palenque was returned to its temple. When that happened, he said, this ancient center became alive again, just like it was in the time of his ancestors."

In the weeks that followed, David and I visited numerous other Mayan ceremonial centers nestled into the rain forests of Central America:

places like Tikal, Kopan, Kirigua—places of amazing sculptural and architectural achievement, places of natural magnificence, resounding with the chatter of spider monkeys and the calling of toucans. Each place had its own unique qualities, yet they all shared a common essence and a common language encoded in stone. It was this that made them Maya.

I felt even more at home in these ancient places than in the contemporary centers of indigenous culture. I was in my element here. I functioned differently, more like the person I felt I truly was. But how to bring that ancient spirit of my true self into the present? To add to my query, I could not consider my personal quest apart from the greater collective needs of transformation and liberation. If I, a foreigner, was so deeply touched by the ancient Maya, then what might be their potential to touch the hearts and minds of the peoples of Central America in the late twentieth century? Could the harmony of the past provide clues for healing the turmoil of the present?

These were the vital questions that I carried with me as I continued on my journey into the tiny country of El Salvador. There, thanks to a scholarship, I was to be part of a research team based at an ancient ceremonial center called Cihuatan. The group was combining archaeological and ecological studies to see how the lessons of the past might speak to the future.

Interestingly, the research group chose to approach this issue from a very different perspective than I had previously considered. They questioned not so much what might be learned from the achievements of the ancient Maya as what might be learned from their possible mistakes. Particularly, they sought to understand whether human-caused environmental problems had triggered the so-called Mayan Collapse. This term was based on the theory that following the ninth century A.D., the Mayan civilization went into a relatively dormant phase—and according to some, actually disappeared.

It is true that after this time, there was a dramatic and sudden decline in both the quality and quantity of art and architecture produced by the Maya. The scholarly explanations included popular revolt, militarization, starvation, agricultural failure, and overpopulation. Amazingly, each of these proposed causes were in fact the very real causes of the systemic collapse facing El Salvador when I visited in 1978.

Upon my arrival there, I discovered slogans calling for a popular uprising painted on buildings and bridges throughout the country. The director of our expedition predicted that revolution would break out within a matter of months. She said that the vanguard of this revolution were farmers who had been dispossessed of their land by the newly built Cerro Grande Dam, intended to provide electricity to the burgeoning capital of El Salvador.

Clearly, the roots of a Salvadoran revolution could be found in the use and ownership of the land. Cash crops such as sugar cane, bananas, cotton, coffee, and cattle occupied El Salvador's most fertile lands, forcing subsistence farmers onto marginal lands and seriously adding to problems of deforestation and erosion. What's more, the profits generated by cash crops went almost entirely to the wealthy elite and multinational corporations. Sadly, El Salvador's problems were exemplary of those of all Central America. And so I wondered if perhaps the archaeologists' theories of the "Mayan Collapse" were in part projections of a contemporary Western reality superimposed onto an ancient, non-Western reality. What were the indigenous explanations of the "Mayan Collapse"?

The Mayan people I knew in Guatemala all felt strongly that the Spanish had intentionally lied in their accounts of pre-Columbian civilizations. They said that the Spanish, in attempting to cover up their own barbarism, pretended that the Maya had already vanished by the time of Columbus. They even tried to attribute the outstanding achievements of Mayan civilization to other ethnic groups. And to make the Maya appear more savage and brutal than the conquistadors, the Spanish had grossly exaggerated the accounts of Mesoamerican human sacrifice. Still later, they said, archaeologists distorted interpretations of the complex esoteric temple imagery of the Maya (which in reality depicted humans at different levels of spiritual attainment), leading to the Eurocentric deduction that the Maya had kings, queens, and slaves.

According to the Maya I knew, their real history was this: They had not disappeared, nor had they gone dormant. They had simply changed their forms and locales of creative expression. The spiritual intent of a certain style of ceremonial center in the dense jungle lowlands—those of the so-called Classic Maya—had been achieved over many hundreds, even thousands of years. Their civilization had then gone on to build other ceremonial centers with new approaches in such places as the Yukatan, which were in active use when the Spanish arrived in America. If anything had caused a Mayan collapse, it was *that* arrival—and all that ensued thereafter.

The Maya understood that everything changes. They saw time as a succession of cycles, and they strove to be in harmony with these cycles. Just as the Navajo will destroy a beautifully intricate sand painting once its healing function has been performed, so, too, did the Maya surrender their own creations to the forest. Unlike Western culture, they were not obsessed with preserving the human-made. As the Maya themselves so eloquently expressed it in the Pop Wuj:

> All moons, all years, all days, all winds
> reach their completion and pass away.
> So too does all blood reach its place of quiet
> as it reaches its power and its throne.

Yet in another way, the Maya did seek sustainability. Again in dramatic contrast to Western civilization, it was the preservation of the natural world that was of foremost importance to indigenous Americans, including the ancient and modern Maya. This they considered to be the greatest achievement of their ancestors—far greater than the building of the pyramids. And still in the late twentieth century, while Ladino peasants in Guatemala and El Salvador farmed steep lands without serious regard to the long-term effects, the Maya painstakingly terraced the hillsides they farmed. This prevented the worst erosion, preserved the topsoil, and allowed for a good, sustained yield of crops. I became convinced that this practice was directly attributable to the ancient ecospiritual ethic they had inherited from their ancestors.

I felt fortunate to find people in El Salvador who would speak openly of their indigenous roots, especially since the subject there was somewhat taboo. This was the result of fear instilled by a tragic event known as "El Masacre." In the 1930s, there was an attempted popular revolution against the government, organized by students and intellectuals and backed by Indians who had been promised recognition of their land claims and their cultural and human rights. The revolution failed, and the leaders fled to Guatemala. The Salvadoran government, hungry for revenge, chose its next most logical target: the Indians. They issued a decree that all Indian men would be killed—period.

The only alternative for male Indians was to quickly adopt Ladino dress, speak only Spanish, and do nothing indicative of their native culture. By the time El Masacre was over, nearly a hundred thousand Indian men had been killed and tens of thousands of Indian women had been raped. The government effectively wiped out all outward expression of El Salvador's indigenous culture, turning the Indians into peasants. Today, with few exceptions, only old women are seen wearing native clothes.

Knowing of this history, I became even more concerned over what fate might hold for my Mayan friends in Guatemala. They still had what the Indians in El Salvador had lost, but they were being drawn into a revolutionary movement that could just as easily backfire on them. Fundamentally I questioned the idea of a Marxist alternative. Marxism had been born out of the beginnings of the Industrial Revolution in Europe. It was not a legacy of the American earth, nor did it address indigenous sensibilities any more than capitalism did. Why, I wondered, couldn't indigenous forms of goverment become models for social reform in Central America?

On my way back to Guatemala via Honduras, I was reminded of Don Adrian through a dream. . . .

We are walking together through Don Adrian's village of San Francisco El Alto, and fires are burning all around us. It appears that the village is having a big fiesta with lots of bonfires and fireworks. People are laughing and celebrating. At the same time, though, I hear gunfire and see houses burning all around me. People are crying and mourning. I am confused. I can't tell if this is a time of peace or a time of war. Children are laughing and crying simultaneously. I can't tell if the people are happy or sad.

Don Adrian tells me to keep walking. We walk through many villages for days and days. Everywhere we walk, there is fire and the same paradoxical reality. . . .

We come to a clear, shallow river in the forest. It is quiet here except for singing birds and the sound of the moving water. Don Adrian tells me to take off my shoes and step into the middle of the river. As I do so, he does the same. He faces me and speaks: "This river could not exist without the two sides that form its banks. For many suns you have walked across the lands of my ancestors, and in all your experiences you have seen how everything has two sides, just like this river. To see life in terms of good and bad limits our ability to create and be whole. Embracing polarity is necessary to bring about creation. Like the river, we could not exist without polarity.

"Were it not for darkness, would we still seek the light? Were it not for shade, would we not get burned? Find the gift that each side has to offer. Let those gifts be married within you. Free yourself of judgment. Become like the river."

As Don Adrian says these words, he places a palm on my forehead. With his other hand, he supports the small of my back. Pushing with one hand and lifting with the other, he turns me horizontal and lays me in the river face up. He lets go.

I am floating in the river. I float past Don Adrian. I float for what seems like an eternity. All I can see are sparkles of light reflecting in the water.

I was awakened by a shrill whistling sound outside the window of my hotel room. As I came to full consciousness, I realized it was the screeching of brakes. I looked out the window and saw that the bus to Puerto Barrios had just pulled up. I knew it would be leaving in less than fifteen minutes, so I threw my things into my pack as fast as I could.

I was on my way out of Guatemala, and I had never gone back to see Don Adrian. Somehow, with all the other things I had wanted to do, I had kept putting it off. Now it was too late. I felt depressed, like I'd missed an opportunity, but I was glad at least for the dream. It was strange that my experience at Don Adrian's apartment was so much like the end of my dream. Then again, maybe it wasn't strange at all.

From Puerto Barrios I took a boat up to Livingston, the other town along the Caribbean coast of Guatemala. There I stayed in the home of a fat old preacher who had a television. We watched the news of the surging revolution against the Somoza regime in Nicaragua.

The next two days I spent stranded in Livingston trying to get to Belize. I was totally frustrated. Finally, early the third morning, I boarded a tiny, motorized canoe that plowed its way through the ocean to Punta Gorda, the southernmost town in Belize. From there I hopped a bush plane that was going to Belize City.

To my dismay, halfway to Belize City we landed in the middle of the jungle. On the landing strip was a man holding a black suitcase. The pilot said I had to get out because this man had a reservation. I protested vehemently, explaining that I didn't have any idea where we were—and besides, I'd bought a ticket to Belize City. The pilot said only that we were in Stann Creek and that I had to get out.

The plane took off, leaving me on the landing strip with my backpack. I knew the man with the suitcase must have come from somewhere, so I started walking until I found a dirt road. I didn't know which direction to take, so I guessed. I walked with high trees on either side of me and nothing else in sight.

Finally I came to a clearing with a couple of broken-down shacks and a handful of people sitting around. I asked them how to get to Belize City, and they pointed down the road in the direction I'd been walking. "Isn't there a bus or anything like that?" I asked. They shook their heads.

I started walking down the road again, hoping that a vehicle—any vehicle—would pass by. After about three hours, a rickety old truck full of mangoes came bouncing along. I didn't even chance thumbing it; I just stood in the middle of the road so that it had to stop. The driver didn't want to take me. He said that his axles were too weak and couldn't handle the extra weight. But I knew this was my only ticket out of the jungle before nightfall. I persisted, pleading with him. Finally, when I pulled a few dollars out of my pocket, he let me ride in back with the mangoes.

A couple of hours later, I got off at a Y intersection. The driver said, "Belize City that way. I goin' this way." It seemed like every time I thought I was home free, I was in for a new surprise. As I began walking again, I noticed that my skin had red bumps and itched all around my waist. I was sure I had contracted some rare tropical disease.

Now I was even more desperate to get to Belize City. It was getting dark, but at least the road was paved and cars were passing by every few minutes. Finally I got a ride.

Once in Belize City, I found a funky little hotel. I was looking forward to taking a cold shower to cool the burning from my mysterious rash. Then I discovered that the plumbing was out. Feeling absolutely tortured, I decided to go out and find a restaurant. Maybe food would help me forget the itching.

On the way to a restaurant, I suddenly became aware that I was being followed. The voices sounded like those of teenagers. I overheard one of them saying that he thought I must have a lot of money. I quickly glanced behind me and saw four teenage boys with large sticks less than a block away. I continued walking steadily, turned the first corner I came to, and immediately tore out at a rapid pace, zigzagging through the streets. Once I was sure I had lost them, I found my way back to my hotel room and collapsed on the bed.

By morning my rash was gone. Then I remembered that mangoes could cause a rash that was similar to that caused by poison ivy. I felt relieved that I didn't have a rare disease, but I was still drained from the previous day's ordeals. I decided that in my last days before going back to North America what I really needed was a vacation. So I took a boat to a place called Key Caulker, where I knew I could just lie on the beach and relax.

Key Caulker was a quiet little island about a quarter of a mile in width. Old wooden houses painted in pastel colors and raised on stilts lined the sandy streets, adding to the island's Caribbean charm. I found a local homeowner named Tony Vega who rented his beachfront property to camping tourists. I gave him the one-dollar fee and hung my hammock between two palm trees.

The wind kicked up dramatically during the late afternoon. Dark storm clouds moved in across the ocean from the northeast. I soon forgot about relaxing. I wanted some kind of climactic conclusion for my journey to the south. Intuitively I sensed that it would come that night.

Reflecting on where I still felt incomplete, I knew it had to do with fear—with being chased by forces outside my control: vicious dogs, hungry vultures, street muggers. Already I had concluded that I must face my fears. If not now, when?

By sundown, the howling wind had set the palm trees creaking. Dark clouds waited impatiently across the eastern sea. I stepped to the edge of the water and removed my black cross crystal from its medicine pouch. Holding it in my right hand, I raised my arms to the sky. I felt as powerful as the impending storm. My fears would not get the better of me. Defiantly I declared, "Whatever is out there, I'm ready to face you!" Then I climbed into my hammock, eventually falling asleep.

I am awakened by a crashing sound. I jump out of my hammock. The waves are practically at my feet. I see that the crystal has dropped out of my hands. It is not in the hammock, nor can I find it with my flashlight anywhere in the sand. Losing the one thing that might protect me from unseen forces, I feel panicky. But there is no time to indulge. A massive downpour begins. The rain is blowing hard against my face, and the waves are almost upon me.

I rush to untie my hammock, grab my backpack, and run for shelter. I duck underneath Tony Vega's house and tie my hammock between the stilts that support it. I climb back into it, listening to the rain and wind. Falling asleep once more, I begin to dream. . . .

I see myself walking naked on an asphalt road that winds through dry, mountainous terrain. Even though it is a road for cars, there are none. As the road winds, it also rises upward. I come around a bend to find a red bandana that belongs to me. I reach down to pick it up, but the road sucks it in. A few hundred yards more and I find my yellow shorts, but the road takes them, too. Finally I see my white socks and sneakers. The road takes these, as well, just as I am about to pick them up. I feel that what is rightfully mine is being denied me. I am very upset.

Suddenly I awake and realize that I am in my hammock and that the storm has died down. My eyes still closed, I hear voices mumbling, two men talking in the distance. Through my closed eyelids, I see their shadowy forms. They are shaped like humans, but they are not human—they are spirits. They are coming down the sand path toward the house. Their language is alien, but I understand it.

As they approach the house, they stop walking and become silent. I know they can see me now, and I am afraid. I hear them talking about me; they are wondering who I am. They are angry because I have violated their territory. One of them says to the other, "Let's kill him."

The two men walk slowly up to the house and come underneath it. I am utterly terrified. They come right beside my hammock and stand on either side of me. I am paralyzed with fear. I can neither move nor speak. One of them starts laughing, while the other begins swinging me in the hammock. Both of them are talking about how they are going to kill me. I want to do or say something, but the most I can get out of my mouth are feeble grunts.

Suddenly, I know they are about to take my life, and everything changes. My strength rises like an explosion from within. I break through the shell of my fear, screaming primally and demanding that they go away.

Now all is silent. My hammock is still. I open my eyes, and no one is here. The storm is over. All is still.

In the morning I was awakened by the predawn light. I felt like I'd been through hell and back; I was exhausted. Then I remembered the black cross crystal. I had to find it. I walked out to the place where I'd first strung my hammock. Sure enough, it was lying in the sand, plain as day. But it hadn't been there before; I was sure of it. I had looked in that exact spot, and it wasn't there. Now it was.

A short while after my return to North America, I received a letter from Hilario informing me that Don Adrian had passed away. I was very sad. I knew that there was something more he had wanted to impart to me, and I felt badly that it had not happened. The opportunity had passed me by, and now it was too late. My only consolation was that maybe he'd completed his exchange with me through the dream. When he set me in the river and I floated past him, I think he was saying good-bye.

I also remained shaken by my experience at Key Caulker. I realized how foolish I had been to so brashly expose myself to the unknown. The next day I had gone snorkeling in the ocean for the first time in my life. On my way back to the boat, I was followed by a shark. Obviously I had not freed myself from my fears. When would they stop chasing me? The answer came in another dream.

I am walking with a friend down a path in a dense forest. Suddenly we stop in our tracks. A short distance ahead is a black jaguar lying on the trail, writhing around and growling. I know it will attack us if it sees us, but we have to get past it because this path is the only way forward.

We walk a bit closer to the jaguar. I tell my friend that if we move very slowly and quietly, maybe we can sneak around unnoticed. We try this and succeed. Relieved, we continue walking ahead on the trail.

But something feels terribly wrong. I feel like I've cheated myself. I turn around and look at the jaguar again. It's still in the same place, just as before. I realize that the only way to honestly continue on the path is to first go back and face it. I tell my friend to wait for me, that I'll return.

I walk back and stand in front of the jaguar. I wait patiently until it sees me. Then it leaps up and attacks me. I surrender to it without resistance. I feel it ripping my body to shreds, but amazingly I am not in pain. I feel it consuming me, but my demise actually feels good. Finally I am inside the jaguar—or is the jaguar inside me? Regardless, I feel whole and complete. No longer are we separate beings.

THE HUMPBACKED
FLUTE PLAYER

WEST

I will forever remember the brilliant colors of autumn that set the Massachusetts woods ablaze. In that season, during my senior year at Amherst, I discovered the joy of running barefoot and half naked on deserted forest trails. I didn't care that the sensitive soles of my feet came down on rocks and branches; I rejoiced in raw sensation.

I liked best to run when the sun was setting—to feel its warming rays against my sweating skin, simultaneously caressed and cooled by the briskness of the air. The rhythm of my feet, the beating of my heart, and the pulsing of my breath were all catalysts for a multitude of sounds that accompanied this impassioned running. At the same time, I would throw up my arms and flap like a bird, leaping and whirling through the atmosphere. I was primal energy in motion.

Rarihokwats had been right. My journey to the south was like a genetic trigger, causing me to become more connected to my body. As a result, I was finally primed to experience the pleasures of sex.

Unknowingly I had set myself up for a rare gift of ritual initiation. I had moved down the road from Amherst to Hampshire College, where I found the students and the ambience more conducive to my alternative lifestyle. A group of us on campus had begun to gather on special occasions to do ceremony at sunrise. As the harvest moon approached, I realized that it was also time to give thanks for the fruits of the Earth and the rhythms of the moon. Thus I called a ceremony to honor the Goddess of all creation.

The night of that ceremony, we assembled in an empty field beneath the full moon and encircled ourselves with a ring of smooth, round river stones. The women poured water over the heads of the men, and we drank from each other's cups to harmonize ourselves with the ebb and flow of the tides. We danced and chanted and howled by the moonlight, celebrating the great luminescent body that guides us through the night.

When the moon was directly above, we returned to our dormitories, and Linda invited me into her room. As a man, I had at last honored the Goddess, and now the Goddess was about to honor me. As she opened herself to receive me, I could see the full moon shining in through her window.

Thus did I enter a new and unknown dimension. Contrary to some religious beliefs, I found that my spiritual and creative life was actually enhanced through exploration of my sexuality. I wrote more songs and more poetry. I had increased vitality and visionary awareness. I also found that I could direct this new energy into my theatrical epic about the Ghost Dance, the longtime object of my creative passion.

The summer prior to my Central American trip, I had gone to New Mexico. I had stayed with Blue and Red and prayed with the black cross crystal before I went to bed. This was the only way I had of connecting with their Lakota grandfather, John Fire Lame Deer, for he had passed on before that summer arrived. And so I sought his guidance about the Ghost Dance through my dreams.

The west was a good place to dream. It made me go deep inside. And there I realized that in some strange way I, too, remembered the time of the Ghost Dance. I drew up those memories until they became conscious, and from that place the words and music flowed. Sometimes they flowed with tears, sometimes with rain. And when the summer lightning came, songs, rain, and tears all flowed together. My voice became the thunder, crying for vision and strength. The storms played through my hands on the keyboard and the drum. I cried for us all to be one—for the return of the Buffalo Nation.

That same summer I had participated in my first purification lodge ceremony, which the Lakota call the *inipi*. It was in New Mexico's Gila Wilderness at a World Family Healing Gathering. Manitonguat was there, and he took me into the lodge—a deep, dark, unknown space like the Dream-time. The ancestors were singing inside, and I was singing with them. The Buffalo Nation was in there, too; I could hear them all. When I came out again, it was like crawling out of a womb. For *Buffalo Nation* to be born, I saw that I would have to enter the lodge many times and come to know that space as deeply as my dreams.

So it was that more than a year later, when Amherst's autumn colors were hidden by the snows, Manitonguat came and built a lodge. But I did not enter the lodge with him alone, for a whole community of friends had joined to give *Buffalo Nation* its first expression. This family prayed and laughed and cried together many times in the lodge. And outside the lodge, Manitonguat directed us in the first performances of *Buffalo Nation*.

Our multiracial, sixteen-member cast was accompanied by an equally large chamber orchestra, musically bringing to life the history of the La-kota resistance from the time of Custer's Last Stand to that of Wounded Knee. Though the staging was stark, our intention was nevertheless to create a circle of warmth between ourselves and the hundred-or-so audience members who came to each show. Just as the ancient shaman's charge was to guide his community through a transformative experience, so did we seek to transform our audiences. More than theater, *Buffalo Nation* was a ceremony—almost like an *inipi*—in which all could be purified and receive new vision.

After a cycle of five performances over the course of two weekends, we held one last lodge together to celebrate the arrival of spring. On the way to that lodge—on equinox morning at the opening of the season of the east—I saw two shapes circling in the distant sky. As I got closer, I could see that they were bald eagles. They circled in silence. Even so, I heard their song, and I took it with me into the lodge.

> In a dome of covered branches on the Earth,
> people huddle close together.
> It is dark.
> No clothes.
> No possessions.
> Just us.
> Human beings,
> no different from our distant ancestors.
> Just us,

the way we came into this world.
Just us,
praying for life.

Our naked bodies sink into the soil
and mingle in each other's sweat.
It is hot.
The fire in the earth turns the water to vapor.
The Four Winds carry it upward and inward,
cleansing,
healing,
revealing even that which we hide from ourselves.
Now everyone will see.

Out there the machine keeps going,
        keeps growing,
        keeps claiming more victims
        and still is not satisfied.
Hopelessness hangs heavy on the people.
We have relinquished our power,
become the machine.
We keep it going,
and yet we too are the victims.

Still we awaken.
We awaken once again.
Even while caught in the cacophony of confusion,
we awaken.
We awaken to the sounds of other voices,
voices that are ancient but alive,
voices that can only be suppressed for so long.
For deep within our being lie the memories,
the memories of the songs of our forgotten relatives.

When exiting the purification lodge, a person says, "O Mitakuye Oya-sin," meaning "All My Relations." Even at the place of the door, between out and in, you can hear the songs of your relatives. At the same time, you start to hear the machine again. It's still outside, still going, and you know you have to face it.

On the night of March 26, not long after our equinox lodge, I went with Linda and some friends to see a new movie called *The China Syndrome,* about a nuclear power plant that malfunctions and comes close to having a meltdown. For myself and my college friends, the story had real immediacy because we all lived near a nuclear power plant in Rowe, Massachusetts. We were also members of an antinuclear activist group called the Clamshell Alliance, trained in nonviolent civil disobedience. For the past two years, we had engaged in protest actions attempting to either shut down existing nuclear plants or to keep new ones from going into operation. New Hampshire's Seabrook plant was our best-known target. Many of us had been arrested there before.

But by all outward means of measuring strength, we knew we were no match for such a technocratic giant as the nuclear industry in cahoots with big government. Perhaps it was that inescapable feeling of powerlessness that left us sitting silently in the movie theater after everyone else had gone. We were numbed by the film, by the thought that maybe a meltdown would occur somewhere soon in spite of our best efforts. The bottom line was that we all realized our movement was failing to get across to the people on the street. We were still in the minority, still the "radical fringe." What would it take to shift the scales?

I see a land with rolling green hills and clusters of big deciduous trees. On one hilltop is a tipi, a wind generator, and solar collectors, where many people have gathered. On the opposite hilltop is a nuclear power plant. I am inside the plant with a lot of other people, part of a big protest.

All of a sudden, the plant starts shaking and everybody panics. People are running wildly in all directions, trying to escape. I can feel the plant heating up, as though it is going to explode. I start running, too, down the road leading away from the plant. I come upon people with survival gear and makeshift tents. Their possessions are piled up all around them. They look like refugees. Over the hill we can see that the nuke's still shaking, and we're all really frightened. We're hoping that someone will come soon to rescue us, to take us far away from this place of danger.

All during that night and into the next morning, I kept dreaming different versions of the same nightmare. When I finally woke up, I was exhausted and my bedsheets were drenched with sweat.

The next day, Linda knocked at my door with the news that there had been an accident at the Three Mile Island nuclear plant in Pennsylvania. She said the authorities were insisting there was no need for alarm, but that people on campus were talking about an evacuation.

I kept flashing back to my dream, wishing that was all it had been. Then, after consulting a map, I realized to my horror that Three Mile Island was only eight miles from Rarihokwats's new home at the School of Living near York, Pennsylvania. This was the hilltop I had seen in my dream!

I picked up the phone and dialed him immediately. "Are you OK?" I asked nervously.

"I'm very good, younger brother," he answered. "And how are you?" He told me that he had been planting his large, circular garden on the hilltop when he heard the sirens at the nuclear plant, whose cooling towers were visible from that spot.

I didn't see how Rarihokwats could be so calm. "Aren't you concerned?" I asked. "Aren't you going to evacuate?"

"Of course I'm concerned, Jim. I'm very concerned. But don't you see? There's no place left to run. We've got to find our land, all of us, and make our stand—take responsibility for where we are. My responsibility is here now, so I'm going to stick with it. The trees can't evacuate, so why should I?"

"Well," I said, "I understand what you mean. I do. But what is it going to prove if it's a matter of being self-destructive?"

"How can I separate my own destruction from that of the Earth?" he answered. "I'm part of it; it's part of me. If we really love this planet, then we've got to stop abandoning it every time we screw up."

"I really do admire you, Rarihokwats," I said. "I guess this time I just can't live up to your standards."

"It's all right, younger brother. You do what you need to do. But no need to worry about us down here. We're prepared to deal with whatever happens."

Later that day, I called my parents to see if I could convince them to leave New York City, which was only two hundred miles from the nuclear plant. They were skeptical of the danger and insisted on taking a "wait and see" approach. I kept trying to explain that this was what everyone was doing—that if they waited and a meltdown did occur, they'd never make it out of New York City. When I told them I might never see them again, my mother started crying and said maybe they should consider leaving. Then Dad insisted we were both being ridiculous, and Mom backed down. Realizing that was the end of the conversation, I told them I loved them and hung up the phone.

Meanwhile, back on campus about four hundred miles from the nuclear plant, we weren't being much more decisive. Most of us just figured we'd wait and see if a meltdown was actually going to occur. For the next three days, we tortured ourselves with the question of whether we should evacuate. At one moment a meltdown seemed likely; at the next, almost impossible. Many of us cancelled our normal activities. Emergency meetings were held constantly. The possibility that we might become refugees was a staggering concept.

In any case, I had to do something. By the second day of the crisis, I had written a song called "Buying Time," which I recorded and got on the college radio. The chorus was my desperate cry:

> Will you melt or will you wait?
> Down in Middletown they're gambling with our fate.
> And is a meltdown the price that it will take
> To get the people to awake?

Unpleasant as the circumstances were, I saw how all the pieces of my reality were starting to fit together. Rarihokwats had recently told me that I had entered the west direction of my journey around the Medicine Wheel. He said that it was going to be a very emotional time and that my music would help me to move through those emotions. He said that I needed the western waters to cool my eastern fire; otherwise, I would burn out. I imagined the analogy of a nuke on the verge of melting down because its water-cooling system had failed. I began to wonder whether the whole world was like a purification lodge, waiting for someone to pour healing waters over the red-hot rocks.

What actually happened at Three Mile Island is still a matter of debate. The general belief was that it was brought under control before it became very serious. Yet many reports indicated there had been a 25 percent meltdown of the reactor core. There is no question that dangerously high levels of radiation were released into the atmosphere during the first days following the accident. But how dangerous? No one could say.

One thing was for sure, though: Like the Wounded Knee occupation, the Three Mile Island nuclear accident catalyzed a movement. The number of people opposed to nuclear power grew by quantum leaps, and those who were already opposed to it became far more determined and active. I was one of these. I had seen my friends get arrested for civil disobedience, but I had always found an excuse for not putting myself on the line. Now I had no more excuses.

It is June 3, 1979. I am marching with six hundred other people—men, women, children, babies, grandparents, and even the disabled—toward the construction site of the Shoreham Nuclear Power Plant on Long Island's north shore. Instead of guns, people carry guitars. I carry my flute. Most of us wear backpacks with the supplies essential for our survival.

The ground is muddy from last night's downpour, and a gentle rain is still falling. As we approach the chain-link fence, we see the police waiting on the other side. Beyond them looms the 80 percent-completed nuclear plant. I think about the dream in which I willingly surrendered to the jaws of the black jaguar. That's just how I feel now. We all know we will be arrested, but we are not afraid. We are making this day a celebration, for we know that by giving ourselves to our adversary, we will trigger a transformation.

When we reach the fence, the police warn us not to climb over or we will be charged with criminal trespass on the property of the Long Island Lighting Company. We simply smile and proceed. Some women actually lift their babies over the fence into the waiting hands of the police.

Once on the other side, we sit on the ground. To us this is not private property—it is our Mother Earth. Nevertheless, we've broken man's law, and we are under arrest. When the police try to escort us to buses, most of us choose to go limp, and they have to carry us. We explain to the police that our intention is not to give them a hard time, only to stop nuclear power.

We've been trained to transform our rage into active love, and I'm amazed at the effectiveness of this approach. Inside the bus, many of the police openly tell us that they understand what we are doing and wish they didn't have to arrest us. They say they don't like the idea of their children growing up near a nuclear plant, either—especially after the Three Mile Island incident. This is a revelation to me. In choosing to see our adversaries as human beings, we have given them room to express their humanity. . . .

Inside the detention center, we refuse to cooperate with their order to form separate groups of men and women. Explaining that we are not doing this to hassle anyone, we turn a potential confrontation into a music jam. The next thing we know, the police are singing their own chant: a demand for overtime pay! Everyone starts laughing. It is no secret: we all want justice; we all want to go home. Finally we're taken to the local jail, booked, and released.

Throughout the world on that same day, thousands of people had been arrested and tens of thousands had protested as part of International Antinuclear Day. Those in our protest group felt confident that our action had contributed to real change. And indeed it had: our own protest had laid the foundation for the eventual dismantling of the Shoreham nuclear plant and its conversion to a non-nuclear energy facility. Out of crisis, hope was born.

For me, however, an even greater challenge came on the home front. At about 3 a.m. on June 4, the day after the demonstration, I quietly unlocked the door of my parents' apartment. My mother was still awake worrying. Possibly her conscience was troubled, too, because she and my father were stockholders in the Long Island Lighting Company, which had requested that my compatriots and I be arrested. There we were in one family, a microcosm of the opposing forces on the nuclear issue.

Later that morning when we talked, I found out that my parents were actually neither for nor against nuclear power. They saw both sides of the issue. Like me, they were concerned about its inherent dangers, but they were also concerned about their investment. I kept reminding them that their investment was helping to create a threat to future generations, their own grandchildren included.

Even more than money, though, it was my parents' investment in their lifestyle that kept them sitting on the fence. They couldn't imagine living without electricity. They believed the energy companies' reports that solar and wind power would never be economically viable. I tried to explain that these companies had a vested interest in keeping people dependent on resources they could control.

In spite of my efforts, my parents were not ready to believe anyone but the "experts." I tired of trying to convince them otherwise. Yet I continued to be frustrated. If I couldn't resolve this dilemma in my own family, how could I ever hope to see it resolved in a larger arena? Still, I was sure of one thing: the nuclear issue had to be resolved soon; otherwise it would resolve itself, as it had almost done near Middletown, Pennsylvania.

March 1979 had been a momentous month, coming in with *Buffalo Nation* and going out with Three Mile Island. It was also in that month that a young Indian from Nebraska named John Hawk came into my life. I had invited him to speak at a performance of *Buffalo Nation* after hearing about him from one of the women in the cast. She felt that we had an important connection, because John was deeply devoted to the return of the Ghost Dance. He had been given a vision of how it would come back as a universal movement to unite all races in a moment of collective crisis.

As it turned out, there was a whole circle of creative people working with John who shared his vision. They called themselves the Earthkeepers. I began to attend their meetings, and I was impressed. These people saw the return of the dance as inseparable from the dance grounds. They saw their spiritual practice as inseparable from their response to the needs of the Earth itself. Out of this came their commitment to defend sacred lands and cultural ways. It was through this group that I learned a new term: "National Sacrifice Area."

A Cherokee woman named Starfire first told me about it. She said that among native people in America, certain geographic areas have traditionally been recognized as spiritual and natural energy centers—areas that help to generate weather patterns for the entire continent and that have become focal points for prayer and pilgrimage.

"There is a hidden cause for these interactions, which our ancestors were aware of long before the development of modern science," she said. "Beneath the surface of these areas lie the greatest concentrations of uranium, oil shale, coal, and other mineral resources. They contain the power to both create and destroy."

In North America, Starfire said, there are two areas considered vital to the health of the continent: the Black Hills of South Dakota and Black Mesa in the Four Corners area of the Southwest. "The government mapmakers didn't know what they were doing when they drew the borders of the four states to meet in the center of that sacred land," she said. "But we know that it is a true Earth center. That is why the Hopi people, who are its guardians, refer to it as Tuwanesavi, which means 'the spiritual center of the universe.' "

Starfire explained that the U.S. government, in an attempt to gain complete control of these centers for mining, had designated them "National Sacrifice Areas." "For years they have been ripping apart the body of our mother to get what they want," she said. "They pull her uranium out of the ground and leave the radioactive waste exposed to the elements. It blows in the wind. It washes into the waters. It gets inside the plants and animals. It finds its way into our bellies and lungs. It poisons our people.

"Even after they have taken the uranium away, they try to send everything they've poisoned back to us," she went on. "They propose to bury it in remote regions that they say are unpopulated. But these regions are the very places where our people still survive, and the government knows this well. Perhaps it is their wish that these places will become unpopulated in the future.

"In the traditional ways of native North Americans, only the one making a sacrifice has the right to choose it," said Starfire. "So now we must ask: Who has chosen to sacrifice our spiritual lands? Who is it who has declared our most sacred places to be 'National Sacrifice Areas'? We cannot allow these things to happen. It is our responsibility to protect these sacred spiritual centers for all life. This we know. But unless all peoples can see that finally we are *all* being sacrificed, the destruction will continue. It will continue until natural law forces a change upon humankind. Then we will all know the full meaning of sacrifice."

As Starfire spoke, I thought to myself how her words told the other half of the nuclear story. Previously I had not much considered where the uranium came from or where it went to; I was too preoccupied with the dangers of its actual use. Now I realized that its whole cycle was deadly. There was nothing it did not touch in some way. On the other hand, as Starfire had stated, the dangers of radiation exposure gave us all cause to see our oneness. And each of us had a responsibility to use our special talents to awaken people to unity.

"You, Brother Jim, must make that call for unity through your music," she told me. "You must put your heart into it completely, without doubt, without fear. I see that you will soon be journeying west to the lands of Tuwanesavi. When you go, do not forget to take your flute with you. There is a sacred teaching that it carries for you on this journey, and John will help to prepare you."

There was no way that Starfire could have known that her advice paralleled that of Yellow Robe, who had previously instructed me to take my flute to the spiritual center of the Black Hills. Yet both women had intuited that this instrument was necessary for me to fulfill my task of uniting with a directional center. I could only trust their guidance. When the time was right, I would journey west with my flute.

But for the moment, there was still music for me to perform in the East. Though I had graduated from college, I had decided to stay on for another year in the Amherst area to further develop *Buffalo Nation* and to complete the composing of other works. One of these was a song I had begun after my ascent of Mount Saint Helens in 1972, called *The Song of Native America*. It had grown gradually over the years, and its words had inspired my illustration of the body of America for *East West Journal* and *Akwesasne Notes*. (See figure 7.) Finally, in March of 1980, came the inspiration for the last lyrics of the song:

> Volcanoes in snow,
> quiet for years,
> will blow if they have to,
> will blow if they have to.

Though I wasn't sure why I had written those words, I thought that maybe they were triggered by my lucid dream of Starfire in that same month. As she came up the stairs to my room, she let loose with a bloodcurdling scream, like a desperate cry of the Earth in pain. Whatever the source of the words, I could feel that the song was whole at last. A few days later, rumblings began near the base of the supposedly dormant Mount Saint Helens. Then on May 18 of that same year, she erupted with tremendous force.

As I would later learn, the Indians in that region had foretold this event as one of the signs that the Earth was about to cleanse itself in preparation for a new era. I remembered my fiery vision at the base of the volcano, and then I understood why "The Song of Native America" had chosen to be born there. Like the explosion of the volcano, it was a call to humanity from the bowels of the Earth—shouting a warning, asserting a power, announcing a change. It ended with these words:

The condor soars on thin air.
The *ketzal* cries alone in the night.
A silent eagle circles far above,
Watching,
Waiting.

For me, the eagle would forever be associated with that magical moment of transition into a new cycle of existence: the turning point from north to east, from winter to spring, from the height of the storm to the glory of the sunrise. It was a symbol of the spiritual power to transcend all physical obstacles to the realization of a dream. That eagle spirit was often with me when I sat at the piano, calling in the inspiration for *Buffalo Nation*. I felt that through my music, I was striving to lift the weight of a tragic past and liberate it into the promise of a prophecy fulfilled.

During my last year in Amherst, my piano was the only thing I kept in the back room of the old farmhouse where I lived. Sometimes in that same room, I would see the shadow of a tall man standing in a corner. At other times I would feel the shadow behind me when I played or watching me from across the room. The shadow seemed heavy, weighted by the same tragic past that my songs sought to free. I knew that this was an Indian spirit and that, like the eagle in my song, it was silently waiting for something to happen.

After I moved out of that house, I discovered a most astounding article about the Charles Eastman family, who had lived in Amherst at the turn of the century. They were not by any means a typical New England family. Charles Eastman was a Santee Dakota who went by the Indian name of Ohiyesa. Born in the mid-1800s, he had been raised with the traditions of his people in the woodlands of Minnesota and Manitoba. But he was later to become a bridge between worlds, earning a degree in medicine at Boston University. Five months later, he was appointed agency physician at the Pine Ridge Reservation in South Dakota.

Shortly thereafter, a woman by the name of Elaine Goodale arrived to set up her winter quarters as the supervisor of education for the Sioux reserves. The two met and fell in love—during the very time that the Ghost Dance movement was spreading like wildfire across the prairie. They became engaged on Christmas Day, 1890.

Four days later came the event that was to set the course of the rest of their lives together: the massacre at Wounded Knee. The Eastmans were sent in to direct the medical rescue team—he to treat the injured survivors and to lead the party that uncovered the hundreds of Indians dead from the snow, she to nurse the dying as they and their dream faded before her eyes.

The ghosts of Wounded Knee stayed with them, and their marriage became a shared devotion to heal the rift between red and white Americans. Together with Elaine, Ohiyesa wrote numerous books and articles to awaken people to the true humanity of indigenous civilization. Such books as *Indian Boyhood* and *The Soul of the Indian* established him as the most renowned Native American author of his time.

"I know that our people possessed remarkable powers of concentration and abstraction," he wrote, "and I sometimes fancy that nearness to nature keeps the spirit sensitive to impressions not commonly felt, and in touch with the unseen powers."

The bulk of Eastman's writings emerged after the couple had settled in a stone-and-log house built on land belonging to Elaine's family. The location was on the outskirts of Amherst, in the woods below the Pelham hills. And, amazingly, it was the very land I had been living on during my last year in Amherst. The farmhouse I lived in had been built on the Eastmans' land after their death, and the old house set back behind the trees across the road below my window had been the Eastmans'. I had often wondered if someone lived there, but I'd never seen anyone come or go.

With the history of that house revealed, I felt I knew where the spirit in my farmhouse had come from and why I had unwittingly chosen that place to rework *Buffalo Nation*. Even the fact that *Buffalo Nation* was, in fact, an opera bore an extraordinary synchronicity to the lives of the Eastmans. In the School of the Woods summer camp they had established to impart nature and Indian lore to young people, the most popular camp activity had been its "mini-operas" that revolved around themes of Indian life.

In the summer of 1980, I took *Buffalo Nation* north to Canada to perform it at an international theater celebration of indigenous people. A contingency of the Earthkeepers was joined by a New York–based ensemble of Native American performers to premiere my new version of the opera. Our hope was that by sharing our vision of the Ghost Dance with other native people from around the world, there would be a recognition of its relevance and universality. And this, we thought, might help to spark the process of its global rebirth to unite all peoples around the Sacred Tree.

But once within the celebration, our presentation stirred more controversy than unification. Many people could not accept our eclectic blend of Indians and non-Indians performing a piece about Native American spirituality. Neither could they accept our mix of European and Native American musical styles. As much as some hated it, others loved it. It became the center of a heated debate over cultural politics. Thus we had to reevaluate whether the time was ripe to bring our vision forward.

I was filled with many conflicting emotions. I wondered if my ego was clouding my perceptions. I struggled with self-doubt. A million questions echoed through my mind. In the end, I resolved to put *Buffalo Nation* away until I knew that it was clearly called for. John Hawk counseled me not to be discouraged. He said that he had been carrying his vision since long before I had started my own work, and that he was still waiting to make it manifest.

"I think it would be good for you to spend some time alone," he said. "Maybe a more personal journey with your music is what's called for now."

"I feel that, too," I told him. "And somehow I sense that the Southwest is the place I need to go."

"If you want to make your journey west, now is the time," John said. "If you can meet me in California in one week, I will help you prepare for it."

One week later, as I walked with John along the pebbled banks of the American River in California, a large group of hawks appeared from behind a nearby cliff and began to circle above us. "Redtails," he exclaimed, looking up, his long black hair falling smoothly down his back. We counted thirteen of them. John seemed very pleased. "Let's sit by those boulders," he suggested, still eyeing the hawks.

When we reached the boulders, John took off his shoes and rolled his blue jeans to his knees. He told me to do the same. Then I followed him to the river's edge. He dipped his right hand into the water and then touched it to his sunlit forehead.

"I want you to feel this place," he said. "Let the cold water run over your feet. Sense everything around you. But before you step into the river, touch the water to your head as I have done. We always give thanks to the water in this way. We pray that it will continue to flow and be clean, that all living things will always have pure water. It's important to let the river know we respect it, not just to step into it and take from it what we want. It only requires a little bit of consciousness to remember this, but it makes a big difference."

I did as John suggested, then we stepped into the river together. It was a very reverent feeling, like worshiping without words. I couldn't help but be reminded of my dream with Don Adrian. But this place was much more rugged and wild. We watched the hawks soar off toward the west, then I followed John back to the boulders.

"I want to tell you about Kokopelli," said John. "During the years when I was living with the Hopi and training with their elders down inside the kivas, his name came up a lot. I was always very curious about him, because I found his symbol so compelling, so full of vitality. He seemed to me like a herald of the future."

"What did he look like?" I asked.

As John described Kokopelli, he drew an image in the sand with his index finger. "Kokopelli is the humpbacked flute player. The Hopi usually depict him as a stick figure in the act of walking. He's got two antennae on top of his head, and he's almost always bent forward, blowing into a flute that he holds between his hands. His back looks bowed like a hunchback's, but it's not because he's deformed; his back is filled with a sacred cargo."

John went on to explain that Kokopelli is a traveler. Though Hopi by name, his image is universal in the Western Hemisphere. It is found painted and carved on canyon walls from Alaska to the tip of South America. The ancestors of the Hopi, who are known by the Navajo name Anasazi, meaning the "Ancient Ones," left his image at many of their dwelling places during centuries of migrations.

"Of course, Kokopelli was only one of their symbols," John said. "All of their rock paintings and carvings in stone were left as messages to future generations. Through these symbols, they expressed their knowledge of the Creation. If you understand how to read these symbols, you will see that their mythology is based on a living reality." (See figure 3.)

John said that another image of the Anasazi was that of Panayoik-yasi, the ancient Hopi guardian of the underworld. He embodies the potentially dangerous powers within the Earth, which the Hopi knew should be left completely undisturbed. To insure this, they placed effigies of Panayoikyasi in crypts beneath the ground. They buried him face down with his left arm broken off so that he would be unable to wield his power in the world above.

Centuries later, archaeologists began to excavate some of the Panayoikyasi tombs. During this same time, uranium mining began to spread through the Southwest, bringing with it the dawn of the nuclear age. The Hopi's prophesied "gourd of ashes" was dropped from the sky—or, seen another way, the plutonian powers of Panayoikyasi rose from the ground in the form of a radioactive plutonium nightmare.

"As I see it," John said, "Kokopelli is the antidote for Panayoikyasi. He is like the Pied Piper for the Indian spirit returning to this land. He calls forth that energy with the magic of his flute, awakening it within people's hearts. But unlike the Pied Piper, he doesn't lead the masses to their suicide; he inspires the emergence of new life. When I see antinuclear protestors marching with their musical instruments and their packs on their backs, I can't help but be reminded of Kokopelli. Maybe this is one of the ways he has chosen to return."

"Well, I can certainly relate to that analogy," I said, "but what about this pack? You said Kokopelli carries a sacred cargo on his back. What is it?"

John smiled. "It is the seeds of new life. Kokopelli is a fertility symbol. He carries the whole cycle of regeneration within his nature. The seeds in his sack belong to plants and flowers, but metaphorically they are cultural and spiritual seeds as well. It is Kokopelli's responsibility to spread them. Then with the music of his flute, he creates warmth to bring the rain and heal the Earth. This gives the seeds the special energies they need to sprout and grow. Their germination is represented by a sprouting life-energy symbol in the form of a four-directional spiral. This same symbol is used by the Hopi today to represent their migrations across the continent."

"Is it possible that Kokopelli has some kind of parallel in the European horned god Pan?" I asked. "It seems like they both provide a link for humanity to the rest of nature through their music."

"Absolutely. But that's not all that Pan and Kokopelli have in common. Between the one's horns and the other's antennae, they're both pretty horny characters. In fact, Kokopelli is often depicted with a huge erection instead of a flute. Sometimes the flute he's playing actually is his erection—imagine! This aspect of Kokopelli lets us know without a doubt that he's a fertility symbol, as well as a celebration of the erotic part of our human nature.

COLOR
PLATES

Figure 1

THE EAST

Wap Opoteniok, Guardian of the Great Peace

Wap Opoteniok is the Powhatan name for the white eagle. Though this mandala was originally created as a flag for the Powhatan Renape Nation, the white eagle is a sacred symbol for many Native American cultures, representing spiritual transformation and watchfulness for the well-being of future generations.

In Haudenosaunee (Iroquois) legend, a white eagle alighted atop the Great Tree of Peace when it was first planted by the Peacemaker. In other Eastern Woodlands cultures as well, the white eagle is sometimes associated with their legendary prophets and teachers, such as the Pale One of the Tsalagi (Cherokee).

According to the Mexika, the white eagle, known as Iztakkuautli, symbolizes the spiritual evolution of the human being. This concept is beautifully conveyed in a traditional Hopi song:

> The eagle rises.
> His wings swoop upward.
> High toward the sky the great bird moves.
> His plumes are filled with prayers.
> Earth and heaven are one.
> The eagle rises.

In this mandala, the Sacred Tree is rooted on the back of Turtle Island. The ascension of the eagle above the turtle symbolizes the transformation from matter to spirit through the body of the tree: the eagle is returning to its spiritual source in the sun. The rainbow colors emanating from its wings represent the embracing of diversity as the only hope for unity and peace on Earth.

Figure 2

THE SOUTH

Ixim-Yaxche, The Mayan Cross of Regeneration

Ixim is corn, growing in the four sacred colors: red for east, yellow for south, black for west, and white for north. *Yaxche* is the ceiba, or Sacred Tree, growing in the same four sacred colors. Both *ixim* and *yaxche* are symbols of rebirth and eternal life.

The central circle of this mandala represents the inner world of the subconscious—hence the bats over a full moon reflecting in the waters of Atitlan, world navel of the Maya. Surrounding the lake is the body of Imix, the Earth, shown as a giant *cipactli*, or crocodile-like dragon. *Ixim* sprouts from her belly, and hidden within her womb is *balam*, the jaguar, associated throughout Mesoamerica with the subconscious realms. For the Maya the jaguar is also Yumil Ka'ax, the young lord of the cornfields. Thus do the diverse elements of the inner circle tie together.

In the outer circle, quartered by the sacred ceibas, are the temples of Palenque arising from the realms of consciousness. The ceibas and the temple windows have the same T shape, known to the Maya as Ik, which denotes wind or spirit. The T shape also signifies the Sacred Twins, who are shown on either side of the temple doorways much as they appear throughout Palenque. They hold *ketzal* birds and stylized Mayan crosses as offerings to the principle of enlightenment. This is represented by the double cross of *tulix*, the dragonfly, as a living symbol of Kukulkan, the feathered serpent.

Beyond the temples are the plants and animals of the jungle, and above them is a stylized Mayan sky. The sacred fifty-two-year cycle of the Maya is woven into the abstract design. The entire mandala is patterned in cellular units, much like the kernels of corn at its center. The resulting visual effect is intended to be reminiscent of the way one perceives when journeying on the *teonanakatl*, or sacred mushrooms, which also grow in the shape of Ik. Outside the mandala are the cosmic realms, the infinite universe that the Maya know so well.

Figure 3
THE WEST
Kokopelli, The Humpbacked Flute Player

This mandala is a prayer that the waters of life may continue to flow in supporting the delicately balanced desert ecosystems of the American Southwest. Kokopelli appears in his guise as a fertility symbol, playing his flute to warm the Earth, which brings the rain that makes the seeds grow—the very seeds he has spread.

His music is carried down through the water-serpent kivas into the central circle, symbolic of the kiva pit. There the rattlesnake awaits its release into the desert, at which point the calling forth of the rains is completed.

Descending deeper through the *sipapu* of the kiva, we enter the underworld, which is guarded by the ant people. This is the abode of Panayoikyasi, who is placed upside down so that his dangerous powers are kept below, where they belong.

Above ground, butterflies and hummingbirds are depicted cross-pollinating a Native American garden of corn, beans, squash, and sunflowers. These animals, like Kokopelli, are fertility symbols. The mesa walls where Kokopelli plays are a synthesis of Monument Valley and Canyon de Chelly. Beneath them are the remains of Chaco Canyon, where the Anasazi culture attained full flower. The geometry of the mandala is inspired by the Hopi shield of the Four Directions and the Zia sun symbol used on the New Mexico state flag.

Figure 4

THE NORTH

Ta Tunka Wian Ska, Return of the Buffalo Nation

Ta Tunka Wian Ska is White Buffalo Calf Woman, who long ago came to the Lakota bearing the gift of the Sacred Pipe. She appears here coming out of the clouds, wearing a crown of moons and stars. Accompanying her are buffalo of the four sacred colors, representing the returning native spirit of the four races of humanity.

Lightning flashes as a sign of the dynamic changes these buffalo spirits are bringing. The black-and-white bird at the top of the mandala is the magpie. It is the medicine bird of the Ghost Dance, which according to prophecy will bring back the buffalo.

The eagle and crow appear in the east (right) and west (left) quadrants of the mandala as messengers of the Ghost Dance (see page 189). In the south quadrant, fourteen ghost dancers circle the Earth, so that a sacred nation might again be born in America. The Sacred Tree is rooted in the heart of the continent and blooms in the colors of the Four Directions.

The white bird beneath it is a dove. Along with the two Sacred Pipes, it signifies humanity coming together to make peace. The buffalo skull in the center signifies the concept that out of death comes new life. The rainbow shield that surrounds it brings the hope of fulfillment to this sacred dream.

In the outer ring, the solar and lunar cycles are depicted. Sixteen suns represent the four seasons of each of the four great ages, according to Lakota tradition. The twenty-eight moons represent the lunation cycle of days, being the multiple of the numbers *four* and *seven*, which are both especially sacred in Lakota symbology. One moon is red and one sun is blue, because these are prophesied to be the signs in the sky of White Buffalo Woman's return.

Figure 5
THE CENTER
Ketzalkoatl, The Morning Star of Anahuatl

In the center of this mandala is the sacred *ketzal* bird. Spiraling around it is *koatl*, the snake. Ketzalkoatl is the feathered serpent, representing the divine union of duality. His spine is blue for the sky, his belly green for the Earth. Ketzalkoatl is also associated with the planet Venus, especially as the Morning Star, which shines in the heart of the *ketzal*.

Like Ketzalkoatl, pyramids and volcanoes join Earth and sky. The Great Pyramid of Cholula was dedicated to Ketzalkoatl and aligned to the nearby volcano of Popokatepetl, where Ketzalkoatl is said to have disseminated his teachings to the Four Directions. The erupting volcanoes of the mandala are a metaphor for this dissemination, affirming the transformative process from destruction to renewal. Thus the smoke of cataclysmic Earth change spirals into the mouths of the conch shells, symbol of Ketzalkoatl's return and humanity's rebirth. There it is purified to become the breath of life, awakening the holy sound of creation.

Ketzalkoatl is credited with bequeathing the sacred calendar to ancient Méxiko. This mandala is encoded with many of the numerological formulas of that calendar, although the encoding was not consciously planned. The crests of the conch shells and the steps and doorways of the pyramids number thirteen each. This is the number of heavens in Mesoamerican cosmology, as well as the number of months in the ceremonial year. Thirteen multiplied by four (that is, all the conch shells or all the pyramids) yields fifty-two, the number of years upon which Mesoamericans base their larger calendric counts. The smoke and wind circles in the outer ring of the mandala are twenty in number, as are the purple areas surrounding Ketzalkoatl's body. Twenty is the number of days in the ceremonial month, and twenty times thirteen yields 260, the number of days in the Mesoamerican ceremonial year. These are but a few of the calendric calculations that can be made from this mandala.

Figure 6

THE CONTINENT

Mettanokit, The Sacred Heart of Mother Earth

This mandala is based on many of the sacred teachings of the North American continent. It is a form of "x-ray art," where the viewer is able to see through physical forms into deeper and deeper dimensions.

The first form is the Sacred Tree, which flowers in the colors of the Four Directions. This tree is rooted on the back of a four-headed turtle representing Turtle Island. The turtle's shell is composed of twelve sections, symbolizing the twelve great clans, tribes, or nations of the peoples of Earth.

Within the center of the turtle is depicted an abstract four-chambered heart as a symbol of its enduring strength. Within this heart burns the eternal flame, the fire of truth, light, love, and healing. It is generated by the *naui olin* ("four movement") symbol of the Fifth World and of the migrations of indigenous people across Turtle Island. The *naui olin* is rainbow colored because it is a force of unifying light. It is the activator of *olin yolliztli*, or "movement of the sacred heart," within Mettanokit, the sacred heart of Mother Earth.

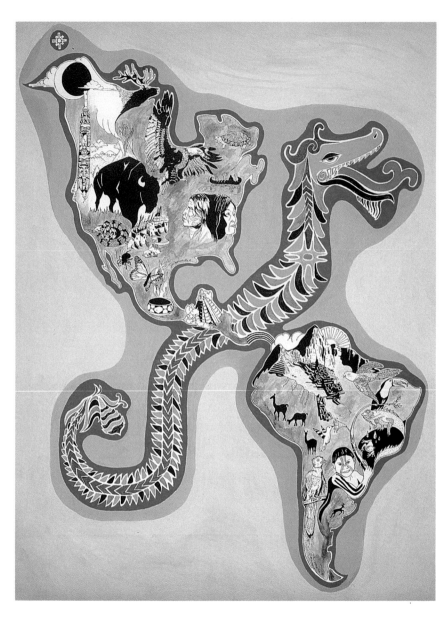

Figure 7

THE HEMISPHERE

Amaruka, Land of the Serpent

In the ancient Quechua language spoken by the Inca, *amaru* means "snake" or "serpent." *Ka* signifies "location" or "place." Amaruka is a very old name given to the Western Hemisphere by some of its indigenous inhabitants, long before Amerigo Vespucci sailed across the Atlantic to its shores.

This painting has been created from the pen-and-ink drawings originally done for *East West Journal* and *Akwesasne Notes*. The feathered serpent that has been added is patterned after the constellation of Scorpio, known to the Inca as Amaru because it looks like a snake in the sky. The bright star in the heart of the constellation is Antares. It is the brightest star close to the Galactic Center and has a primary spiritual influence over the lands of Central and South America.

Figure 8

THE PLANET

Etenoha, Turtle Island

Known to the Haudenosaunee as Etenoha, the Earth is a great living being floating through the infinity of space. She is Gaia to the Greeks, Pacha Mama to the Inca, but whatever her name, the ancient and native cultures of our planet recognize her as a conscious entity.

This painting was created from the pen-and-ink drawing done for *Akwesasne Notes* in 1976. Inspired by the metaphor of Turtle Island, it depicts not just a continent swimming through the ocean, but a jewel-like planet on a journey through a vast cosmic sea.

"I also remember that Pan is somewhat of a trickster," John continued. "This makes me think of our stories about Coyote, who happens to be one of Kokopelli's symbols."

"Are there any other animals associated with Kokopelli?" I asked.

John pointed to the drawing he had made in the sand. "As you can see, Kokopelli looks a little like a grasshopper or a cricket. Because that insect makes a high-pitched music, it has become a symbol of the flute player. And of course the reason it's making that music is because it's calling for its mate. In Native American tradition, the flute is frequently connected to courting. We've learned this association from nature.

"The third animal symbol of Kokopelli is the hummingbird," continued John, "whose long beak looks like the flute coming out of Kokopelli's mouth. This bird, too, plays an important role in cross-pollination and the spreading of joy. It's no accident that it is found from the Atlantic to the Pacific and from the Alaskan islands to Tierra del Fuego."

"So why did you want to tell me all about Kokopelli?" I asked.

"Because he's one of your spirit guides."

"Really?"

"Of course. And he's waiting to give you a song. That's the real reason you've come west."

"How do you know this?" I asked. "And how can I find this song?"

"You need to go inside yourself to answer these questions. Let your intuition guide you. Kokopelli will give you a sign, a way for you to recognize when he is near, but you will have to be very attentive. It will be something so subtle that most people wouldn't even notice it."

I asked John if he couldn't give me more specific information, and he said that my plan to go to Arizona for the Hopi Snake Dance was a good one. "Even the timing of your journey is significant, because in the alternate years that the Snake Dance is not performed, the Flute Dance is performed instead. It's done at this time, in late summer. Everything is working for you, Jim. Believe me, Kokopelli wants to play with you, and he's not the serious type. The best advice I can give you is to just relax and have fun."

That evening I joined John and his small community in a purification lodge, which they dedicated to preparing me for my journey to Tuwanesavi, the Four Corners. The people were from many different North American Indian cultures, and they all prayed strongly. They gave me the sense that I was part of their community, that I was being sent on a sacred mission on their behalf. The lodge was the hottest I had ever experienced—I felt like my skin was melting. But the hotter it got, the stronger we prayed and the louder we sang. In that lodge, I burned through a lot of resistance so that I could be truly open for what lay ahead.

Coming into Hopiland, I was reminded of Jerusalem. A shimmering quality in the atmosphere and a sort of glow permeated everything in sight. I had no doubt I was entering a holy land, a spiritual center, and the birthplace of a prophetic tradition that spoke profoundly to the entire world.

I drove on to Second Mesa, where I was met by members of my spiritual family. Many of the Earthkeepers were there, converging for the Snake Dance. With little previous planning, we all seemed to have been called to this place at the same time. Sheri had just come from the International Survival Gathering in the Black Hills. Gail carried offerings from the people of Taos Pueblo. And Joan had come to continue her research into lightning, which in the summer occurs at Hopi more than anywhere else on Earth.

Joan said that the high content of underground uranium and other minerals in the region was a major factor in the production of lightning. "We are at a focal point on the global energy grid," she said, "a center of elemental activity that actually affects weather for the whole planet. No one really knows the extent to which all the mining here might disturb the delicate balance of forces."

Later that morning, we all sat together in the stone-and-adobe home of one of the Hopi elders in Oraibi—the oldest continuously inhabited village on the North American continent—as these things were explained further. "The Great Spirit has told the Hopi leaders that the great wealth and resources beneath the lands at Black Mesa must not be disturbed," the elder said. "The Hopi were given special guidance in caring for our sacred lands so as not to disrupt the fragile harmony that holds things together. If these places are disturbed or destroyed, our prayers and ceremonies will lose their force, and a great calamity will befall humankind.

"Our ancestors foretold these things," he said, his voice quivering. "They gave us prophecies. Much of what they warned us of has already come to pass. They described a network of giant spider webs that would crisscross the land in all directions. Today we know these are the powerlines that carry our sacred energy away. They spoke of houses that would fly in the sky, and we can see now that these are airplanes. They told us these things would be among the signs that we are coming near the end of this world cycle.

"But the most important signs are the same as the ones we paint on our ceremonial gourd rattles, like the one I am holding here," he said. "When we shake it, we stir the life force, and for that reason we paint the symbol of this force—the swastika—at the top center part of the rattle. It awakens things to grow. The Nazis reversed this symbol. They took the same force and sent it spinning in the opposite direction, against the powers of life."

As the elder spoke, I realized that the swastika was also the sprouting life symbol that the Hopi used to represent their migrations. How amazing that such a potent design could have meanings so diametrically opposed!

"The red design you see here surrounding our life force symbol is a ring of fire that represents the sun," the elder continued. "It penetrates with its heat and light, which causes things to grow. It sends that energy into the seed, which is represented in the center. We know from our ancestors that these two symbols, the swastika and the sun, would come with the first two events to shake the world. After the first event, the first power would rise again with even greater strength to join the second, warning us that the Great Day of Purification was coming close. It is obvious now that the two nations that rose forty years ago to try to conquer the world carried these exact symbols on their flags, so this part of the prophecy has already been fulfilled.

"We were also told that near the time of the rising of the swastika and the sun, a 'gourd of ashes' would be dropped from the sky. Its shape would be just like this rattle. It would burn the land and boil the waters. Nothing would be able to grow where it fell. Today we understand that what our ancestors were describing was the atomic bomb. We know that the first one to ever be dropped was not far from our sacred center of Tuwanesavi. Our elders were standing on the high mesas looking south when it happened. They knew from their dreams that this tremendous power was being unleashed and that our world would never be the same. According to our instructions, this was the last event to signal that it was time to share our prophecies with the rest of the world.

"The final sign that we have reached the Great Day of Purification will come when a power symbolized by the color red joins forces with the powers symbolized by the swastika and the sun. We still don't know how it will happen because, as you can see, these powers can be used either to create or destroy. This is the choice that humanity has before it today. We are praying that humanity will choose the peaceful way. All of our sacred dances and ceremonies are offered with this prayer."

When the elder was finished speaking, someone asked whether he could tell us anything about the Snake Dance. He explained that at one time it was closed to non-Indians. "But then we realized," he said, "that if only one or two spectators with good hearts merge with our prayers, that is good. So I would say that this is the most important thing—how you hold your intention. It will also help to know that the snakes we are dancing with were captured in the desert more than a month ago. They have been inside the kivas all this time, where we have been filling them with our prayers for rain. After the dance, we release them back into their desert homes. They don't forget us. Afterward, the rains always come."

As we left Oraibi, the road climbed up to Third Mesa. The day was exceptionally beautiful, with an intense blue sky and huge cumulus clouds.

Soon we were in Hotevilla. Around the central plaza, people were gathering on rooftops and in front of the bordering homes. Staggered at many different levels, everyone was afforded a view. The village had been transformed into an outdoor theater. The hot summer air sizzled with anticipation. Everyone knew the invisible curtain was about to rise.

The ceremony begins as a pulsation, the steady beat of rattle and drum and the percussive trill of bone rasps held over open gourds. Now comes the sound of men chanting in tight unison. The music hums and buzzes up and down, reminding me of a beehive coming to life.

The snake dancers appear, their bodies painted with mud in different shades and patterns. In their mouths they hold the rattlesnakes they have lived with for the past month below ground. Their dance is hypnotic, trancelike, expressing simultaneously both the stillness and the movement of the snake.

I think about the association between the snake and sexual energy, the kundalini, the same primal life force that courses up and down our spines. This is the energy that can bridge our spiritual and physical natures, that can merge polarities and spark electricity. This is the lightning in our genitals and spines, in the Earth and in the universe: serpent power—the power that awakens the fluids, calls the waters, makes love and rain—the very essence of life.

I feel the trance of the dancers overtaking me. Anchoring to the sound of the chant and the drums, I breathe into the ground. The deeper I go, the higher I rise. I think of my flute and the breath I blow through it, and of Kokopelli blowing through his own flute. I imagine the Flute Dance, its same primal energy—Kokopelli's power—moving through the spines of the dancers, calling the lightning and rain. Then I realize that the serpent's dance and the flute player's song are one.

As we left Hotevilla in late afternoon, dark clouds had already begun to form in the western sky. From the distant San Francisco Peaks where the *kachina* spirits dwell, a wind was blowing across the mesas. A storm was brewing. The dance had done its magic; the prayers were being answered.

Soon the sky was blacker than any daytime sky I had ever seen. As we descended Third Mesa and passed Oraibi, lightning struck in all directions. Thunder crackled and exploded with awesome power. Large raindrops began to fall on the windshield. Within less than a minute, we were driving through a torrential rain. On the car radio I heard warnings of flash floods throughout the Four Corners region.

My pilgrimage in search of Kokopelli had begun with a torrent. I rode the wave of the storm to my first destination: Canyon de Chelly in northeastern Arizona. There, smooth red and orange cliffs dropped dramatically to a sandy bottom. Thanks to the recent rains, a shallow stream now flowed in the narrow space between the canyon walls. Cottonwood trees and other native plants shared the canyon with the peach orchards and cornfields of the Navajo, who had made this place their home since the departure of the Anasazi around A.D. 1400. But the cliff dwellings of the Ancient Ones still clung precipitously to the distant past, nestled into sandstone caves and ledges with great organic and aesthetic sensibility.

I sat at the edge of the canyon and began singing to the opposite cliff. The echo was astounding. Not one, but four or five echoes rang out as my voice bounced back and forth between the rock walls. As I continued singing, I thought I heard another musical voice responding from the canyon floor. But from my perch a thousand feet above, I could see no one.

The next morning I returned to the same spot to pursue the echoes further. I discovered that there was indeed an entity living inside the canyon—inside the ancient rock. I, the newcomer, was its echo. From this realization, the first part of Kokopelli's song was born.

Walking away from the cliff, I discovered a stick that fit my grip and height perfectly. It became my staff, which, as John had told me, was also one of Kokopelli's symbols. Now I was ready to enter the canyon. Over my shoulders was the Mohawk birchbark pack basket that Rarihokwats had given me. I slid my flute inside my belt, along my right hip. And in my left hand I held my staff. I was doing all I could to look like Kokopelli, so he would feel welcome to enter me and teach me.

Three times I hiked into the canyon, where I found many petroglyphs of Kokopelli carved into the cliff faces. On my third hike in under the full moon, I came upon a cave that was filled with his images and magic. I had no doubt he had walked this canyon floor before.

Suddenly I was aware of an unusual stillness, a total silence. The air was not moving, and I knew that I, too, must be still. In a moment I felt the air blowing against my face. A wind rose and swept past me. In this wind I heard the voice of Kokopelli. With it he planted his words and music in my mind. They were simply there, perfect and complete. The composing was effortless. There was no "figuring out"; it was like receiving a song from a friend.

Before I left the canyon the next morning, I stopped at the visitor center. On display was a large wooden flute that had been excavated from one of the cliff dwellings. I read the corresponding plaque, which informed me that during Anasazi times, Canyon de Chelly had been the home of the Flute Clan! Unknowingly, I had been drawn here first, guided only by my intuition.

In the weeks that followed, I traveled throughout the Southwest, encountering the most bizarre of earthscapes and skies unmatched in dramatic beauty. Always when the silent stillness came, I knew Kokopelli was near. And in the new wind he revealed his song. He revealed it one section at a time, as if paralleling the sequential steps of my journey. The only thing required of me was to stay acutely aware.

My awareness rewarded me in other ways, too. One day, in Arches

National Park in southeastern Utah, I chose to walk barefoot in order to feel the heart of the Earth more intimately. As I walked the narrow, sandy trail between sweeping bridges of multicolored rock, I stepped up on a small boulder in the middle of the path. For some inexplicable reason, I paused before putting my foot down on the other side. Only when I looked down did I see why. Curled up beside the boulder, in the very spot where my right foot would have landed, was a rattlesnake.

I stared into the snake's eyes and felt its inner fire. I watched its body slowly expand and contract with the pulse of its breath. It watched me, too, aware now of my presence, waiting for a move. But I was still and had no fear. The snake was part of me, part of the self that I loved.

At last my journey took me to Monument Valley on the Utah-Arizona border. There, three gigantic rock buttes stood apart in a striking triangular configuration. These buttes are popularly known as "The Mittens," but the name doesn't begin to convey the meaning of their design. The two northern buttes are clearly a representation of two human hands, all fingers joined except for the thumbs, which rise separately. The third butte is a solid form without a separate thumb—neither right nor left but a unity of the two. My intuition told me this is no accident; this natural monument is the Earth's commemorative sculpture to the unity of duality in all creation.

Between these buttes, I felt Kokopelli's presence as strongly as I had in Canyon de Chelly. I could almost see him and his clan walking through the desolate valley, the dust rising around them as they moved in procession with playing flutes. It was here that Kokopelli gave me the last words of his song, as well as an opening poem. Then he whispered, "Go sit on the mesa."

I'm sitting on a rock that has called to me. I remove the rattle from my pack basket, pull the flute from my belt, and prepare to sing Kokopelli's song in its entirety.

I take a deep breath and begin. When I come to the line "In ancient times Kokopelli walked the Earth," I begin to shake my rattle. At this moment, a dust twister rises from the valley floor about a hundred feet below. As I continue singing, it builds in height and power. I am aware of a vibrant energy throughout my body that is pulsing through my arm and hand into my rattle and from there outward to the whirlwind. As I shake the rattle, I can feel that it is connected to the wind. I feel as if I am hooked in to an invisible power grid. My will to move within it is inseparable from the greater will by which it moves me.

Though observing in amazement, I continue to sing until I have finished the song. The whirlwind rises up the mesa and comes within ten feet of where I am sitting. It encircles me completely, moving in the direction of the sun, and then continues on behind me. Just as I end the song, the wind disappears and the dust falls back onto the Earth.

I have come full circle from the Hopi Snake Dance. I am not merely an observer, but a living part of the human bridge to all creation. I can only thank Kokopelli for allowing me this privilege.

> Land gives lightning to sky,
> gives it back,
> illuminates the crack
> that hides between worlds.

> Just so are we given
> our rain
> and our vision,
> that two worlds may meet.

> Play your flute.
> Play it sweetly,
> Kokopelli,
> Kokopelli.

INTO THE

PART TWO

CENTER

THE MOUNTAIN
OF THE SERPENT

Full of inspiration from my western journey in search of Kokopelli, I returned once more to the East Coast. For a season, I joined my friend Nemattanew in Rankokus, helping to awaken the indigenous cultural renaissance in the unlikely locale of rural New Jersey. Yet this was not so unusual as it might seem, for virtually all places in the Western Hemisphere were once home to indigenous peoples. And now, what remained of those peoples in body, culture, and spirit was everywhere showing clear signs of renewal. New grass was pushing up through the concrete; nowhere could it be held down.

A few hours from Rankokus was the home of Rarihokwats at the School of Living in Pennsylvania. While I had intentionally kept away from there in the year immediately following the nearby nuclear accident, by 1980 I felt it was safe enough again to begin making visits. On the first occasion, Nemattanew and I went together.

As our car reached the top of the hill where the school was situated, I asked Nemattanew to stop. We both got out, and a terrible chill shot through my bones. There in the distance rose the now-infamous cooling towers of the Three Mile Island nuclear facility. The image still held incredible potency for me. In truth, my horror was even greater than it had been at the time of the accident. Now, the archetypal twentieth-century symbol of the uncontrollable monster was not on television or in a magazine but standing right before me. To actually see it was to know it as more than symbol, to move it out of its mythic dimension and finally to accept its grim reality.

Certainly for the people of this region, the encounter with the monster had already passed the abstract phase. In the year following the accident, the three counties surrounding Three Mile Island had reported a significant rise in birth defects, stillbirths, and infant mortalities. Particularly dramatic was the increase in infant hypothyroidism, a problem often connected to radiation exposure.

Among other life-forms, the effects were even more pronounced. Unexplainable deaths and strange diseases had begun to occur in farm animals, dogs, and cats. Widespread local reports indicated an unusually high number of animal breeding problems, miscarriages, Caesarean sections, unhatched eggs, stillbirths, and newborn deformities. Many calves had died from a mysterious disease that waterlogged their bones and left them incapable of standing.

Deer, pheasant, and other free-ranging animals virtually disappeared from the region. Even snakes and songbirds were seen far less frequently than before. Large trees began dying for no apparent reason, and on a farm close to the plant, photographs had been taken of mutated dandelions.

Most of these tragic changes went unreported in the mass media. Like so many other incidents, as quickly as it had captured national attention, the Three Mile Island accident had been forgotten. How many more times would Panayoikyasi have to raise himself above ground and shake his mighty fist? What sort of horrendous event would it finally take to awaken the public?

I had no certain answer. But in the song of Kokopelli's flute was a hope that still sustained me. In the teachings of the Peacemaker was a vision that still inspired me. In the prophecy of Maximón was a dream that still enveloped me. And in the wisdom of White Buffalo Calf Woman was a path that still called me to my destiny.

I knew that I had to find a way to integrate these four sacred powers, the precious gifts that I had received from each direction. These were my answer to the four atomic towers that loomed so ominously on the not-so-distant horizon. Their synthesis was the key to my own transformation, as well as to my ability to serve the greater needs of the planet. Thus, on my last visit to see Rarihokwats in that year, he told me that my time had come to journey to the center.

"You have gained much experience in the few years that I have known you," said Rarihokwats. "But consider the importance of letting understanding seep into every nook and cranny, so that it can emerge through your words and actions. This is one of the hardest lessons for those in Western civilization to learn. People *know* so much, but they reflect their knowledge so little.

"If it is your choice to continue on the journey you have begun, then you must learn to become the embodiment of your knowing."

"Yes, I want to do this," I responded.

"Then you are ready to go to the source," Rarihokwats continued, "to the center of all centers. There you will receive your greatest gifts. And there you will also face your greatest challenges. I will send you to my teacher in México. He lives in a place called Koatlan, beneath the Mountain of the Serpent. We call him 'El Maestro.'

From my first day in Kalpulli Koatlan near Mexico City, each morning began at dawn, with the sounding of *kikiztli*, the conch shell. Five times the shell sounded, greeting Tonatiuh, the sun, and supported by a steady, three-beat rhythm on the tall, tripodal huehuetl drum. With this music, there was always the burning of sage and *kopal* inside an iridescent shell of abalone. Prayers in Nahuatl, the Aztec language, culminated with the group shouting, "Teáhui! [Forward!]"

Such was the ceremonial focus held throughout the day at this community and school that was devoted to the revival of indigenous ways. Kalpulli Koatlan was a continuation of the ancient Aztec communal system of *kalpullis*, an autonomous social organization based on mutual respect and support. As among the Haudenosaunee, decisions were made by consensus, the equal rights of individuals contributing to the strength of the collective body.

But Kalpulli Koatlan nevertheless had a guiding force to whom its members were apprenticed. This was El Maestro, and his teachings spanned a vast range of subjects pertaining to ancient history, religion, and the arts and sciences. Through his years of study, he had earned the title of *tlamatini*, the Nahuatl word for "man of knowledge," or *sabio*, as they are commonly called in México. El Maestro's greatest devotion was to see the brilliance of his ancestors reawakened in the youth of México and the world. To this end, he received all who were open and ready to learn.

El Maestro was short and powerfully built. Though already in his sixties, he had incredible stamina, and his long, straight hair was still jet black. His eyes had a piercing quality, yet paradoxically they seemed very far away. Sometimes, while gazing into them, I felt as if they were pulling on me like magnets, leaving me no choice but to align with my own inner center or be utterly absorbed into their deep, dark pools. It was obvious that he dwelt within a compelling vortex of energy. Some might have called it charisma, but this was much more.

Every morning following our sunrise ceremony, El Maestro would give a teaching focused on some aspect of the ancient knowledge. I soon learned that Koatlan meant "Place of the Serpent," the serpent being a symbol of great wisdom to most Native American peoples, and particularly to the Aztecs.

"The name Koatlan descends from the mountain above our pueblo, which is known as Koatepetl, the Mountain of the Serpent," he explained one day. "Four ridges rise from each of the Four Directions in a wavelike, serpentine pattern. They join to form one peak, and from this natural design the mountain receives its name. It is the place where the serpent paths meet."

El Maestro went on to recount a fascinating story passed down by his ancestors. Approximately seventeen hundred years ago, he said, thousands of native people gathered atop this serpent mountain, Koatepetl, in order to undertake a mission that would fulfill their prophecies. They understood that this mission would take many generations to accomplish. Their task was to begin a migration out of which the spiritual unity of the entire continent of North America would one day be realized.

The people divided into four groups: one facing east, one west, one north, and one south. Four arrows were shot into the air, one to each of these directions. The people were then instructed to follow these arrows by migrating in paths that formed great spirals on the land. As the spirals became increasingly smaller, the descendants of these people would finally be guided back to Koatepetl, their ancestral place of origin. The time for the entire journey would take one thousand and forty years.

And so the journey began. With each culture that was visited, there was an exchange of sacred knowledge. The growing knowledge was passed on from generation to generation. From that fertile place of cultural cross-pollination, new sciences and forms of sacred expression were given life. And out of this tremendous wealth of diversity, there emerged the understanding of a fundamental spiritual unity between all the cultures of the continent.

El Maestro told us that his ancestors went east all the way to the Atlantic, west all the way to the Pacific, north all the way to the Great Lakes, and south as far as Nicaragua. In those days, that country was known as Nikankanahuatl, meaning "Here ends the land of Anahuatl." Anahuatl, he said, is the indigenous name for the continent of North America. Even in the far north, El Maestro added, there is linguistic evidence of his ancient Nahuatl-speaking ancestors. It was they who originally gave the lands by the Great Lakes the name of Michhuahkan (Michigan), meaning "Place where the people possess fish." And a derivation of that same name, Michoakan, was given to a region of many lakes in México.

Finally, in the early fourteenth century, the migrating groups began to return from all directions to converge at Koatepetl. Once all the groups had arrived at the peak of the mountain, final instructions for the fulfillment of the prophecy were revealed. As one great group, they were to journey south to the shores of Lake Texkoko. There they would come upon an island in the middle of the waters, and on this island they would see an eagle. The eagle would be perched atop a nopal cactus, and in its talons it would be holding a snake. This was to be the sign that they had at last arrived at the place where they were to found a new civilization.

The civilization would be based on the collective wisdom of all the native cultures they and their ancestors had encountered in a journey of more than one thousand years. In this way, the Aztec (or, more correctly, the Mexika) civilization was born on the island that became its capital—the ancient ceremonial center of México-Tenochtitlan, present-day Mexico City. "Thus was a sacred dream made manifest," El Maestro concluded. "This is the spiritual root of our people."

Listening to this story, I was once again struck by the archetypal parallels of indigenous history. Like Kokopelli, the traveling ancestors of the Mexika had been the carriers of cultural seeds. And like many indigenous peoples, their migration was an outbreath into the unknown, followed by an inbreath back to the source—a journey of discovery to the corners of the Earth that ultimately became a quest to recover their original wholeness.

Following El Maestro's verbal teaching, we went out into the garden to experience this same sacred knowledge in our bodies. In the middle of the garden was a large circle that had been cleared of plants. Here we began our practice of the Mexika dances. All of the other apprentices were of Mexika descent and had been doing these dances for years. Nevertheless, I was welcomed into the circle without hesitation and supported by my brothers in learning their ancient ways.

The first dance in which I was instructed was called Naui Olin. As El Maestro explained, this dance (whose name literally means "Four Movement") was always done before and after every other dance to honor the Four Directions. Moreover, its design was of four interlocking spirals, the basis of the migration patterns that went out from Koatepetl. When El Maestro drew this design on the ground with his finger, I immediately recognized it as an elaboration on the Hopi "sprouting-life" symbol. Clearly the spiritual cultures of the Mexika and the Hopi shared a common root.

While doing the dance, I saw that the Naui Olin was formed out of the even more universal symbol of the circle and the cross. I also remembered what the Hopi elder had said about the importance of their life symbol moving in the direction of creation rather than destruction. I found it curious that this dance spun the spiral design in both directions. I asked El Maestro what he thought about this.

"For us the movement in both directions is necessary, and both are sacred," he said. "One could not exist without the other. Their interaction represents the eternal dynamic out of which life itself is created. Movement—*olin*—is the very essence of our being. It is the beat and the pulse that sustains us. That is why the dance is so sacred. It enables us to harmonize all the opposing forces within and around us. Through dance we come to understand that no thing is separate, that all things are connected. Through dance, heaven and Earth become one."

In subsequent days, El Maestro focused his teachings on the brilliant Mexika mathematical system known as Nepohualtzintzin. He talked about the cycles of the moon and their effect on human beings. He talked about how the Mexika solar year of thirteen lunar cycles corresponds to the thirteen major joint articulations of the human body. He explained how the Mexika mathematical system was based on the number *twenty* rather than *ten*, partly because people went barefoot and used both their fingers and their toes for counting.

"For these reasons," he said, "our ceremonial calendar has thirteen months of twenty days. Or to put it another way, we multiply the major by the minor articulations in our bodies to come up with the 260-day sacred count."

El Maestro then went on to explain that this is almost exactly the time it takes for a baby to develop in the womb and how both corn planting and human conception were usually timed with the ceremonial calendar. He also demonstrated how the ceremonial calendar and the solar calendar aligned precisely every fifty-two years (four times thirteen) and that on such occasions there was always a renewal ceremony.

At these times, he said, everything was begun over again: new leaders were installed, new projects were begun, pyramids and temples were given fresh coats of paint, and often new structures were superimposed over old ones. As the universe is truly a grand harmonic design, astronomers also took note that every fifty-two years, the stars of the Pleiades returned to their exact same positions in the sky. It was this positioning that had signaled both the beginning and the end of the great migrations—twenty cycles of fifty-two years. So important was this fifty-two-year cycle that the Mexika used it to account for calendric periods ranging as high as twenty-six thousand years.

"The heavenly cycles are written in our very bodies," concluded El Maestro. "We are living computers, the perfect summation of an ordered universe. When our instruments are fine-tuned and in harmony with all organic and celestial movements, we have no need for charts or calculations. All information, all knowledge of time and space, is transmittable to our consciousness on a cellular level. This is the rightful inheritance of every human being on Earth."

As always, there was a strong correspondence between our afternoon dance practices and El Maestro's verbal teachings of the morning. Thus, while learning about the harmonic proportions of our bodies, we also focused on two dances. The first, called Iztakkuautli, or "White Eagle," represented human spiritual evolution. Its movements took us both downward to the Earth and upward to the sky, and it had a highly exuberant and expansive quality. In contrast, the following dance was called Tezkatlipoka, meaning "The Smoking Mirror." Its movements, though equally intense and powerful, were decidedly more elusive and contained. In between these highly aerobic dances, we would catch our breath as El Maestro explained their many layers of symbolic meaning.

"Iztakkuautli, the White Eagle, carries the force of the solar logos," he said. "It is the clear, white light that awakens our vision and illuminates our future. Tezkatlipoka, the jaguar, balances this as the guardian of the realms of darkness. He holds up his smoking mirror to the shadow side of our nature. The mastery of both these powers is necessary for true awakening to occur."

At last we were ready to plunge into the core of Mexika cosmology. In the central room of Kalpulli Koatlan hung a large poster of the Mexika Sun Calendar, known traditionally as Kuauhxikalli, the "Eagle Bowl." Within its complex mandalic design were elaborated the fundamental cycles of the Nepohualtzintzin mathematical system. As we pursued our study of the Kuauhxikalli, El Maestro began to teach us about the history of the previous "Suns," or world cycles.

In the center of the calendar was the face of the Fifth Sun, surrounded by the symbols of the four Suns, or worlds, that preceded it. El Maestro told us that the last inhabitants of the First Sun were consumed by jaguars. At the end of the Second Sun, he said, a tremendous wind swept over the face of the Earth. The Third Sun concluded when the Earth was pummeled by a fiery rain. And the Fourth Sun came to an end with a great flood.

El Maestro also told us that the Mexika language holds keys to the ancient past. "Our word for 'water' is *atl*," he said, "and we know that our ancestors migrated to this country from Atlan, the 'Land Surrounded by Water.' The Spaniards changed this name to Aztlan, and from that word is derived the word Aztec. But to clearly understand the past, we must go back to the original names and words."

With that, El Maestro told us of an ancient island continent, the center of a great civilization. This island, named Atlantis by the Greeks, was destroyed through a series of cataclysms culminating in a massive flood. Those who survived fled by boat for other lands.

"This corresponds exactly to our own remembrance of the island of

Atlan," he said. "This knowledge is also preserved in our ancient name for the Americas. We call it Itzachilatlan, meaning 'Land of the Great Red Ones from Atlan.'"

El Maestro then went on to explain that the memory of Mexika origins is so imbued in their language that a very high percentage of their words contain the root word *atl*—for example, *tlakatl* (man), *cihuatl* (woman), *mazatl* (deer), and *koatl* (snake).

"The importance we give to *atl* also reflects our scientific knowledge that water is an essential element in the makeup of all living things," said El Maestro. "Now, as we come to the close of the Fifth Sun, known as Naui Olin, we must explore all the permutations of meaning within the word *olin*, or 'movement.' This will give us the understanding we need in order to prepare to enter the next Sun."

El Maestro explained that the possible forms of *olin* include earthquake, axis shift, volcanic eruptions, and all other forms of earth movement above or below the surface. *Olin*, he said, can also manifest as war, revolution, social unrest, hunger, disease, or anything that burns.

"This is because movement generates heat," he said. "Though it begins as a synthesis of the four primary elements, the resulting effect of *olin* is strongly polarized toward the element of fire. Thus it is the element of fire that rules the end of the Fifth Sun.

"But," he hastened to add, "this does not mean that the Fifth Sun must end in cataclysm. The creative and spiritual arts are also manifestations of *olin*. They have the ability to channel the energy for transformative purposes. Movement is the very essence of music, dance, and ceremony. Above all, it is *olin yolliztli*, the 'movement of the sacred heart,' that provides us with the greatest hope that we can make the transition to the next Sun in a peaceful way. *Olin yolliztli* is the power of our love."

El Maestro concluded: "Already the force of *olin* is rising on this planet. Inevitably, its combined powers are preparing the way for the dawning of a new Sun. However it manifests, the secret of working with *olin* is to move with it and through it. The secret is not to resist the momentum for change, but to embrace it—to become part of the dance."

The culmination of my first phase of study with El Maestro came when he introduced me to the being known as Ketzalkoatl, the plumed or winged serpent. This teaching was a synthesis of all the others that had preceded it.

"Ketzalkoatl is the heart and essence of the ancient spirituality of our ancestors," El Maestro declared. "He represents the duality within and around all things."

El Maestro explained that the name Ketzalkoatl is derived from the words *koatl* (snake) and *ketzal*, the exquisite red, green, and turquoise bird symbolizing that which is most precious and sacred. So Ketzalkoatl, he said, not only means "plumed" or "winged serpent" but also "precious serpent."

"*Kikiztli*, the conch shell, is one of the most important symbols of Ketzalkoatl," he went on. "The interior of the shell is in the shape of a spiral, similar to the spiraling pattern made by a snake in movement. It is this movement that governs all things in our universe. Galaxies form in spirals, and so do the ocean waves when they crash upon the shore. Thus, like the conch, which comes out of the sea, Ketzalkoatl is a link to our primordial origins. So do we blow our vital breath into the conch shell to signal the rebirth of humanity and the return of Ketzalkoatl." (See figure 5.)

El Maestro told us that in ancient Mesoamerica, those who attained the highest level of spiritual evolution were given the title of Ketzalkoatl. It was a title of highest honor, equivalent to that of a saint or a bodhisattva. Among the many Ketzalkoatls who lived during those times, one was particularly renowned. His name was Ce Akatl Topiltzin, and he was born in the tenth century near a village called Tepoztlan.

Ce Akatl Topiltzin Ketzalkoatl became a great leader of his people, the Tolteks, and established their new capital in a place called Tollan. It is said that this Ketzalkoatl wore a jade and turquoise mask as a symbol of his enlightenment and that from a beautiful palace he lovingly guided the Tolteks to new heights of civilization, prosperity, and true humanity.

But one day another force entered into the city of Tollan: a man by the name of Tezkatlipoka, that same one we'd heard of before who mirrors the shadow part of ourselves. Being the trickster and magician that he was, this particular incarnation of Tezkatlipoka began to win favor among the people of Tollan. Yet secretly he was bent on conquest and control.

Ketzalkoatl took little heed of this until one day when Tezkatlipoka came to him and said, "Come, Ketzalkoatl, remove your jade and turquoise mask. Gaze into my mirror and see your true self."

Ketzalkoatl was reluctant to remove his mask, but Tezkatlipoka persisted, and finally Ketzalkoatl gave in. When he saw his true face, Ketzalkoatl fell back horrified, for it was covered with sores, scars, cuts, and boils. He became so ill at the sight of his ugliness that the people feared he might die.

Then Tezkatlipoka transformed himself into an old man and said, "Come, Ketzalkoatl, I will cure you. Just drink of my magic potion."

The drink was an intoxicant made from the fermented juice of the maguey cactus. Again, Tezkatlipoka had cleverly tricked Ketzalkoatl into acting against his own better judgment. Ketzalkoatl took a taste of the drink and soon felt much better—so much better, in fact, that he asked for more. Before long, Ketzalkoatl was extremely happy and extremely drunk. Finally he fell asleep.

Once more Tezkatlipoka transformed himself, this time into the beautiful sister of Ketzalkoatl, whose name was Ketzalpetlatl. Then he came to Ketzalkoatl in his feminine form, awoke and aroused him, and seduced him. Indeed, they slept together.

When Ketzalkoatl awoke in the morning and realized what had happened, he was overcome with shame. He went to look out his window, only to find that all of Tollan was in a state of decadence and chaos. The sight caused him such great pain that he exiled himself from the capital, bearing all the burden of blame himself. Thus began the rule of the Dark Lord, Tezkatlipoka, in Tollan. But upon leaving, Ketzalkoatl prophesied that he would someday return to undo the work of Tezkatlipoka and reestablish his capital in balance and peace.

As Ketzalkoatl journeyed south along the shores of Lake Texkoko, his spiritual and creative genius left its mark on every village and person he met. Finally he and his followers, many of whom were dwarves, arrived at the base of the twin volcanoes Popokatepetl and Iztakcihuatl. They began to ascend the slopes, but when they reached the higher altitudes, they were met by a great snowstorm. All but Ketzalkoatl froze to death.

Now Ketzalkoatl had reached his heart's end. Wishing only to die, he sank into a deep despair.

Just then, four holy men appeared to Ketzalkoatl and tried to lift him from his sorrow. Ketzalkoatl perceived in these men a great purity of spirit. Feeling renewed hope, he presented the holy men with the four sacred tablets that were inscribed with his teachings.

"Perhaps there is still a people who will understand my teachings and take them to heart," he said. "Find these people if you can. From them will grow the Tree of the World, and they will know true peace."

And so the holy men set out to the Four Directions, carrying the tablets of Ketzalkoatl. Meanwhile, Ketzalkoatl himself continued eastward down the slopes of the twin volcanoes and on to the place known as the Celestial Waters (today called the Gulf of Méxiko). There at the shoreline, Ketzalkoatl gathered grasses, twigs, branches, and many large logs. A crowd of people gathered around, curious to see what he was planning to do.

Ketzalkoatl piled all the dry kindling and wood together and set them ablaze. Then he spoke to the crowd of people, again prophesying his return. He said he would return in the year of his birth, Ce Akatl, or "One Reed," and that he would come from the east. Finally he stepped into the flames, sacrificing himself for his people and the world.

According to El Maestro, the Old Ones say that as Ketzalkoatl burned, his ashes rose skyward and turned into all the precious birds. *Ketzal* and macaw, hummingbird and eagle—birds of every color of the rainbow were seen rising upward into the sky.

For eight days the fire burned and the ashes rose—just as Venus disappears for eight days between the Earth and the sun before it reappears as the Morning Star. When the ashes were all gone and the last of the birds had risen, finally the heart of the *ketzal* appeared from the smoldering coals and slowly ascended toward the Heart of Heaven.

Witnessing this, all the people knew that Ketzalkoatl had gone to the sky. Thus, the Old Ones say Ketzalkoatl was changed into the Morning Star, and that this star first appeared after Ketzalkoatl died. And thus they call him the Morning Star of Anahuatl, the "Lord of the Dawn."

Hearing this story of Ketzalkoatl, I remembered the first time I ever saw the Morning Star from atop Harney Peak. Now, almost seven years later, I could feel it beginning to shine brightly in my life again. It was illuminating the same path as before—an unbroken path that had guided me through four sacred directions and in toward the all-unifying center. But here the path had a new and different appearance. It wound in waves and spirals. It was made of feathers and scales, paved in patterns more intricate and paradoxical than I had ever experienced.

Who was this Ketzalkoatl? I wondered. Who was this man who was said to be the most enlightened teacher ever to walk the Americas? I wanted to walk where his feet had walked, touch the places he had touched, for in his footsteps I could hear the echo of my own heart. Not since my exposure to the teachings of Black Elk had a system of spiritual knowledge touched me so deeply.

Within the walls of the *kalpulli*, living only with others who shared a similar view of reality, it was easy to become immersed in the ancient ways and forget the world outside. Yet a mere hour away by bus from the village of Koatlan was the nation's capital and the world's largest metropolis: Mexico City. And it, too, was a source and center for much of what I had been learning with El Maestro. I soon began venturing into the city often, in order to supplement El Maestro's teachings with my own research and direct experience.

Mexico City was an overlay of three cultures: the ancient, the colonial, and the modern. During the ancient time when it was known as México-Tenochtitlan, its pyramids, temples, markets, and dwellings covered an island in the middle of a vast turquoise lake. This was the same island where the first Mexika pilgrims had found the eagle eating the snake.

In all written sources, both indigenous and Spanish, México-Tenochtitlan is described as a city of exceptional aesthetic beauty. Back in Europe, its sophisticated network of plumbing, irrigation, and canals earned it the title of "the Venice of the Americas." Five causeways led from the shores of Lake Texkoko to the shores of the island capital, which was divided into four sacred districts in accordance with the Native American worldview. Each district was composed of five *kalpulli*s, so that a total of twenty on the island corresponded to the cyclical twenty-day count. The total estimated population of the city in 1519, when Córtes arrived, was approximately three hundred thousand, making it the largest city in the world at the time. Nevertheless, it was orderly and clean. This astonished the Europeans, many of whom had come from the filthy and disease-infested cities of Europe's Dark Ages.

In every respect, nature seemed to provide the perfect complement to Tenochtitlan's aesthetic appeal. Its idyllic, high-altitude lake floated against the massive backdrop of the two snow-capped volcanoes where Ketzalkoatl had finally sent his teachings to the Four Directions. These same volcanoes were regarded by the Mexika as Tlalokan, a heavenly paradise on Earth and the abode of the divine powers. Thus they were somewhat akin to the Greeks' Mount Olympus. Mirrored by the lake under once-clear skies, the view of the volcanoes beyond the temples of Tenochtitlan must have been an exquisite sight to behold.

Correspondingly, the waters of Lake Texkoko were teeming with fish and frogs, while the hills and forests around it were home to a vast variety of indigenous animals, including rabbits, deer, coyotes, and jaguars. All sorts of brightly colored birds filled the air. Trees and flowers ranged from tropical to temperate, and fields of corn, amaranth, squash, beans, tomatoes, chile, and cotton graciously yielded their bounty all year round. No wonder human beings found the Valley of México such an attractive place to settle and grow.

Regarding culture, a few Spanish chronicles tell of orchestras of up to ten thousand people playing a wide range of drums, rattles, conch trumpets, ceramic flutes, and ocarinas on special ceremonial occasions. Equally dazzling were the enormous processionals and circles of dancers outrageously costumed in feathers, beads, shells, skins, silver, gold, colored cloth, and precious stones.

But these reports won little notoriety back in Europe. Instead, what piqued the imaginations of the "civilized" countries were reports of ceremonies involving human sacrifice. It was these reports, filled with gruesome details of blood and gore, that sent chills through the European spine. And it was these reports that eventually aroused a sense of horror sufficient to justify the wholesale destruction of an entire people.

Even today, long after confirmation of the Aztecs' artistic and scientific brilliance, the word Aztec continues to conjure images of human sacrifice. In fact, the two terms have become virtually synonymous.

It was this grisly impression that El Maestro was trying so hard to overcome. Many of the native people I had met in Guatemala told me that the Spaniards had severely distorted their accounts of human sacrifice in order to paint their adversaries as the ultimate savages. But El Maestro went much farther: he insisted that there had never been any human sacrifice in México, not even among the Aztecs! Rather, the offering of the human heart to the sun, he said, was an esoteric symbol of the human ability to give complete love to the Creator on behalf of all creation.

El Maestro's perspective was appealing to me, but I was hesitant to believe it completely. I was still fairly new to Mexikan history and felt it would be best to learn from as many sources as possible. Fortunately, in Mexico

City there was no shortage of such sources, including some of the world's most fabulous museums, as well as a wide range of people who had devoted their lives to the understanding of Méxiko's heritage.

In my research I found no definitive answer about human sacrifice. But one thing on which there seemed to be universal agreement was that Ketzalkoatl's name and priesthood were always associated with the spiritual path of giving the heart as an act of love, rather than in some bloody rite. If nothing else, this reaffirmed my own sense of personal alignment with Ketzalkoatl and made me all the more determined to seek evidence of his legacy, both within and outside of Mexico City.

One of the places I went was the Zocalo, the large colonial plaza in the center of Mexico City. Nearby, I had learned, there were once two tall, white pyramids glistening in the sun. In their place now was a dark, gloomy church. Opposite the pyramids had been a conical temple dedicated to Ketzalkoatl.

Walking around the Zocalo, I came upon one of the distinctive serpent heads of Ketzalkoatl carved in stone. It had obviously been moved from its original location and now formed part of the cornice of a colonial government building. Its obsidian eyes had been taken out, and it appeared to be crushed by the weight of this alien bureaucratic structure.

As I imagined Ketzalkoatl's spirit trapped within that head, I wanted to throw off the alien rock and free the ancient memory that was buried beneath it. Just as vision had been plucked from the serpent's eyes, I, too, felt blinded by the oppressive force hanging over Tenochtitlan. I desperately wanted to see through the smoky haze of this city to the volcanoes where Ketzalkoatl had given his teachings. But they were forever hidden by the most choking, burning smog I had ever experienced. How was I to receive the revelation of this sacred place?

I soon found myself having the same sort of apocalyptic visions in Mexico City that I had received as a child growing up in New York City. The Earth and all her ancient, primal forces would appear to me reclaiming what had been taken from them. One day, while walking near Alameda Park, El Maestro and I passed by a church that was sloping down to one side. El Maestro explained that it was one of many such cases—that slowly the city was sinking back into the lake. I asked him if there were prophecies regarding these changes. He said yes, that it was all part of the awakening of *olin* at the end of the Fifth Sun. He said that tremendous volcanic eruptions and earthquakes would rock Mexico City and shake a new awareness into the people who survived.

El Maestro also told me that I was receiving messages from Tepeyollotl, the "Heart of the Mountain," whose animal form (like Tezkatlipoka's) was the jaguar. He said that Tepeyollotl ruled earthquakes, volcanic activity, and all subterranean movements. El Maestro cautioned me not to fear my visions, but to observe them carefully and remember them. Such an opportunity came the following day.

I am walking alone on Avenida Insurgentes near the university in the southern part of the city. For some unexplainable reason, I stop in my tracks and look up. Just ahead of me a massive form seems to be floating mysteriously in the sky. I realize I am looking at one of the twin volcanoes. Finally the atmosphere has cleared enough for me to see it! As I stare at it, it begins to move, and I feel its power coming inside my body. I am oblivious to the passing crowds and traffic. All I can hear are these words:

> I am Iztakcihuatl,
> the Woman Who Sleeps.
> Now you shall see me rise.
> My snow-lined body slides downward
> and stretches against the sky.
> Shall I dance upon the people
> and melt them with my feet?
> If they must be remade,
> then it must be so.
> Who shall know?
> Teahui!

Suddenly I feel a hand grab my left shoulder and pull me back. At the same moment, a taxi whizzes past me with its horn blaring. Unknowingly, I have stepped off the curb. As soon as I am on the sidewalk again, I turn around. But in the place where I am sure I will see my savior, I see no one.

Then I feel something like gravity pulling my head to look across the street. In the midst of the moving crowds is a muscular, bare-chested man wearing nothing but a loincloth! He is looking right at me with intense green eyes, and his face is the face of a jaguar. Once more, all other sounds disappear as I hear the words:

I am the Heart of the Mountain jaguar.
I roar from the depths of time.
I, mighty warrior, lift my chest.
I call upon the waters of the moon.
Soon they will ripple.
Soon they will rise.
The city will surely swim.
The Lake of Texkoko reclaims its shores
as turquoise forever ascends.

A few days after my urban encounter with these powers, El Maestro said he wanted to take us far from the city to a Nahuatl-speaking village called Chalma. Two of the apprentices, brothers named Tekpatl and Topilli, were from this village, and I assumed that we were going to visit their family. As it turned out, however, El Maestro had something else in mind.

Chalma lay nestled in a deep, lush valley filled with fruit trees and fields of corn. Its remoteness made it all the more appealing to me, as I was feeling burned out from too much time in the city. Inside the village, Tekpatl and Topilli's parents lived in a small adobe house with a thatched roof that reminded me of the Mayan homes I'd seen in Guatemala. They were very happy for the rare opportunity to see their sons, whose education they had entrusted to El Maestro. He clearly knew this and didn't want to monopolize their time together.

Thus, not long after we arrived, El Maestro told me that Tekpatl and Topilli would stay with their parents for a couple of days while the rest of us went elsewhere. Shortly, he flagged down an old pickup truck. We all climbed in back and descended still deeper into the valley.

The next village we arrived at was called Malinalko, meaning "Place of Grass." From there we hiked down a trail through the forest, past huge trees with vast root systems that tangled all over the rocks. It was a very hot day and much more humid than I had grown accustomed to. As the trail gradually wound its way up the mountain slope at the forest's edge, I wondered what the reward was going to be for all my buckets of sweat.

Finally we came to a cleared area overlooking the valley. It was obviously the remains of a small ceremonial complex. In the center was a pyramidal platform of thirteen steps topped by a squarish stone temple. The temple had a thatched roof much like that of the native houses, and the entire structure appeared to have been carved right out of the solid-rock mountainside.

El Maestro's eyes flashed with excitement as he gathered us together, and his head quivered as it always did just before he revealed something of great importance. He said he had brought us here to continue our teachings on the animal powers. As we walked up to the temple entrance, I could see that the doorway was actually a carving of the open mouth of a snake. Its flat, protruding stone tongue provided a symbolic stone mat upon which to enter.

El Maestro said, "Like our *kalpulli*, this place is a *koakalli*, a 'serpent house.' Whenever we come to a temple with one or more carvings of snakes at the entrance, the Old Ones are telling us that we are entering a sacred place of knowledge and wisdom. So leave your shoes outside and step barefoot on the tongue of the snake. Go inside the body of the serpent."

Once within, I was amazed to see that the interior of the structure was circular in design, not square or rectangular like the other pyramid temples I had seen in Mesoamerica. Even more surprising, there was a low ledge for sitting that ran along the perimeter of the circular space. This made it quite similar in appearance to a kiva, the ceremonial chamber found among the Pueblo peoples of the American Southwest. Carved into this ledge, directly opposite the entrance, was the round head and flattened skin of a jaguar. Spaced widely on the ledge to both right and left were the beaked heads and flattened bodies of eagles. A third eagle was carved on the floor in the center of the temple.

El Maestro told us to be seated on the ledge and to go into silence. A few minutes later, he began to speak.

"This place is one of the most important ceremonial sites for the native people of America," he said, his head quivering as before. "It may not be very large, and it may not be very famous, but it is unique. This temple is part of the living evidence of our extensive migrations and cultural links with the people to the north. It is the perfect synthesis of pyramid and kiva—of the temple that rises toward the sky and the temple that reaches into the Earth. It is also a perfect synthesis of linear and circular structures, which together symbolize the union of matter and spirit."

El Maestro explained that for hundreds of years before the arrival of the Europeans, this temple had been used for spiritual initiations by peoples from as far away as the Hopi mesas. So that the elders would be clearly guided in the giving of sacred names, the temple had been designed with symbols of the three animals that represent the essential attributes of the human psyche: the snake, the jaguar, and the eagle.

"The snake, connected to Ketzalkoatl, is the symbol of consciousness or cosmic intelligence," El Maestro went on. "Because we entered through its mouth, we are actually within it, and this tells us that the other powers are contained within its totality. We might think of this chamber as the snake's head.

"At the back of its head, opposite its mouth, is where the jaguar sits. This position corresponds to the occipital point, the indented area where the back of our neck meets our head. In the brain it is the area of the medulla. Its function is memory, and its attribute is the subconscious. So do we find the jaguar directly opposite the snake's mouth, farthest from the outside.

"The three eagles symbolize the third eye, the power of vision. The attribute of the eagle is superconsciousness, the ability to see beyond what we already know or have experienced. As the jaguar is the past, the eagle is the future, and both are contained within the movement of the snake, which is time itself."

As I listened, I strained to absorb the meaning of all that El Maestro was saying. But he did not stop for us to reflect. "The snake is the current that moves up and down our spine, from the root to the crown," he continued. "As this temple is its head, in its roof is the place where the powers of eagle and snake unite. There the serpent has wings. There is the place of Ketzalkoatl. But disconnect it from its foundation, from its root deep in the Earth, and it is nothing; it is without worth.

"Perhaps you find that all these symbolic meanings are entangled in your mind," El Maestro said, correctly reading my confusion. "They can become like a snake that is wrapped and coiled around itself. In such a state, it is difficult to see the beginning or the end. But that is the infinite quality of this teaching. Our cosmology is not neat and linear. It is intricate and round like this world. It is full of apparent contradictions. But everything finally seeks to become a part of the original oneness. There is no use in fighting it."

Up to that point, I had not told El Maestro about my encounter with Tepeyollotl in downtown Mexico City. It disturbed me, and it had thrown me off balance for days. It was not that I couldn't accept what Tepeyollotl had said. Rather, it was the unsettling feeling that I didn't know what to do with it. Only now, within this temple, did I even feel capable of verbalizing my predicament.

Knowing that this was the time, I recounted the entire experience to El Maestro. When I was done, he told me to get up from where I was seated and move over to the position of the jaguar at the back of the temple.

"You must allow yourself to merge with the presence of Tepeyollotl without resistance," he said to me. "Because this temple has been carved from the living rock, here we are physically within the Heart of the Mountain. Particularly where you are now is the position of Tepeyollotl."

El Maestro told me to sit on the jaguar's skin with my legs crossed, then lean forward and place my arms in front to support my body. He told me to turn my hands in toward each other, fingertips touching and palms flat on the stone, then to arch my neck away from my chest and let my eyes roll into the back of my head.

"Breathe deeply," he said, "circulating your breath up the front of your body and exhaling down your spine. This is the meditation of the jaguar."

With that, El Maestro announced that he and the other apprentices were going to leave me alone for a while so that I could go into the silence. "Go deep," he admonished—"very deep. Tepeyollotl has yet another message for you." Then he left.

No sooner was I alone and in the jaguar pose than I felt as if I actually *were* a jaguar. I felt like I was inside a much larger, thicker body, and my breathing even took on the low-pitched purr of a cat. I kept following the cycle of breath through my body until my body and consciousness seemed fused into one. When I reached that place, I was filled with a deep, cellular knowing.

When at last I released my neck and refocused my eyes, El Maestro was standing directly opposite me, in the doorway of the serpent's mouth. All I could see was his silhouette. He asked if anything had been shown to me.

"Yes," I said, "it was very clear. It was like remembering something that is my future. I have to go to some volcano and stand at the crater's edge. But there is one thing that I do not understand. I was shown that this volcano must be very young. It can only have been born within recent times. How could that be possible?"

"You have seen well, and you have seen correctly," said El Maestro.

"The volcano you must go to is called Parikutin, and it is in the state of Michoakan. There you will learn its story. You must go today."

"Today!" I exclaimed. "Why so soon?"

"Better than to wait," responded El Maestro. "We will leave Malinalko and get you on the first bus to the town of Uruapan. Isn't there someone you know who lives near there?"

My first inclination was to say no, but then I remembered a beautiful young woman I had met at the Indigenous Peoples Theatre Celebration in Canada back in 1980. Her name was Lucinda, and she was a Purepecha Indian from the village of Pamatakuaro in Michoakan. She had actually invited me to visit if I ever had the chance, and I had fortunately saved her address.

When I told El Maestro about Lucinda, he immediately said, "Go find her. She will take you to the volcano of Parikutin."

I arrived in the isolated village of Pamatakuaro after a long, dusty bus ride from Uruapan through the dark, rugged forests of the Sierra Madre of Michoakan. Emerging from homes here and there, smoke curled skyward against the morning light. When I asked someone to direct me to Lucinda's street, I was at once surrounded by a throng of children. Thus my personal search quickly became a village processional, replete with shouts and laughter.

At the door of Lucinda's house, I was greeted by an old woman with long, gray hair woven into braids. She seemed strangely unsurprised to see me. She said Lucinda had gone to another village but would be back soon. Then she invited me in.

For two days, there was no sign of Lucinda. By this time, everyone in the village knew I was at her house waiting for her. A rumor had begun to spread that I had come to take her away to marry her. The villagers could not imagine why else I, a young foreigner, would have come there from so far away. The mother superior of the local church also made a point of getting to know me, hoping to insure that I would "rescue" Lucinda from her "primitive" Indian background. I finally gave up trying to explain my purpose in coming. No one would ever believe that the real passion that drew me here was not a woman but a volcano.

At last, on the third day, Lucinda came home. Unlike her grandmother, she was very surprised to see me. I explained to her that I hoped to climb the nearby volcano of Parikutin, and suddenly she became very silent. Her wide eyes and high cheekbones seemed to sink behind her long black hair. I wondered if I had insulted her, and I hastened to say that of course I had also come to visit her.

"I know that, Jim," she said. "It's nothing about you." But she wouldn't explain further. All she said was that if I wanted her to take me to Pariku-tin, we would have to leave early the next morning.

Before dawn, we boarded a bus to the village of Angahuan, about an hour's ride from Pamatakuaro. On the bus she told me the story of Parikutin.

Forty years ago, she said, Parikutin did not even exist. Instead, beneath the black lava that now covers the land around the mountain, there were once two villages. One was called San Juan; the other was called Parikutin. For decades these two villages had been caught in a bitter feud over the ownership of land along their common border. By the early 1940s, the feud had escalated to the point where some villagers were actually getting violent with each other.

Then one day, a local farmer whose land lay right on the disputed border noticed a strange new hole in the ground. Even stranger, there was smoke coming out of it. The farmer shoveled some dirt into the hole and covered it up, thinking that would be it. But the next day, he came upon the hole again. It was even bigger and spewing more smoke.

Once again the farmer filled the mysterious hole with dirt. But it didn't disappear; each day it kept growing. Soon earth began to push up around the hole, and before long there was a cone-shaped mountain growing in the farmer's field. It grew so big that eventually there was nothing left of the farmer's field, and a large part of the border area was taken over. In spite of this, the two villages continued fighting each other over who had rightful control of the land.

Finally, though, the fighting came to an abrupt halt. The smoking mountain burst alive, erupting with deadly power and burying both villages under molten lava. Some of those who survived still argue over the land, but as Lucinda said, "These people have never understood that the land belongs to no one but the Earth herself."

When we arrived in Angahuan, Lucinda suggested we first go to the marketplace to buy food and drink for our hike. While we were there, she also bought a large bundle of flowers, which she wrapped in her dark-blue shawl. I asked her what they were for. All she would tell me was that it was a personal matter.

Lucinda seemed very different to me than she had been in Canada. There, she had always been spirited and happy. Here, by contrast, she seemed serious and withdrawn. I sensed a deep sadness in her. But since I didn't know her well, I was reluctant to ask many questions.

From Angahuan we began our hike toward the volcano. Before long, the terrain was completely devoid of plants. All around us were nothing but fields of lava and an occasional dead tree. In the distance rose the massive black cinder cone of Parikutin. As we walked, I thought about the amazing history Lucinda had shared with me on the bus. Here we were in the very midst of that history's legacy. It was so immediately present that I could almost feel it searing and crackling beneath my feet.

Soon we began our ascent, climbing the switchback trail to the top of the crater, a couple thousand feet above the eerie lava plains. I wondered why Tepeyollotl had wanted me specifically to come here, but I had no doubt there was a good reason. I knew I must look into the mouth of the volcano and listen to the unspoken words.

Reaching the crater's edge, I burn an offering of cedar and *kopal*, and Lucinda and I peer down to see sulphur steam still rising from the crater floor. As I gaze into the volcano, I have an important realization: Here is a power that not only destroys but renews. It dawns on me that volcanoes are the cry of the Earth Mother, the roar of the jaguar, the impassioned call to awakening. When all else has been denied, repressed, and disempowered, volcanoes will rise to shake free the hidden past and make clear the way for the coming of a new era.

There can be no more immediate encounter with these perceptions than by meeting the untamed Earth as a newborn volcano. Here, in this territory that is absolutely and undeniably hers, I again hear the voice of Tepeyollotl. I enter the Heart of the Mountain.

> House of lava,
> silent, dark, waiting,
> like a jaguar that crouches
> in the jungles of night;

> Anahuakalli,
> ready, ripe, waiting,
> ripe and potent with primal force.
> Emerge from the darkness,
> O powers of Anahuatl.
> Emerge and take your place.
> We must be ready to receive you,
> Volcano,
> the voice of the Earth.

As I conclude my ceremony, smoke still rising from the melted sap of *kopal*, two young Mexican boys arrive at the top of the crater. One takes his empty Coca-Cola can and throws it into the abyss. The other follows suit with his candy wrapper. Neither perceive their act as a violation, though smoke still rises from the depths of Parikutin.

Thus do the patterns of ignorance continue, I am thinking. But the story is still unfolding. Those of us who choose to must continue in a sacred manner as best we can, continually cleansing the pain of violation from our hearts. Oh, how patient is the Earth!

Lucinda and I gathered our things together and silently departed. After a few miles along the trail, we came to a most bizarre and profound image. Buried at least fifteen feet deep in rock-hard lava were the remains of the church of San Juan. We stood at the base of its two solitary steeples—all that was left of a once-thriving village.

At this moment, Lucinda was clutching her shawl, and I saw a tear roll down her cheek. As soon as I took her hand, she burst out sobbing. Whatever deep sorrow she had been carrying, I knew now that it was connected to this place.

After many minutes had passed, Lucinda laid the flowers on the ground, knelt beside them, and began to speak.

"Today is February 20," she began. "Thirty-eight years ago, on February 20, 1943, the volcano erupted and sent lava flowing toward this place where we are now sitting. My grandmother, whom you met at my house, lived here in San Juan at that time. So did her daughter, who was my mother. So did her husband, the grandfather I never knew. He was buried here in the lava while praying in this church. Despite my grandmother's pleas, he refused to leave. Finally, she fled with my mother in her arms. They barely escaped.

"When my mother married my father in Pamatakuaro, my grandmother moved in with them," Lucinda went on. "A year later I was born. Every year on February 20, we used to come here to leave flowers between the steeples of this church in memory of my grandfather—except ten years ago, just after my brother was born. My parents felt that he was too young to travel, so they asked me and my grandmother to stay at home with him while they traveled by bus to leave flowers at the church.

"On the way to Angahuan, the bus went off the side of the road. Everybody was killed. I've never come back here since that time, because I've never been able to forgive the volcano for taking so much of my family away from me."

Lucinda began crying again, but she struggled to continue speaking, her copper skin glistening with fresh tears. "A couple of years ago, my grandmother had a dream that a young man was going to come to the village and bring me back here to make peace with the volcano. I refused to believe her. I swore I would never come back. I resented her because she had been able to find her own peace, while I never could . . . until today.

"I never really thought I could forgive the volcano," she said, "but without knowing, you challenged me to make it so. Today, at the edge of the crater, where I had never dared to go before, I watched you pray with so much love and sincerity that I found the power within myself to heal my wounded heart. Thank you, Jim. It was not I who guided you here; it was you who guided me."

From Michoakan I traveled back to Koatlan, arriving just in time for a major ceremony marking the Mexika new year. This ceremony usually fell in late February, but its precise date was determined by the rising of the star Sirius in exact alignment with the peak of Koatepetl. El Maestro watched for the nearing of this event, upon which members of many other *kalpulli*s in the area were called to converge in celebration.

On the morning before the dawning of the new year, about fifty dedicated pilgrims made a procession to the top of Koatepetl. The two-thousand-foot climb took close to four hours, the trail winding like a serpent to the highest point. On our arrival, we burned *kopal* and sounded conch shells to the Four Directions. We then continued beyond the rocky peak to a forested area, where we set up our camp.

That night, around the fire, El Maestro shared more about the ancient history of this very special mountain. He told us that it was the birthplace of Huitzilopochtli, the sun—or, in its animal form, the hummingbird. He explained that like many other spiritual traditions, the Mexika have a cosmic trinity: sun, moon, and Venus; bird, feline, and snake; Huitzilopochtli, Tezkatlipoka, and Ketzalkoatl. These spiritual powers, which represent will, memory, and intelligence, also manifest as action, reflection, and energy. He explained that in ancient times, each of these powers was important enough to have its own separate temple in the center of Tenochtitlan.

At this point, a member of one of the other *kalpullis* asked El Maestro a question: If it was true that Huitzilopochtli was the war god of the Aztecs, as most archaeologists and historians would have us believe, then how did this fit in with his other seemingly more divine attributes?

"As the members of Kalpulli Koatlan have been learning, there are violent warriors and there are spiritual warriors," El Maestro explained. "Huitzilopochtli is the model spiritual warrior. Like the hummingbird, he acts instantly from a stance that is all knowing. His movements are rapid, precise, focused, and clearly directed. Like the sun, Huitzilopochtli is dependable. He never falters. His actions bestow blessings upon his entire community, upon all the children of the Earth. Huitzilopochtli aligns his will with the greater will of the Creator."

Just before we went to bed, El Maestro concluded: "As we dream this night upon the mountain where Huitzilopochtli was born, may each of us be guided to understand the true task of warriorship in our lives."

The following morning, all the celebrants came together in a large circle surrounded by rocks and boulders. Everyone wore garments of white, and many carried offerings of flowers or had brilliantly colored feathers in their hair.

The dawn view from the top of Koatepetl was spectacular. High above the dense smog of Mexico City, I could at last see Iztakcihuatl and Popokatepetl set against a shimmering sky. As the sun rose behind them, the sound of conch shell trumpets signaled the opening of the new solar year and plumes of *kopal* smoke wafted through the air.

Simultaneously, the best of the Mexika dancers came into the center of our circle, stamping their feet in unison to the thundering beat of the big huehuetl drum. Bursting into vigorous movement, with hundreds of ayoyotl ankle rattles percussively accenting every falling leap, the dancers spun out their cosmic choreography on behalf of all creation.

At the conclusion of the ceremony, El Maestro stepped into the center to deliver a message. "This morning marks not only the ending of an old year and the beginning of a new one," he said. "It is also the anniversary of the death of one of our greatest leaders: Kuauhtemok.

"It was Kuauhtemok who led the strongest defense of Méxiko-Tenochtitlan and who put up the final resistance to Cortés's army of conquistadors. The Spaniards translated his name as 'Fallen Eagle,' as if to say he was defeated. But the true translation of his name is 'Eagle Who Descends.' He was the impeccable warrior, targeting his prey with pure focus and intent in the manner of Huitzilopochtli."

El Maestro went on to deliver Kuauhtemok's long and eloquent final speech. He spoke of the tragedy that had befallen Méxiko-Tenochtitlan, as well as of its former brilliance. He said that although the Mexika had been outwardly defeated, spiritually they had remained strong so that they could endure and rise again.

El Maestro said that Kuauhtemok had instructed the Mexika to bury their sacred books, their holy objects, and even their pyramids. He told them to cover these with earth so that the Spaniards, in their destructive fervor, would pass them by. He encouraged them to take the power and wisdom of these things and guard them within themselves. In the secrecy of their own homes and communities, they were to pass on the sacred teachings to their children, for as long as the oppressors remained in control.

But one day, said Kuauhtemok, the Mexika would know that the time had come to bring all these things out into the open again. The sacred books and relics would come forth, the ceremonies would return—even the pyramids would be revealed again in their full splendor. On this day, he said, the Mexika would shine once more like the sun, and their greatness would be known before all the world.

As El Maestro concluded Kuauhtemok's speech, there were tears in many eyes, for we all knew that our own times had begun the fulfillment of Kuauhtemok's prophecy. But there was more.

"After Kuauhtemok's last speech," El Maestro said, "he was captured by the conquistadors. They tortured him to try to get him to tell where the Mexika had hidden their gold. But he would not tell. Even when they burned off both his feet, still he would not tell. He knew that the gold was in the hearts and minds of his people, and he would never betray them. Even if he had spoken the truth, the Spaniards would never have understood.

"Amazingly, Kuauhtemok escaped from the conquistadors," continued El Maestro. "Hobbling on the bloody stumps of his legs, he walked across our country all the way south to the Yukatan. The physical strength of this man was beyond belief. Wherever he went, in every village and community, he warned the people because he knew what was coming. So did he give them the same message that he had given to the Mexikas: 'Hide all outward physical evidence of our ancestral spiritual knowledge. Instead, place it fully inside yourselves, and teach it to your children. Our day of rebirth will come.'

"Finally, the conquistadors found Kuauhtemok living among the Maya. They captured him and placed him in prison, where he died not long afterward. But they never defeated him. Spiritually he was too strong. He was as much eagle as he was man."

Like Koatlan, the ancient ceremonial center of Teotihuakan lies to the north of Mexico City. It was built by the Tolteks, and its designers were obviously master architects and artisans. The massive dimensions of its pyramids and walkways give the impression that it was inhabited by a race of giants.

According to El Maestro, Teotihuakan was not a city but rather a university. It was one of the great mystery schools, or learning centers, of the Americas. The famous pyramids of the sun and the moon, like most of the pyramids of ancient Mesoamerica, were complex calendars and observatories of the entire heavenly realm.

I was fortunate, in my first visit to this great center, to be accompanied by El Maestro and his other apprentices. Arriving on the day just after the beginning of the new year, we entered the site sounding conch shells and offering burning herbs. As we approached the main pyramid, we gave thanks to the Ancient Ones who had built this place, that we might honor them and benefit from their wisdom.

In sharp contrast to our approach, many of the tourists and Mexican visitors behaved as if they couldn't care less about the religious nature of the site. To these people, it might as well have been a playground or an amusement park. At the Temple of Ketzalkoatl, I saw two adult North American men place their arms inside the stone jaws of the serpent heads on the building's facade. They screamed and made panicked facial expressions as their wives captured the mock dramas on video cameras. Meanwhile, Mexican teenagers ran up and down the Pyramid of the Sun all day long, blasting rock and disco music from large portable cassette decks. Beside numerous sacred structures, trash and human feces littered the ground, and the whole site was ringed with a tall and incongruous metal fence.

Under such circumstances, it was difficult to connect with the true spirit of Teotihuakan. I knew that El Maestro and other traditional Indian people were very disturbed by the gross behavior of certain visitors. For them, the site was an active, living spiritual center—not at all a "ruin," as commonly thought.

El Maestro explained that although most of the sacred books had been burned by the Spanish, the ancient teachings were yet written in these stones. By deciphering the stones, one could gain access to tremendous astronomical, calendrical, and mathematical information. The greatest books of this treasure house of knowledge still remained for those who held the keys to their translation.

At the base of the Pyramid of the Sun, El Maestro instructed us to climb it in a zigzag pattern, like the movement of the serpent of knowledge. He said that to climb straight up was considered arrogant because it did not respect the degree of spiritual power represented by the highest position of the pyramid. That is why the steps were built so shallow and steep, to discourage a direct ascent. To climb it correctly, he said, it was necessary to meditate on raising our internal energy while connecting with the serpent's path.

Once on top of the pyramid, we had a commanding view of the entire ceremonial complex as well as the surrounding valley and mountains. There, El Maestro shared further secrets.

"We consider this pyramid to be a scale model of the Earth," he said. "Its base corresponds to the equator, and where we now stand is the North Pole. In between are the points that correspond to the entire Northern Hemisphere. Just as the Earth is like an observatory in space, so is this pyramid like an observatory. Depending on where we stand, our view of the stars will be different. Here, with this one structure, our ancestors made accessible a vast range of celestial observation.

"For every pyramid that is built above the Earth," he continued, "there exists an inverted pyramid of energy beneath the Earth. In this case, that inverted pyramid corresponds to the Southern Hemisphere. For a physical pyramid built in the Southern Hemisphere, the entire relationship is reversed. But the base always corresponds to the equator.

"In all cases, the complete form, combining physical and energetic structures, is a three-dimensional diamond with four sides. This diamond corresponds to the rounded sphere of our planet. Its force field projects all the way down to the core of the Earth and all the way up to the Heart of Heaven. It forms a chain of invisible diamonds, much like the DNA ladder in our cellular structure. The pyramid activates our genetic memory and aligns us with the designs of our future evolution. It connects us to our infinite potential as co-creators in the universal web of existence."

On the way back to Koatlan, I thought again of the teaching I had received from Don Adrian about the meaning and purpose of the pyramids. I saw how the explanations of El Maestro did not contradict but rather complemented those teachings. Whether the pyramid was a scale model of the universe, the Earth, or the human body, it was clear to me now that it was really all the same. The divine, hidden structures that permeated our existence could be found on every level, from the cellular to the galactic. Just as with the spiral design, the pyramidal form was encoded into the fabric of our lives by the grandest architect of all: the one, omnipresent Creator.

The next day, my fellow apprentice Tekpatl invited me to join him on an excursion to Tula, another ancient ceremonial center a couple of hours to the north of Teotihuakan. This site had been built long after Teotihuakan was established.

After we had made our offerings at the site, I climbed with Tekpatl to the top of the main pyramid. There stood four enormous, evenly spaced statues of men in elaborate ceremonial dress. Supposedly, they had once served as pillars here supporting the roof of a temple.

Tekpatl told me that these statues were known as "Atlanteans" and that they carried much ancestral power for the Mexika people. He explained that the abstract symbol carved on their chests was a butterfly, which represented the returning spirits of the departed. By focusing one's attention on the butterfly, it was possible to access the ancestral memory of the Atlanteans.

"Do you come here often?" I asked Tekpatl.

"Yes," he said. "I have been coming here on every new and full moon ever since El Maestro initiated me with my name."

"What does your name mean?"

"A *tekpatl* is a ceremonial obsidian blade or knife. It represents the power to cut through obstacles and to bring forth the most precious gift that we have hidden within ourselves."

"What a beautiful meaning," I said.

"Yes, but there is another side to it," responded Tekpatl. "According to the archaeologists, it was the *tekpatl* that our ancestors used to cut out the still beating human hearts of their sacrificial victims atop these pyramids. Of course, El Maestro denies that this ever happened."

"Well, what do you believe?"

"The Atlantean ancestors have told me that it is true," he said. "There was once human sacrifice in this place. It was not widespread, but it did happen. It happened through those powerful priests who distorted our sacred teachings for their own personal gain and strange pleasure."

"Are you saying there was a spiritual knowledge about sacrifice that existed before Tezkatlipoka came here?"

"Yes. The original teaching of sacrifice is the teaching of the snake who sheds his old skin in order to grow. Like the snake, what we must sacrifice is not our physical body but our old skin—our limitations and attachments. We must sacrifice our fear of the unknown. As El Maestro has told you, the real sacrifice is not to cut out a human heart but to willingly give from our own hearts as an act of love. This love comes from the conscious merging of fire and water. We call this mix of passion and compassion Atl Tlachinolli, or 'Burning Water,' and it is the greatest gift we have to offer."

Tekpatl went on to say that even the terrible pollution we see from oil refineries, exhaust fumes, and oil spills are modern manifestations of Burning Water. He intimated that the powerful priesthood that distorted Tezkatlipoka's teachings has continued through a technocratic priesthood of corporate, government, and military leaders. And he feared that it was getting much worse. But, he added, just as the return of Ketzalkoatl is prophesied for our time, so there will also be a new Tezkatlipoka—a god of darkness who is aligned once again to the highest meaning of spiritual sacrifice.

"Maybe it is because of El Maestro's genuine connection to Tezkatlipoka that he cannot consciously accept the history of human sacrifice," Tekpatl concluded. "It is too close, too personal; for like Tezkatlipoka, El Maestro's greatest gift is as a wizard of the night sky, of dreaming, and of all that belongs to the jaguar. Still, I thank him for giving me the name Tekpatl, because it has forced me to cut through many obstacles to my growth. I understand now how to use the sacrificial blade, and I am no longer afraid of Tezkatlipoka, for I know who he really is."

Shortly after my visit to Tula, I had a startling dream.

I am in a large room, apparently the interior of an ancient temple. A multitude of ritual objects surround me, and many beautiful weavings cover the floor. I'm sitting on one of these weavings in front of a large stone table.

El Maestro enters the room holding a big plate in his hands. He brings it to the table and sets it down in front of me. On the plate is a beautiful snake.

With an obsidian blade, El Maestro slices the snake down the middle. Then he neatly removes the meat from the interior and hands it to me. I eat the whole thing, and I greatly enjoy it; the taste is wonderful.

The next morning when I awoke and remembered the dream, I was very disturbed. More than eating the snake itself, what bothered me was the fact that I had enjoyed it. I was a vegetarian at the time and didn't like the idea that even on a subconscious level I could take pleasure in consuming the flesh of another animal. I decided to tell the dream to El Maestro, hoping that he might help me to understand it.

"This is a very good dream, for which you can be thankful," he said. "It has nothing to do with partaking of the physical flesh of the snake but rather of its energy, its essence. Remember that here we are in Koatlan, the Place of the Serpent, which is also the house of knowledge."

El Maestro explained that in my dream, I had been given a sign that I had received the knowledge of this sacred place, that I had taken it into myself fully, and that it had pleased me greatly. "Now that this is accomplished," he said, "you must meditate for the next step to be shown to you. Realize that what you have seen is not only a message about your past, but about your future."

As El Maestro spoke, I was already filled with the knowing of what I had to do next. The dream was letting me know that, at least for now, my purpose in coming to the *kalpulli* had been fulfilled. It was time for me to move on. It was time for me to take one of the serpent paths that spiraled out from Koatepetl and follow it to its completion.

The path that called me was to the south. It was the path by which I would retrace the journey of Ce Akatl Topiltzin Ketzalkoatl across the Mexikan landscape. I had already visited his ancient capital at Tula. Now I would make pilgrimages to all the sites where this inspired prophet had left signs of his luminous presence. In so doing, my intention was to touch the very heart of this sacred teacher and thus to find his essence within myself.

THE WINDOWS
OF PERCEPTION

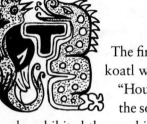The first stop on my pilgrimage in search of Ketzal-koatl was the ceremonial center of Xochikalko, the "House of Flowers." This ancient site lay slightly to the south of the colonial city of Cuernavaca, and it clearly exhibited the combined creative efforts of Mayan, Zapotek, and Toltek craftsmen. Especially exquisite was the main pyramid dedicated to Ketzalkoatl, carved on all four sides with enormous bas-reliefs of a dragonlike feathered serpent.

According to El Maestro, Xochikalko was built by the major cultures of Mesoamerica, roughly in the tenth century, for the purpose of synchronizing their various calendars into one harmonious system. And according to legend, it was here that Ce Akatl Topiltzin Ketzalkoatl was conceived by his mother, Chimalman.

There are at least two versions of how this occurred. One says that the Chichimeka chief Mixkoatl fell in love with Chimalman, fathered the sacred child, and was subsequently killed by his envious brothers. The other story says that Ketzalkoatl was born of an immaculate conception resulting from a precious stone that Chimalman swallowed. This stone was jade, the symbol of everlasting life throughout Mesoamerica.

Whatever the case, the birth of Ketzalkoatl was prophesied by the astronomer priests of Xochikalko, and it was known that Chimalman would bring him into the world. However, she died in childbirth, and Ketzalkoatl was instead raised by his maternal grandparents near Tepoztlan. At an early age, he was sent back to Xochikalko for training by the priests into the sacred knowledge.

Following Xochikalko, I continued on to Tepoztlan, faithful in my intention to trace the prophet's path. Here I found bizarre rock formations, not unlike sand castles, embracing a network of lush, green valleys. In the ancient days, Tepoztlan was an important center for the arts, and it still is today. The alternative-minded community is also home to many spiritual seekers of numerous paths, as well as to Nahuatl-speaking Indians who have retained many of the old ways.

From the sites of Ketzalkoatl's beginnings, I journeyed on to those places he touched following his exile from Tollan. Traveling east, I headed toward the twin volcanoes. I was profoundly moved when Popokatepetl first came into view. More than any other, this seemed to be my personal sacred mountain. Just seeing it was sublime; I felt as if I were looking upon the very face of God.

By the time I arrived in the village of Amekameka at the base of the volcanoes, it was close to sunset. As the last clouds cleared from the peaks, both volcanoes were bathed in a warm, amber light. In that romantic hour, I was reminded of an old Nahuatl legend about the volcanoes being a pair of immortal lovers.

But my own romance in this realm was of a far different nature. As the jaguar Tepeyollotl had called me to Parikutin, now the feathered serpent Ketzalkoatl was calling me to the summit of Popokatepetl. And so I took a taxi to the twelve-thousand-foot base camp of Tlamakas, in the saddle between the two mountains. The following morning before dawn, I began my ascent to the top of the eighteen-thousand-foot volcano. Alone but determined, I raised my hands to its snowy summit and spoke these words:

> You, like bald eagle with white-capped head;
> You, like bald eagle with black-winged body;
> You rise from the Earth, Popokatepetl.
> You are the Earth, and yet you are more;
> Something beyond, something awesome.
>
> Let me climb your shoulders and soar to your heights.
> Let me stand at the crest of your gaping mouth.

I will hear what you have to say.
The clouds are your white feather collar.

But I was not to reach the top—only fifteen thousand, five hundred feet. Just as Ketzalkoatl's devotees of long ago, I was not adequately prepared for the cold. What's more, my head was pounding—an early sign of altitude sickness. In my religious fervor, I had tried to ascend eleven thousand feet in less than a day. Resolving to return in the near future, I reluctantly started back down the snowy slopes.

On my descent, though, I noticed a small, weathered, white object lying beside a rock outcropping. On closer inspection, I realized that it was an animal bone. I asked the mountain for permission to take it, and placed it in my bag. Later I showed it to the old man who had rented me my climbing gear in Tlamakas. He said it was the wrist bone of a cougar. To me, this was a sign that the feline spirit of Tepeyollotl was close. Though I had not reached the summit, I had once again touched the Heart of the Mountain.

My ride down to Amekameka the following day provided another synchronicity: as it turned out, the driver was going on to the very place that was next in my eastward pilgrimage. Together we rode to the city of Cholula, former site of a vast network of ancient pyramid temples. At its heart was a massive pyramid dedicated to Ketzalkoatl. Scientific measurements of its remains have proven it to have been the world's largest pyramid by volume, surpassing even the Great Pyramid of Giza in Egypt. And atop this pyramid, say the chronicles, there was once a magnificent, solid-gold sculpture of the feathered serpent.

All that is gone now. When Cortés arrived in Cholula, he vowed to destroy every pyramid and raise a church in its place. Tragically, he kept his vow. Cholula's temples were burned to the ground, its devotees massacred, and its treasures stolen. Today, what is left of the great shrine is heavily overgrown. It looks more like a big hill than a pyramid, and on top is a yellow, blue, and white church.

Thus, the only way to really appreciate the pyramid is by entering a doorway that leads to its interior. An extensive maze of tunneling passageways runs through its base, but why they were built is a mystery.

One thing, however, was clear. I discovered that when I stood beyond the east end of the pyramid and faced west, its shape aligned perfectly with the pyramidal contours of Popokatepetl; while I stood on the west side and faced east, it aligned perfectly with the volcanic contours of Poyauhte-katl (known today as Orizaba). This led me to conclude that the pyramid was intended as a scale model of the sacred mountains—and that perhaps one of its functions was to allow devotees to symbolically reenact Ketzalkoatl's ascent of México's two highest peaks.

From Cholula I knew I must follow the path of Ketzalkoatl eastward to the shores of the Gulf of México in the modern state of Veracruz. But precisely where, I didn't know—until a dream, in which I was instructed to go to the volcanic crater lake of Katemako. Beyond this lake, the jungle-covered mountain slopes descend to the Gulf of México. There, I was sure, I would gain new insight into Ketzalkoatl's departure from the world.

I arrived at a virtually untouched stretch of coastline known as Montepio. A clear, flowing stream wound its way through buttress-rooted mangroves where bare-breasted native women bathed unashamed in the soft waters. The stream emptied into the gulf sea, and white, sandy beaches extended beyond the horizon both north and south. There I prepared my offering of sage, cedar, and *kopal*, kindling it to remember Ketzalkoatl's final transformative act of self-sacrifice nearly a thousand years before.

No sooner had the herbs begun to burn than I heard a voice. I turned to see an old woman, her long gray hair falling in two tightly woven braids.

"What are you doing?" she asked.

As I told her the story of my pilgrimage, she seemed quite entertained by my gringo passion for ancient Mexikan history. Smiling silently, she listened until I had finished. Then she spoke.

"What you have recounted is but one version of the story of Ketzalkoatl," she said. "All along this coast, his departure is remembered, for part of Ketzalkoatl's greatness was his ability to be in many places at one time. Some saw him burn and later arise to become the Morning Star, but others saw differently. As you have come here to this place, it would be good for you to know the story we remember."

The old woman explained that long ago, when Ketzalkoatl stood by these waters, the whole village came to see him. They came because he had wrapped many snakes around himself, and they were curious to see what he would do with them. Suddenly, by his magical command, all the snakes lined up, one beside the other. Together they slithered across the sand and into the waves, forming a raft for Ketzalkoatl to stand on. Thus he appeared to float on water, and all the people were amazed.

Ketzalkoatl spoke, telling the people he was traveling across the Celestial Waters to the Land of the Sunrise. He said he was going to the place of light and wisdom.

"But when will you be back?" the villagers asked.

"You will know by my signs in the sky," he replied. "I will come across the waters. I will come from the east. I will return in the spring, in the year of my birth." Then the waves lifted around his raft of snakes, and Ketzalkoatl floated off toward the horizon.

I asked the old woman whether she knew anything more about where he went. She said that the Maya remember the arrival of Ketzalkoatl in the Yukatan, where he became known as Kukulkan, and that he built a special pyramid at a place called Chichén Itzá.

"Every year on the first day of spring, the shadow of the celestial serpent of Kukulkan descends the steps of this pyramid," the old woman said. "The energy of Kukulkan enters the Earth, and a new year of life begins. It is something that I have heard is very wonderful."

As the old woman spoke, I realized that it was only three days to spring equinox. The timing was perfect; my direction was clear. I had to go to Chichén Itzá to conclude my pilgrimage in retracing the path of Ketzalkoatl across México. And there was no time to waste. I thanked the woman profusely. Then I made my way to the dirt road out of the village, where I hitched a ride back to Katemako.

After two days of traveling, I arrived at Chichén Itzá, leaving me a full day to explore the site before the equinox. Throughout what is known as "New Chichén Itzá," the Toltek architectural influence was unmistakable, lending credence to the possibility that Ce Akatl Topiltzin had indeed landed in the Yukatan and guided major building projects at this site. Interestingly, the greatest architectural feature at Chichén Itzá was the exquisitely symmetrical pyramid of Kukulkan, whose sophisticated design served as both a calendar and a cosmic computer. I did not want to pass up the chance to visit its interior while there were still relatively few tourists.

Ascending a long, low, and narrow passageway that led from the outside, I slowly worked my way through the darkness to the central inner chamber. There, dimly lit, was a beautiful, orange-painted stone effigy throne of a jaguar with spots and eyes of green jade.

Breathtaking as it was, it came as no surprise. From all I had learned with El Maestro about Mesoamerican animal symbolism, it seemed entirely natural that the jaguar was deep inside the temple, the hidden place of the subconscious. Clearly, here was a representation akin to Tepeyollotl, the Heart of the Mountain jaguar.

The next morning began a day of major celebration at the pyramid and throughout Chichén Itzá. Even the president of the Republic of Mexico showed up for the festivities. But to me, the real royalty were the dignified Yukatek Mayan villagers whose ancestors had built this place and who had celebrated here for centuries.

In the late afternoon, the serpent began to descend the pyramidal staircase. In the midst of a huge crowd, I watched as the light crossed the northwest edge of the pyramid, casting an undulating shadow onto the west-facing side of the northern staircase. As the sun dropped lower, the shadow formed into seven distinct waves, each perfectly matched by seven waves of light. Then, at the bottom of the staircase, the serpentine mix of shadow and light joined with the carved stone head of the feathered serpent, Kukulkan.

The symbolism was abundantly clear: Kukulkan was the essence of the equinox, bringing all opposites into balance. Before my eyes, he was impregnating the terrestrial world with his fertilizing celestial power. Returning was the lightbearer of consciousness, counterpart to the jaguar who dwelled in the depths of the subconscious at the center of the pyramid. Paradoxically as always, the feathered serpent was returning as both the light to balance the shadow *and* the light in balance with the shadow.

When,
in all places,
the belly is upon the ground,
the spine upon the sky,
and the core of being
lies equally
between
the two worlds
of night and day,
heaven and Earth,
north and south,
woman and man;
when at once

shining
is the Morning
and the Evening Star,
look upon your heart
and you will see
Ketzalkoatl.

As the crowds departed, I made my way to the north side of the pyramid and ascended its ninety-one stairs to the top. There, I circled the temple in a sunwise direction, coming around to face the west. I placed offerings in my abalone shell and set them ablaze. Facing the setting sun, I raised the shell from Earth to sky and back again, laying it before my feet.

I stare into the sun, arms outstretched, hands open, the smoke of *kopal* curling around me. By now, the sun is a brilliant red-orange disk poised on the edge of the perfectly flat plains of the Yukatan, like a ball balanced on a tightrope. As I gaze, the sun seems to draw me in, impregnating my consciousness just as Kukulkan impregnated the Earth. I hold my gaze, breathing in the light.

Suddenly, in a striking vision, I see seven black suns descending to the Earth in a zigzag, serpentine pattern. They descend at an angle, starting at my left and finally entering the physical red sun that is aligned to my center. No sooner do these suns come down than another set of seven black suns begins to ascend from the red sun on the horizon. They rise at an angle, zigzagging up to the right and finally disappearing like a celestial serpent into the sky.

Finally the red sun sets, and day turns to evening, but the serpent suns are still pulsing in my mind. They have inscribed in me the image of an inverted pyramid, the pyramid of energy beneath all physical pyramids. Thus am I awakened to the diamond nature of all being—to the infinite ladder of genetic remembrance that stretches between the Heart of Heaven and the Heart of the Earth.

Following my equinox experience, there was only one place I wanted to go: Palenque. Like an impassioned romantic who could not forget his first true love, I gave in to her call. My first night in the campground there, I could hardly sleep. I crawled out of my hammock and wandered barefoot over the roots of tall trees, gazing through their leaves to the full moon and stars. I was obsessed, lovesick. I so desperately wanted to merge with this realm of primordial magic.

Going deeper into the forest beyond the campground, I could hear the occasional eerie hooting of owls. Soon the flying silhouettes of bats flashed before my eyes. "O guardians of the night," I whispered, "have you no answer to this strange mix of pain and bliss?"

Even as I asked the question, an answer was given:

"Owls and bats," the Nightbird sings,
"Now in darkness, see all things.
Find the inner light to shine,"
sings the Nightbird to the mind.

"The Mayan moon is soft and clear.
The jungle people have no fear.
The forest and themselves are one.
The moon is equal to the sun.

"Heart of the Mountain jaguar
roars from the depths of time.
Now is the reawakening.
Embrace your primal being."

Embrace my primal being! That was *exactly* what I wanted to do—but how?

The next morning, I met a young man named Jorge who joined me for a tropical breakfast of mangoes and papayas. He told me that he had been living in the camp beneath the temples for many months, but that only now was he beginning to access the true essence of Palenque.

Jorge said he had traveled throughout the world, working his way across Europe, Asia, and South America. Wherever he went, he always found himself drawn to sacred sites. Finally his quest had led him here, to the place built by his ancestors. And here, at last, he had found what he was looking for.

"Didn't you know about this place before you started traveling?" I asked him.

"No," Jorge responded. "Although my grandparents were Maya, I grew up in Mexico City. My parents were ashamed of our background, so I had to discover on my own what it means to be Maya. Until I found Palenque, I didn't even know that I cared."

I felt a strong brotherhood with Jorge. Though of different races, we both had been called out of the cities of our birth to reconnect with something more at the core of our common humanity. In different ways, Palenque was part of our shared heritage. I sensed it would also become an important part of our shared future.

With considerable fervor, Jorge explained that Palenque had been an ancient mystery school that at one time drew people from all over the Americas. More important, he said, its wisdom was still alive—not only in the temples, but in the rocks and trees. But to receive this wisdom, he added, one must look with new eyes.

"How does one get such eyes?" I asked.

"There are many paths to perception," he responded. "It is a question of what is appropriate in the moment."

Jorge told me that if I had a genuine desire, he would introduce me to the beings at Palenque who had gifted him with clear vision. "They are known to the Maya as *akox*," he said, "and in the Nahuatl language they are called *xochitl*. This word means 'flower,' but it also refers to all the consciousness-expanding plants through which it is possible to communicate with Teotl, the divine power of the universe. In this case, I am referring to mushrooms."

"So you have tried *xochitl* yourself?" I asked.

"Of course," he answered. "Many times the flowers have assisted me in my readings. For Palenque is a book of poetry carved in stone. If you would like to read it without a translator, then come with me tomorrow to the fields, and we will gather the *xochitl* together."

Naturally, I was excited about seeing the world from an entirely new perspective. In considering Jorge's offer, however, I was faced with a new dilemma. I had always prided myself on being able to access visionary experiences without the use of mind-altering substances. Many times I had been offered drugs of one sort or another, and I had always refused them.

Now, for the first time, I began to see that my path was not so narrowly defined as I had previously believed. I felt that I needed to drop some of my rigidity. Besides, listening to Jorge speak about the poetic and spiritual traditions associated with the *xochitl*, I simply couldn't place them in the same category as drugs. He had spoken of *xochitl* as sacred medicines, natural sacraments provided by the Creator for the enlightenment of humanity. Indigenous cultures had learned their safe and proper usage over thousands of years. With these things in mind, I resolved to let Jorge be my guide.

The following morning at sunrise, Jorge and I hiked out to the fields. After an hour of searching through the grass, I began to think we might not find any mushrooms. Nevertheless, Jorge assured me that we would both find the *xochitl*. They would appear when we least expected it, and they would be the exact ones that were waiting for us.

He was right. Just at the point when I was ready to give up, I stumbled on a cluster of four beautifully formed beige mushrooms, each about three inches high. Almost simultaneously, Jorge encountered his medicine. We thanked Xochipilli, the lord of flowers and poetry, for the gift of the sacred plants. Then we gently picked them, placing them inside the personal pouches we had tied around our waists.

Jorge suggested we hike back to the waterfalls that flow down from the temples of Palenque. On my previous visit to Palenque, I had not seen these waterfalls, and I was astounded by their beauty. Clear, aquamarine water cascaded from one limestone pool to another, forming a sort of living sculpture in the midst of the rain forest.

"These waters have tremendous cleansing and healing power," Jorge said. "Before we eat the *xochitl*, we must purify ourselves in the water and ask the spirits of Palenque to bless our journey."

Jorge removed his clothes and dove in. I followed. The water was just cool enough to be refreshing. Early morning sunlight filtered through the tropical foliage and sparkled on the water's surface. Birds sang exotic songs in the trees above us.

Jorge swam back to shore and removed the *xochitl* from his bag. He asked me to do the same. Then, at the center of the lower pool, we stood waist-deep in the water, facing each other with the precious "flowers" in our hands.

"This is a blessed moment of renewal and rebirth," Jorge said serenely. "The spring equinox has just passed, and the sun has just risen. It is a new season and a new day. All powers are aligned to support us on our sacred journey." So saying, he dipped his hands into the water and sprinkled it over the *xochitl*.

"Is there anything you wish to say before we take the medicine?" he asked.

"Yes," I responded. "I would like to offer it to the Four Directions and the Earth and sky, to call in the Six Powers of the Universe, and to dedicate our journey to all that lives."

Thus we held forth the mushrooms as we turned in the water to face each direction. Finally we held the medicine to our hearts, praying for all powers to be united in our center, and for our center to be one with the will of the Great Spirit.

"May the ancestral Maya of Palenque be our guides," Jorge said as we raised the first mushrooms to our mouths. The taste was strong and strangely rich, but not unpleasant. Slowly, very slowly, I chewed, meditating on the *teonanakatl*, this most holy food, its divine flesh becoming my own flesh. Afterward, I had no desire to do anything but sit quietly in the water, where I contemplated the serenity of my existence.

> The shade is like a drink.
> It refreshes me from the intensity of the world
> and lends my soul a place to rest.
> Here, beside the whirlwind movement,
> I am still and floating on the ripples of the waves.
> Nothing can disturb my peace,
> because I Am,
> and that is enough.

As I sat in the water, a butterfly fluttered into my field of vision. I simply observed as it came and went. Then my gaze was caught by Jorge's eyes, and in my mind I heard him speaking:

> The butterfly passes
> like a thought
> framed
> in your mind.
> It pauses
> as a thought
> of contemplation.
> Sometimes it enters
> and goes back

to where it came from.
Sometimes
it moves on
to other places.
Should it stay,
undecided where to light,
give it patience.
It will find its place.
You will find your way.

With these unspoken words, I stood up and said, "Come, let us go to the temples."

"Yes, it is time," Jorge affirmed.

Silently we dressed and gathered our few things together. Then we hiked alongside the waterfalls up toward the temples. As we walked, I was aware of a heightened sense of all my surroundings. When we reached the top of the trail, stretching before us we could see the cleared, grassy plateau and the beautiful white pyramids of Palenque. No guard awaited us, since we were coming in through the back way, yet it seemed clear that this was the proper entry for pilgrims such as ourselves.

Jorge asked me if I knew the original name of Palenque. I answered no. "My ancestors knew it as Nah Chan," he said. "Palenque was once called the Red City of the Serpents, meaning that it was a place of great knowledge."

On these words, we made our way toward a large, rectangular building at the center of the site. We walked up its steps and went in. "This is the Temple of the Windows," Jorge explained. "Its windows represent the open pathways of our senses, by which we perceive the world. On that level, this temple is you, me, and potentially anyone who enters here. We *become* the temple, and it teaches us to see in a new way.

Looking around, I saw many openings in the stone walls shaped like the letter *T*. "This is the shape of the Mayan glyph known as Ik," Jorge said. "It represents wind and spirit. It is a window through which you can see from one reality into another."

"Last month when I was in Mexico City," I said, "El Maestro introduced me to two Huichol yarn painters who began to teach me about the *nierika*, which they told me was like a passageway between worlds. They said that by using peyote, they were able to journey between these worlds and see the unseen dimensions. They depicted these dimensions in their yarn paintings. Many of them had mandala-like designs with symbolic openings in the center. By meditating on *nierika* such as these, they said, it was also possible to travel into the other world, much the same as with the peyote."

"Yes," Jorge responded, "that is a universal understanding for the native cultures of Mesoamerica. In fact, the Huichol *nierika* is often shaped like a peyote button, while the T-shaped windows of Palenque are the same shape as the mushrooms."

Next Jorge guided me down a shaded corridor to a place where one of the T-shaped windows had been built into the wall. He told me to stand directly in front and look through it. When I did, I was astounded to discover that it lined up exactly with two other T-shaped windows, all of which focused the eyes precisely upon a T-shaped door lintel at the opposite end of the temple.

"What you are looking at," Jorge said, "are the pathways of perception within your own consciousness. You are seeing through the windows that can take you both inside and outside yourself. When you align these windows perfectly, you will discover that the view is infinite."

As Jorge talks, I lose all sense of time. I am transfixed on the distant image of the Ik. Waves of energy move through my body. I feel as if I am melting into myself. When I finally step away from the window, I am suddenly aware of the rain forest everywhere. Its weird, hypnotic sounds and verdant presence surround the walls of the temple. Where just a moment ago I was completely absorbed in my mind, now I feel totally expanded, as if the whole outer world is entering inside of me.

I take a deep breath. Jorge looks at me and smiles. He knows the medicine has just taken effect. He says:

> Jungle in fog,
> fragrant and rich
> with the smell
> of sweet morning dew.
> Oo steamy ecstasy.
> Green, oh so green,

vibrant and vital,
silent, unseen.
You are the paradox.
We hear your call.
You are the mystery,
Master of All.

As Jorge finishes his poem, my gaze fixes on an enormous mahogany tree whose luxuriant branches seem to writhe like dancing serpents. Never has a tree appeared so alive to me. Then it begins to speak:

I am the Earth.
I grow here like this.
How do you feel me?
Where I roll and lift, are you glad?
Where I stretch and fall, does it please you?
Do the trees impart to you their secrets?
Can you hear their spirits whisper?
What does your heart say?
Will it sing tomorrow or today?

"It seems that you are ready," says Jorge as the tree finishes speaking. "I'm going to leave you now." My first impulse is to feel abandoned, but almost immediately I realize the perfection of his decision. He has guided me through the window. Now I will have to continue the quest on my own.

I gesture farewell as Jorge turns to walk down the corridor. Now I, too, stand and turn, for the first time noticing the exquisitely detailed bas-relief carving on the wall behind me. It depicts a beautiful Mayan man in full regalia, seated on a double-headed jaguar throne. To his side, seated cross-legged, is a slightly smaller man who appears to be holding up a feathered offering to the man on the throne. It seems to me that these two must represent the archetypal teacher and student. I realize that I am both these archetypes, as is Jorge—as is every other human being.

At last the tourists begin arriving. Seeking more seclusion, I walk through a doorway into another section of the Temple of Windows, where I find a grouping of small, roofless rooms. Feeling content and secluded, I nestle myself into a corner and begin to dream with open eyes. . . .

I can see many forms in the rocks. I can see that I am one with them and with the lush green plants surrounding the temple. I "become" the stones, the walls, the plants, the temple; there is no separation.

I pass my mind through the Window of Perception to the carving of the teacher and student teaching each other. In this great school, I see all language as patterns of energy in motion, like dragonflies flying on feathered serpent wings, weaving the warp of the world. I pass into the time of the reptiles, where everything is green and primeval. As my evolution unfolds, I transform from man to monkey to bat to eagle. My wings flash lightning. From a volcano I arise on fountains of flight.

Beyond where I stand is the Temple of the Sun. Its roof vibrates with light, as the temple calls to me in song:

> We are the ancestors.
> We are alive.
> We are the ancestors.
> Come forward and meet us.

Over and over again I hear this song. The temple keeps calling me, and I know I have to go. So I rise and glide toward it, walking effortlessly. All around me, the world is vibrating like a feathered serpent, like the wings of a dragonfly. Everywhere I look, it is all Ketzalkoatl. Everything I touch, hear, or smell is Ketzalkoatl. None of my senses are separate. I perceive all things from inner unity.

As I enter the Temple of the Sun, I see the ancient stone carvings there in their original forms. I place my forehead on the carving of the disk of the sun, and I hear the ancestors singing inside. They are still alive! Together we sing:

> We're cracking through stone
> to the mysteries of life.
> We're cracking through stone
> to the mysteries of life.

Many people are entering the temple now, and I invite them to sit with me. Oblivious to how I must appear, I say, "Here we will understand together, foreheads to the ground, the rock, the Earth. Seeing through, seeing to the truth, visions of the other world." Then I begin singing again:

> We're cracking through stone
> to the mysteries of life.

A young man with a straw hat steps forward to greet me. He holds out his hand and smiles, asking where I am from.

"Turtle Island," I tell him. "And you?"

"Europe," he says.

"Welcome, people of Europe!" I call out. "That is what the stones are saying to all of you who've come here—to all of us with white skin, and the yellow, and the black. The red people built this place, but now people of all different colors are coming here to learn, to understand."

My new friend smiles again. "Will you come with me to the other temple?" he asks.

I happily agree. We climb many steps, and when we reach the top, I know we have arrived at the Temple of the Cross of Palenque. This is the temple whose central panel is missing, the one carved with the image of the Tree of Life. Still remaining on the temple's right side, though, is a relief carving of an old man smoking a big cigar. His smoke rises and fills my mind with a scene of the forest burning.

Up until now, it has all seemed like paradise. The land and everything around me has been an abundant expression of corn, like interlocking kernels or the honeycombed cells of a beehive stretching off to infinity. (See figure 2.) But now my throat and insides begin to constrict as the world grows dry, brown, and shriveled. I see fires burning on the plains, and everywhere helicopters are circling like dragonflies, weaving the new warp of the world. I feel like everything is going to die. I see the water going away from the world and the people losing hope. Yet somehow I know I must have faith that things will survive.

Then the rocks speak again:

> See that man? He's a Maya.
> But he's afraid,
> afraid of the reality of being Maya.

In my memory I see them: seventy men to a truck, three trucks a day, being carted away like cattle to work their stolen land. I see young boys torn from the arms of screaming mothers by faceless men with uniforms and guns, who once had been these same young boys. In every city, on every street corner, they stand stiff and silent, pointing their weapons at the flesh moving by; blind to the eyes, the hearts, the souls; waiting for someone to step out of line. These same men who once were the guardians, whose fine curving physiques were carved on the temples—these same men now stand stiff and silent, guarding the fortress of foreign control.

And where is the corn that once fed the people?

> O cry for the people,
> O cry for this land,
> for here there is hunger,
> for here there is war.

I stand in the cornfield. The leaves are brown and the roots dry. How can this be the same world that was once so green? Only moments ago, I felt the joy of growing life. "Oh, hear me, Yumil Ka'ax, Young Lord of the Corn! O hear me, Lord of the Forest!" I cry out. Thus am I answered by Yumil Ka'ax:

> Go to the river and heal yourself.
> Drink of the water and know it.

I follow the voice and go to the river. I let it run over me and flow within me. Slowly the pain in my chest begins to recede. The water is so clear, so beautiful, so full of light. I feel as though I am seeing the water for the first time. Then I know I will survive. I know the people will survive.

I follow the river into the forest, to a place I have never been before. I go high above the river to a small temple in the shade. And here I sit down to rest. I lie down to sleep and to dream. . . .

Awakening, I go to a tree beside the temple and nestle my body between its great roots. Soon I see a man coming up the trail—a Mayan man, but this one is not afraid. He says hello and asks where I am from.

"Turtle Island," I say. "And you?"

He points deeper into the forest, and we both smile.

"And this temple—do you know its name?" I ask.

"It is a place of much force," he responds. "It is the Temple of the Jaguar. Tell me again where you are from."

"Turtle Island," I repeat. "North America. New York City. It's a different world."

"No, no," he counters, "it's the same. There's just a funny little line that separates Mexico from the United States. It doesn't really exist."

I think for a moment, then say, "Yes, of course, you're right. It doesn't exist—the separation is an illusion." We shake hands, and he continues up the trail.

Prior to my journey to México in 1981, friends and relatives had desperately tried to discourage me from going. Many of them had had dreams or strong intuitive feelings that I would die in México. Some even saw me coming back in a casket.

The warnings had become so frequent that I had begun to feel uneasy about making the journey. Yet whenever I had attuned to my own inner guidance about the idea of going south, I had always received a resounding "Yes!"

A few days before I was to leave for México, I had lunch with my Aleut actress friend, Jane Lind, who had worked with me on *Buffalo Nation*. I told her about the warnings.

"In my culture, when someone who loves you has a dream that you're going to die, it's considered a very good omen," she said. "It means that some part of you is going to fall away, that you're going to move beyond your limitations, that you're about to experience a rebirth."

Jane could not have been more right. The intensity of my first months of training with El Maestro had prepared me for the death of which she spoke. My solo pilgrimage to the south had magnetized me to the archetype of the feathered serpent, who like the phoenix willingly entered the flames in order to die and be reborn.

Now I had finally passed through the *nierika*, the window of Palenque, and there was no going back. My old self had died, and in its place was a much stronger and yet more innocent self. Thus were new powers unlocked from within my body. During my medicine journey and forever after, I was able to undulate my torso from side to side like a snake—something I had never been able to do before. During that journey and forever after, I was able to sing two notes at the same time—also a new experience. Perhaps this was all the essence of Ketzalkoatl beginning to free me into a new way of being, to the synthesis of polarities within myself.

Indeed, I had no doubt now that I had found Ketzalkoatl. I had found him through my body, through the Earth spirit and the medicine plants, through ceremony and sacred architecture, through all the things that Rarihokwats had said I would find in the south. At last, I had found Ketzalkoatl.

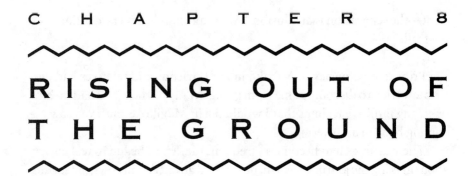

RISING OUT OF
THE GROUND

At Palenque I experienced a reality that seemed to have no limitations: a divine interconnectedness with all life-forms and levels of consciousness minus the constraints of time and space. Everything I could imagine was simultaneously present. I was master of my realm. It was a taste of enlightenment.

Yet it was also a test. Unless I could integrate the divine nature of that experience into a relative world of physical laws, my journey would be worthless. Thus, as my awareness expanded, I found myself wanting more definition in my life. After years of travel, I craved stability.

In my final month of travel, I received a letter from Rarihokwats that spoke to this need. He advised me to "put down roots—good, deep, long roots" as a means of balancing my fast-moving nature. At last I was motivated enough to do it. The question was, where?

The answer emerged through synchronicity. At the Hopi Snake Dance in 1980, my friend Gail had invited me to her home in Taos, New Mexico. She had urged me to come see a unique structure called the "Growhole," built into a nearby hillside. Thus, at the end of my journey in search of Kokopelli, I had gone to Taos to visit Gail and the Growhole. Afterward, I couldn't get it out of my mind; I knew I would live there someday.

By the time I reached the Yukatan seven months later, the Growhole was appearing frequently in my dreams. At Palenque it became an obsession, perhaps because the architecture reminded me of the unusual Taos structure. And on the day of my first medicine journey, I met a young couple who turned out to be two of the Growhole's early builders. Later at the beach of Tulum, I met another couple from Taos. Indeed, throughout Mayaland I was continually meeting "Taoseños," many of whom had helped to build the Growhole.

Every day for a week after my return from México to New York, I tried calling Gail in order to discover the current status of the Growhole. All I got was a recorded message saying her phone had been disconnected. Later I found out that her house had burned to the ground. When I finally did get ahold of Gail, she said the original owners of the Growhole were planning to move back in. Still she thought I should come out, and in spite of her own devastation, she offered to help me with a place to live.

By early June, I was ready to head west from New York City. I stuffed all my possessions into my parents' old car, which they had sold to me for a dollar. Another of the Earthkeepers named Ernest joined me for the drive, and off we went toward the setting sun.

On our last day of cross-country driving, we hit 101-degree weather in the Texas Panhandle. My old new car kept overheating—there was obviously something wrong with the radiator, but repair was out of the question since it was Sunday. Fortunately, I remembered the advice of a friend.

"Get in the car," I told Ernest. "We're going."

He protested, insisting that we couldn't make it.

"Trust me," I said.

Ernest reluctantly climbed in. As soon as we were moving, I turned the heat on full blast. The additional heat made us sweat like dogs, but at least the engine stayed cool. Thus we cruised all the way to Santa Fe in our traveling techno-sweatlodge, purging our bodies and psyches before our arrival in the sacred lands of the New Mexican altiplano.

Trial by fire remained the theme during my first few weeks in Taos. An unusual heat wave with temperatures in the nineties and hundreds lasted for most of June. At night, I literally slept on the ashes of Gail's old house, while during the day I coped with her reconstruction crew, none of whom I got along with very well. In spite of the outwardly hostile conditions, though, I was determined to put down roots in this area. I knew that a good burn can promote new growth, and like a phoenix rising from the ashes, I would rise to the occasion.

Meanwhile, across the gully on the other hill, something else was rising from the ground. The owners of the Growhole were busy laying flagstone floors and replastering adobe walls with fresh mud. I visited with them often, and as I got to know them, I gradually learned the eclectic history of their remarkable creation.

The Growhole had begun as an experiment in environmental living in the early seventies. Adrienne, a native New Mexican, had provided the land for this most unconventional experiment, while her husband, Nick, was the visionary architect. He wanted to recreate the habitations of ancient people—dwellings in which the natural environment was an integral part of the dwelling itself, where indoors and outdoors were dynamically interwoven.

Together, Nick and Adrienne had initially enlisted the help of about twenty-five people to create the Growhole. The remains of Anasazi cliff dwellings had provided them with direct inspiration for many design features. Chacoan-style doorways opened into a vast central room with a sunken stone-and-adobe kiva. Directly overhead was an exquisite, wood-beamed ceiling of carefully interwoven *vigas* and *latillas*. Pre-Columbian pottery shards that had been found in the Growhole's very foundation were artfully laid into the adobe walls, interspersed with a multitude of rocks of all shapes, sizes, and colors.

But the Growhole's inspiration was not limited to Anasazi sources. It extended as far back as ancient Lemuria (where Nick believed that humans had lived partially underground among a rich diversity of plant life) and as far into the future as orbiting space stations (where an astronaut might peer out through the glass of his or her sleeping compartment into an infinity of stars). Hence, the entire subterranean section of the Growhole opened into a greenhouse where fruits, flowers, vegetables, and herbs were grown in great profusion. And the entire upper section was marked by what Adrienne called "window-beds," sculpted sleeping areas built into the walls at ground level and covered by skylights affording spectacular views of the heavens.

Of all the architectural features of this outrageous structure, I most admired the octagonal-walled, pyramidal-roofed meditation chamber at the lower end of the greenhouse. Its stonework was almost identical to that of Palenque. Thus was the Growhole part Mayan temple, part Lemurian cave, part Anasazi cliff dwelling, and part spaceship.

From the initial group of twenty-five who had begun to raise its form from the bowels of the Earth, almost two hundred people had become involved in constructing the Growhole by the end of the second year. As it had grown, it had eventually become a pottery school where students experimented with pre-Columbian techniques and motifs. Other residents explored the application of alternative technologies for heating, lighting, plumbing, and raising food.

But the experiment in collective living had been wrought with interpersonal tensions. The Growhole eventually reverted to Nick and Adrienne, who had used it as a home to raise their growing family. Finally they had left, too, and for the next few years the structure had been rented out to another young couple—the ones who had been living in it when I visited in 1980.

All this time, the Growhole had never really been structurally finished. It had remained for Nick and Adrienne an unfulfilled dream. Now, at last, they had come back to make it complete, intending at the end of the laborious process to reinhabit their creation. The last of the exposed adobe bricks were covered with mudslip, propane lights were installed, the greenhouse windows were redesigned to focus more radiant heat, and the tall wind pump outside was at last made functional. It seemed that the Growhole's aesthetic appeal was finally being balanced by practical concerns.

Just the same, the weeks were passing, and I had to attend to the very real issue of making a home for myself, since the Growhole was obviously not available. So I decided to get a tipi. I had the canvas shipped from California and the poles from Colorado. I passed the next few weeks stripping and sanding seventeen lodgepole pines, preparing the canvas, and clearing a tipi site on the edge of Gail's property.

One Saturday night, as I got ready to go to sleep on the newly cleared site, the sound of a high-pitched drum began echoing across the land. Through the trees I could see that the neighbors to the south had raised their own tipi, its amber glow reflecting the warm fire within. I realized also that the sound was that of the water drum and that this was a peyote meeting of the Native American Church. I fell asleep imagining the ceremony.

As I dreamed, the spirits of the people in the peyote meeting came to me one by one. Each of them gave me a teaching about the nature of duality. Often I would awaken to the rapid beating of the water drum, only to be transported by the sound into yet another phase of dreaming.

I am walking through a middle-class suburban community with two-story homes, green lawns, paved streets, and toddlers on tricycles. But in the center of this seemingly idyllic community, something sinister is going on. Sheltered inside a square building without windows, a group of scientists are secretly conducting genetic research. Somehow, perhaps accidentally, the genetic material has escaped into the atmosphere outside the sealed building . . . .

Before long, there are signs that the community's gene pool is being adversely affected. Many women are giving birth to deformed babies. Some of the scientists begin to question the wisdom of their experiments. At the same time, though, one segment of the population seems to be unaffected by the genetic leakage that is causing so much suffering. These people are existing on a different plane of consciousness. They have freed themselves of hate, fear, and anger. They are openly loving with one another. Their vision of the future is clear.

I find myself among these people. Soon I walk with them through the streets of the community. Everywhere, we pass grief-stricken parents struggling to cope with their deformed children, doing their best to make the nightmare seem normal. As we walk, I am aware of a golden glow surrounding us, keeping us immune from the spreading disease. We keep walking down the paved streets, maintaining our sacred space while emanating compassion toward all we meet.

Finally we come to the edge of the community, and the paved road turns to dirt. We enter a vast, green land of rolling hills and meadows. It is now that I see the buffalo. They are rising out of the ground everywhere, through the soil and grass, out onto the Earth. There are thousands of buffalo—millions of them—repopulating the entire continent, the entire planet.

On the day I finished sanding my last tipi pole, Adrienne came walking up the gully to Gail's hill to see me. "Jim, we have news," she began. "Nick and I have decided that our family is just not ready to move back into the Growhole. We'll be returning East in less than a week, so if you're still interested in renting, we'd love to have you live there."

I was overcome with my good fortune. As Nick and Adrienne put the finishing touches on the Growhole, I moved myself, tipi and all, from Gail's hill to theirs.

I discovered that living in the Growhole was not without its challenges. Far from my urban origins, I had to adjust to living each day according to the forces and rhythms of nature. Minus electricity, my hours of work and sleep were almost entirely determined by the sun. Growing plants year round and regulating the interior temperature through design features, I became much more attuned to the weather and the changing seasons. I watched carefully for the winds to tell me when I would have enough water for a bath. I couldn't leave food around without considering what insects or animals might get into it.

During the winter, great storms swept across the altiplano. I could see them coming from more than a hundred miles away. They would cover the mountains in a white blanket, and the world would become pure silence.

But one morning after such a storm, the noise outside was deafening. Ice had frozen around the pipes of the wind pump, and as the wind blew stronger, the pump was pulling the support tower from its foundations. I rushed outside to see if I could do anything, but there was no way to stop the spinning wind wheel. So I gave in to the inevitable. Finally the pipes broke, the noise came to an abrupt halt, and the wind wheel spun around uselessly, no better than a symbolic decoration.

After that came almost three months of heavy snows. It was impossible to drive across the steep, narrow gully from Gail's hill to mine; all supplies had to be transported in and out by foot. Hauling twenty gallons of water in this way each day over a quarter-mile distance, I learned a difficult lesson about the preciousness of water.

I also discovered many other things about the Growhole that I hadn't anticipated. For one, I found that among the dozen or so species of spiders that inhabited the Growhole was the poisonous black widow. Every night before going to bed, I had to remember to check through all my sheets and blankets with a flashlight, since this was one of the places they seemed to enjoy most. And this was not the only curious feature of the exotic sleeping areas. During periods of heavy rain and snow, the skylights over the window beds leaked. Being awakened by large drops of adobe mud splattering on my face became an all-too-common occurrence.

By the middle of winter, it had gotten so cold in the Growhole that even with the woodstove fully stoked, I had to wear gloves to play my piano.

Otherwise my fingers were too stiff to move. Then in the early spring, as the snows began to melt, the kiva space flooded. An elaborate system of pumps and hoses had to be rigged to redirect water out of the house and down the hill.

In spite of these and many other problems, I never regretted moving into the Growhole. Living within the Earth, I felt more connected to the ancient spirits than at any place I had ever been before. The inspiration this provided was a boon for all my creative work. Nor had I ever known such deep and restful sleep as I knew in the Growhole. Without any internal electronic hums or external sounds of traffic, without a single artificial light source to scar the natural darkness of the night, I slept in the womb of a total void, in perfect black silence. My dreams were never more magical.

Hundreds of eyes are staring at me—deep pools of wisdom, each one riveted on my soul. They are the eyes of the ancestors, and I feel naked before them. Nor have I any hope of hiding, for they are in my house. Within the ruins of their own ancient village, they stand staring silently up at me, giving no indication of whether they are angry or pleased that I am now dwelling here. There is no emotion in their stares—only raw, eternal power.

These ancestors see me. They see all that I am doing. In my house I am not alone.

This dream was but one of many signs of the unseen presences that I felt in and around the Growhole during the time I lived there. Often at night I would awaken to the sounds of footsteps and low, mumbling voices just outside my window bed. I never saw anyone there; still, I knew that the Ancient Ones were close.

Finally I learned from Gail that the hills where we lived had indeed once been the site of a large pueblo community and that a great disaster had befallen them: one day, many of the women and children had drowned in a flash flood by the river below the pueblo. They had been picking berries when suddenly the waters came and swept them away. After that, the community had chosen not to dwell any longer by the site of their grief. Instead, they had moved south to Taos Mountain where, along with another recently arrived community, they had built the multistoried pueblo that stands there today. That was eight hundred years ago.

Thus did I come to understand more about the people I saw in my dreams and whose fragments of pottery adorned my living space. Once again I found myself in a home of native spirits still weighted by past sorrows. What karma, I wondered, drew me to such places?

I remembered the last thing Adrienne had said to me on the day I moved in: "Listen, if you would, Jim, for a new name for the Growhole. That name seems so heavy now. Our dream here is still earthbound. Listen for something that can lift it, that can make it more joyful and golden."

Not long afterward, the name came to me in a meditation. It was Xochimoki, "Flower of the Ancient Ones." It was a name for a place with deep roots that could creatively give rise to my highest aspirations. For through Xochimoki, I intended that the wisdom and beauty of the past would be raised out of darkness into light, that the best of ancient times would become the future, that division would be healed through a sharing of diversity, and that sorrow would be transformed into joy.

There was also an important cultural meaning to the name Xochimoki. Its Nahuatl and Hopi linguistic roots made it a link between the indigenous traditions of north and south. And I wanted my home to serve as a spiritual bridge between the cultures of these directions. I also saw it as a personal bridge linking the Mexikan center of my Medicine Wheel journey to the Southwestern center where I had chosen to synthesize all I had learned.

Thus, to the north of the house I placed my tipi and near it a purification lodge. To the south, I cleared a large circle for the practice of Mexika dance and ceremony. Within the house, the Anasazi-style kiva and the Mayan-style meditation chamber were already positioned respectively to north and south. And centered within all these was the large, wooden beam upon which the entire structure rested, reminding me of the Haudenosaunee Great Tree of Peace.

Xochimoki was all of this together—the totality of my journey in one unique, sacred site. The many musical instruments and objects of ceremonial art that progressively came to fill it were the manifested flower of Cem-Anahuatl, the still-living treasures of Turtle Island. To some, Xochimoki most closely resembled a museum. To others, it was like a retreat or an elegant cave. To me, more than anything, it was a place I could at last call home. Thus established, it was finally ready to begin receiving its special guests.

Shortly after spring equinox, El Maestro arrived at Xochimoki with eight of the dancers from *Kalpulli* Koatlan. They came following the path of an extensive cultural pilgrimage. Their purpose was to reenact the northern migrations that had begun from Koatepetl in the third century A.D.

Already it had been a year since I had seen El Maestro, and immediately I realized how strongly connected to him I still felt. It seemed that our emotional and spiritual bond was even more powerful than before. El Maestro had guided me into the center of my life's Medicine Wheel, and now I was receiving him into my new center so that he might see the flowering of the seed he had planted with me.

I organized a gathering, inviting people from the town as well as from Taos Pueblo. At the gathering, El Maestro spoke of the important connections we all shared, including the long history of contact and exchange between the ancient peoples of the Americas.

In the course of the gathering, Gail informed me that John Hawk had quite unexpectedly arrived at her house from Nebraska. I immediately realized that this was a wonderful chance to create a north-south dialogue between John and El Maestro, so I invited John over. Just to see these two sitting side by side, knowing they carried within them the spiritual essences of North and Mesoamerica, was profound. For me they reflected the marriage of opposites that I sought to attain in myself. They were like two streams of my world coming together.

Though I don't remember exactly what John and El Maestro said that day, I know they exchanged much more through their shared presence than through their words. They had no need to talk about ideas that were inherent to those who are born and nurtured with an indigenous way of seeing. They lived their awareness; they breathed it. Thus did they evidence their tremendous faith in the prophetic visions they carried. For both men, the return of their sacred dance traditions was the return of the native spirit to America. And there was no stopping it. In forms both ancient and new, it was already dancing its way back into the world through all of us who had gathered here and through all the growing circles across the land.

For many evenings after El Maestro arrived, I saw him go outside to gaze at the stars. At his *kalpulli* near Mexico City, most of the stars were no longer visible due to extreme air and light pollution. For a man whose entire life was guided by the cosmos, I was well aware of how frustrated he felt over not having clear access to the heavens, and I knew how much he appreciated watching the twinkling skies over Taos.

Late one evening, just as we were about to go down the steps of Xochimoki after returning from a presentation, El Maestro suddenly stopped dead in his tracks. He stared intently into the sky, his face looking very serious. I could tell from his expression that this was more than simple enjoyment of the heavenly view. After a long silence, he spoke matter-of-factly.

"In approximately one week, there is going to be a volcanic eruption somewhere on Earth," he said. "I don't know where, but I do know that it will be tremendous."

Exactly a week after El Maestro's prediction, a little-known volcano in southern México called El Chichonal experienced a series of massive eruptions. Its final explosion was the largest in the Northern Hemisphere since the eruption of Alaska's Mount Katmai in 1912. It pumped more than ten times as much ash into the stratosphere as the eruption of Mount Saint Helens in 1980. The states of Chiapas and Tabasco were covered with gray powder. Palenque lay buried for nearly two months. If I'd had any doubt before, I was now convinced that El Maestro was a living astronomer-priest in the old tradition of his ancestors.

Long after El Maestro's impressive visit was over, I remained certain that my learning with him had only just begun. I knew I would be seeing him again soon. But for the moment, I was about to be visited by another teacher I had not seen in many years.

I am sitting in the living room of Yellow Robe's apartment. I see her coming out of the back room. She is holding the beaded bag with the Sacred Pipe in both hands. She is standing with it in the doorway, dressed in white buckskin.

Yellow Robe begins to walk toward me with the Sacred Pipe. As she does, she becomes less solid. The closer she gets, the more transparent she becomes, until finally she disappears.

Soon I see her again in the doorway. As before, she is smiling kindly at me. As before, she begins to walk toward me with the pipe bag. And as before, she gradually disappears.

This sequence happens over and over again, each time accompanied by the chanting of one of Black Elk's songs:

> A sacred nation is appearing.
> They are appearing.
> May you behold!
> The bison nation is appearing.
> May you behold.

When I opened my eyes, I was lying in my window bed. Immediately I saw the bright, waxing moon shining down through the glass. It was so bright that it seemed like day. It was as if the moon were shaking me, saying, "Get up. Get up! I have something for you!"

The moonlight became so bright that it was impossible to sleep. Suddenly I had a strong urge to grab a pad of paper and a pen. With pen in hand, I sat on my bed beneath the moon and, without thinking, began to write:

> The process of creation bears the thought of lonely vigil,
> while the wisdom of Creator is a path to lead us home.
>
> Beyond the plains of meaning lie the oceans of our rescue,
> and the woman who protects them is a buffalo.
>
> Upon the great expanses, the mind will open outward
> to the truth that is unfolding,
>   that is shining like the moon.
>
> There the horns of buffalo will slowly raise their crescent,
> and the woman who is glowing
>   will be growing till she's full.

The next morning, I was full of energy. I couldn't seem to shake the dream or the poem from my mind. I knew that something special had happened, and I knew that it had to do with Ta Tunka Wian Ska, White Buffalo Calf Woman. I decided I needed to find out as much about her as I could.

Curiously, I had just been given two books by my friends Blue and Red, who still lived in Taos. One of them was entitled *The Sacred Pipe,* an account of the seven rites of the Oglala Sioux as told by Black Elk. The other was a compilation of the words of Blue and Red's adopted Lakota grandfather, John Fire Lame Deer, who had passed away a few years earlier. Both these books spoke a great deal about White Buffalo Woman.

She had come to the Lakota in the distant past, long before the arrival of the Europeans, long before horses or guns were known on the plains.

She was very beautiful. She wore a dress of white buckskin with beadwork finer than any ever seen. Her hair was long and black, her skin red like the earth. She carried a fan of sage leaves in one hand, and on her back was tied a bundle that held a very special gift.

This gift was the Sacred Pipe, and White Buffalo Woman gave it to the Lakota to caretake for all the nations of Turtle Island. Meeting the people in a great lodge constructed especially for her, she explained how the round bowl of the pipe was its feminine part and the long stem was its masculine part. When these two parts were united and the pipe was smoked, the prayers of the people would be carried to the Creator. The red pipestone buffalo that was part of the bowl piece and the twelve feathers of the spotted eagle that were tied to the stem were to remind the people of their oneness with the four-leggeds and the winged. In this way, they would always remember to include every living relation in their prayers. And thus it is Lakota tradition to conclude each prayer with the words, "*Mitakuye Oyasin*," meaning "All My Relations."

Finally the sacred woman prepared to leave the lodge. When she reached the door, she turned to face the chief and said, "Behold this pipe! Always remember how sacred it is, and treat it as such, for it will take you to the end. Remember, in me are four ages. I am leaving now, but I shall look back upon your people in every age, and at the end I shall return."

Then White Buffalo Woman walked through the door and away from the great lodge. All the people watched her with reverence and awe. As she neared a distant hill, she sat down and faced them, transforming herself into a buffalo. She did this many times, each time becoming a buffalo of a different color. Finally she changed herself into a white buffalo and disappeared.

I was struck by White Buffalo Woman's comment "in me are four ages." This seemed to closely parallel the Hopi belief in four worlds and the Mayan concept of the four creations. The Mexika believe we are at the end of the fifth cycle rather than the fourth. But the return of the original mythic teacher in the final days seems to be universal. Whether the Peacemaker, Maximón, Ketzalkoatl, Kokopelli, or White Buffalo Calf Woman, all of them promised they would come back.

Comparing the four great ages to the four legs of the buffalo, the Lakota say that the buffalo has been on its last leg for some time now. They speak of the "Red and Blue Days," believing that at the end of the last age, there will be a sign in the sky—the moon will turn red and the sun will turn blue. When I learned this, I finally understood why my friends Red Moon and Blue Sun had chosen their names.

Two days after my dream of Yellow Robe, just before sunset, I stood outside Xochimoki facing the Sangre de Cristo Mountains to the east.

Behind the mountains rise many layers of cumulus clouds in pastel shades of pink, blue, and violet, reflecting the far more brilliant colors in the western sky. Heat lightning flashes, too, illuminating the clouds from within. Soon the nearly full moon begins to rise through the flashing, colored clouds.

I stare at the moon, its shining body still mostly hidden. Slowly it appears to merge with the changing cloud forms. As it does, it takes on the image of White Buffalo Woman. Her arms are held high as she rises from behind the snow-capped mountains like the herald of a new world. Surrounding her is an entire herd of buffalo made of clouds. When the lightning flashes, their heads and bodies come alive, accompanied by distant rolls of thunder. I feel them all coming toward me, the sacred Buffalo Nation about to reclaim the holy Earth.

That night I slept deeply, but I awoke again when the moon shone through the skylight. This time it was calling me out, so I walked up the hill to my tipi. There I saw the silhouette of a large owl perched in the poles. I stared at it for a long time. Suddenly it took wing and swooped down toward me, passing right over my head.

I walked back to the house and went inside. I was wide awake; as before, I could not sleep. But this time I didn't need to write or sing—I needed to draw. I sat down at my drafting table and began to sketch a mandala showing White Buffalo Woman and the Buffalo Nation as I had seen them in the clouds. Then I added the Sacred Tree surrounded by a circle of dancers. From the center of the tree hung a buffalo skull, and beneath it was a mirrored image of the Sacred Pipe. (See figure 4.)

All this time I was aware of being guided by the spirit of the owl that had just flown over me. The spirit told me that someday I would paint my tipi with this same mandala—that I must do this for the return of White Buffalo Woman.

The next morning I was abruptly awakened by a loud knocking sound that seemed to be coming from the roof of Xochimoki. Getting up to check, I discovered that a number of magpies were pecking at the window sealant around the topmost skylight. Although I frequently saw these funny, crow-sized, black-and-white birds nesting in the cottonwood trees down in the gully, this was the first time I'd caught them up to such mischievous pranks. Remembering that the magpie was considered the special medicine bird of the Ghost Dance, it occurred to me that perhaps there was some connection between their surprise wake-up call and my recent preoccupation with White Buffalo Woman.

Later that morning the phone rang. It was my friend Doug calling from Santa Fe. He had just gotten ahold of some mushrooms, and he wanted to know if I would like to join him the next day for an excursion to a remote place in the eastern part of the state called Porvenir Canyon. I knew the timing would be perfect for another medicine journey, so I gladly accepted the invitation.

Though relatively unimpressive at first sight, Porvenir Canyon (which translated means "Canyon of the Future") proved to be spectacular. Fantastic, sculpted cliff faces rose hundreds of feet on either side of a narrow creek. Evergreen vegetation in the canyon bottom contrasted dramatically with the red and orange hues of the sheer canyon walls. Perfect blue skies and white clouds only added to the remarkable beauty. On that early spring morning, the sense of new life pushing up from beneath the soil was almost palpable.

Doug and I crawled through the thick brush lining the creek. When we reached the water, we sat atop a boulder and meditated. As Jorge and I had done at Palenque, we cleansed and blessed the mushrooms and one another in the water. To help me stay in balance, Doug brushed me with the branch of a cedar tree, and I did the same for him. Then he beat his hoop drum as we sat on the boulder chanting, attuning ourselves and waiting for the medicine to take effect.

Soon I was seeing dragons. The entire world became reptilian, and I was surrounded by a serpentine flow of energy, again reminding me of Palenque. The primal hum of the insect realm carried me deep into an awareness of the origins of Creation, while the pulsation of our breathing planet filled my body, heightening my desire for exploration.

Doug and I left the creek and hiked up the north side of the canyon. Every step became a living prayer. Eventually I was so overcome with ecstasy that all I could do was stand beneath a tree in silent meditation. When Doug finally asked whether we should move on, I said, "Yes, but separately."

Before we parted, though, I held out to Doug one of the two Mexikan blankets I was carrying and said, "Here, I think you should wear this." Although it was my favorite blanket, I knew I was giving it to him for all time. Except for its purple background, it was the mirror image of my golden blanket; both were brightly marked by the colors of the rainbow. Intuitively I sensed that this fact would have an important bearing on our respective journeys.

I continued up the north side of the canyon until I came to a tall, perfectly straight pine tree. The boughs and branches beneath it appeared to have been intentionally arranged in a circle. As I entered the circle, I suddenly became acutely aware of my identity as a Keeper of the Woods. The knowledge of my family heritage was translated into a profound sense of responsibility to all growing things, to all the forest inhabitants of our precious planet.

I took one of the branches and began to gently beat it on the trunk of the tree, as though the tree were a drum. I sang prayers for everything on Earth, and in my mind I traveled everywhere I had ever been or known about.

Whenever I opened my eyes, a mountainous cliff on the south side of the canyon would magnetize my vision. A huge cleft in its center seemed to be pulling me into the world of my ancestors. As I sang for them, I entered the mountain and found myself in the Black Hills, singing for my people and all our sacred lands. At the top of Harney Peak, I raised my arms to the sky and cried for the healing of the Earth. In the midst of my song, I felt overwhelmingly parched and thirsty but surrendered myself to a greater will. Its power sustained me.

After I had finished singing, Doug miraculously appeared in his purple rainbow blanket to offer me a drink. Afterward, I continued up the north side of the canyon while Doug ascended the south canyon wall. Gradually I rose from one plateau to the next. The higher I went, the broader my vision became. I shed layers of clothing like old skins, metaphorically dropping personal baggage along the way. Eventually I reached a clearing defined by a circle of trees, where the spirit of the place said, "Sit down." I neatly folded my clothing and placed it on a large rock in the center of the circle and sat facing south, wearing only my blue jeans.

I fix my eyes on the same cleft in the cliff that called to me before. Heat is pouring out of it, pulsating against my naked chest. It is reaching into my heart like a flaming torch. Finally, I can sit no longer. I stand up and throw my arms into the air.

At that moment, Moses appears in the rock. He is a thousand feet tall. His body is the cleft, his arms the breadth of the mountain, and the mountain is Sinai.

Moses is shaking with the power of the Creator. "Do not forget your people!" he intones. "Do not forget! . . . Do not forget!" His voice echoes in my mind. I fall to my knees, crying.

A small bird landed in the branch of a pine tree and began to sing. Another landed near my feet. Soon many songbirds chirped and flitted in the trees surrounding the circle. Squirrels and chipmunks appeared, too, running about playfully. Butterflies floated on gentle air currents. The loving caress of nature transformed the drama that had engulfed me only moments before. At last I was ready to move on, but knowing I would return, I left my clothes and my golden blanket as a marker to find the spot again.

As I ascended the highest of the northern cliffs, I felt like I was soaring. I was so sure of my footing that I climbed with my eyes closed. Simultaneously, I experienced the many stages of evolution on Earth, from the first one-celled organisms to the dawn of humanity. Then I saw the unfolding of my own life, from birth to the present moment. I saw how every experience in my life had been a necessary preparation for the challenges of my present reality.

With every clear realization, the wind blew stronger. I felt extremely powerful, and for this I knew I must repeatedly humble myself. I was but one strand in the great web. The web, not I, had the power. For that power was interconnectedness, the spirit of the Creator that flowed through all things, the breath shared by all that belongs to none.

At last I came to a place where only a few trees grew, close to the base of a cliff whose walls rose straight into the sky. Far across the canyon, the mountain of Moses continued to emanate a tremendous force. Directly to my right was a partially charred and leafless tree that looked like it had been hit by lightning. Lava rocks at my feet, the sun overhead, everything spoke of fire. Then a voice in my head said, "Go no farther."

I sit on a large rock and turn to face the apparently lifeless tree. I notice a separate chunk of charred and weathered wood by its blackened base. And where the wood is burned a buffalo appears . . . moving, alive. Like an animal rising from its own dead remains, the buffalo comes out of the tree and gives me its song:

> Hey-a-hey, yey, yey, yey.
> Hey-a-hey, yey, yey, yey.
> Rising out of the ground,
> The Buffalo! The Buffalo!

I sing this song over and over, realizing in the process that it is singing me. The more I sing, the hotter the sun grows and the more the wind blows. The dead tree shakes in the wind. Now, out of the west, I see them coming, charging across the enormous cliff face: a whole herd of buffalo carved from the living rock. The Buffalo Nation is returning!

As I watch them appear from above and below, the song still singing me, the wind still blowing, I hear the voice of Ta Tunka Wian Ska:

> I am coming back now.
> Over the whole Earth I am coming,
> and soon the people will be dancing for my return.
> For I am all buffalo,
> and in me is the universe.
> Out of the west we are coming,
> and we will cover this land again.
> Even beyond the ocean to the land of your ancestors,
> where the caves still hold our memories;
> even there we are returning.
> Over the whole Earth we are coming.

When the voice had finished, the wind stopped blowing, the Earth stopped burning, and the buffalo were gone. But the strange piece of wood was still lying on the ground. I went over to lift it up, and I saw that it was the exact size and shape of a buffalo skull. I knew then that this was a sacred gift. I would carry it with me to the bottom of the canyon and into the world.

As I descended with the wooden buffalo skull, I thought of Moses carrying the Ten Commandments in his arms down Mount Sinai to a people hungry and losing faith. When I reached the circle of trees where my vision of Moses had occurred, the paradox of my spiritual heritage was finally revealed to me.

For the Hebrews, Moses was the giver of the sacred laws. For the Lakota, White Buffalo Calf Woman fulfilled the same role. The teachings that each carried to the people on behalf of the Creator were embodied through holy objects: the stone tablets and the Sacred Pipe.

Today, both these law-givers had spoken to me. I had been gifted with an object that might seem simple and of little consequence, yet for me it was profoundly sacred, invested with prophetic visions and revelations. Like the sacred stone tablets, this piece of wood was inscribed with the memory of a holy flame and thus became an object of power. Still, I asked, how could I connect with my Hebrew heritage as a Keeper of the Woods in one moment and in the next be singing for my Lakota grandfathers?

In the center of the circle, the answer was given. Both peoples were my ancestors. Both traditions were my heritage. Genetically of one place, I had been born and raised in another. Spiritually, I was linked to two different continents, each with their respective sacred ways. Both were in my blood and bones.

And what of my spiritual ancestry? Where had I actually been during the long journey of my soul? To what peoples and traditions might I be tied through previous existences, even more powerfully than the linkage of a genetic chain?

I did not know. But I knew that the ancestral Lakota were in my memory. The buffalo, too, were buried in my consciousness like seeds in soil. Under the proper conditions, these seeds were now awakening to new life. In all my recent dreams and visions, the buffalo had been rising out of the ground—even coming out of the mountains and the clouds. They were stampeding into my world of perception like an unstoppable herd. But was their return symbolic or literal?

I recalled a photo I once saw of a buffalo trudging through a fierce blizzard with its massive head and upper body thrust into the wind and snow. For me, that one photo said it all. As I now held the wooden buffalo skull in my arms, it contained the same message. To persist through the storm, to turn adversity into strength, to rise from the flames and the ashes, to burst forth from the ground, to defy extinction—the power of the buffalo was the power to return. And that power was both symbolic and literal.

I had no doubt that the buffalo would cover the North American continent again, as my visions had shown me. As for the closely related European bison, I prayed that the words of White Buffalo Woman were true. But whatever the buffalo's future, it was inseparable from the fate of the planet as a whole. Faced with weapons of mass destruction and an environmental crisis without historical precedent, humanity's own extinction seemed arguably as imminent as that of the buffalo a century ago. Could humanity meet the overwhelming challenge it had created for itself and all its relations? In my mind, this was where the metaphor of the buffalo's resurgence held its greatest power.

Descending the canyon slopes with the buffalo medicine in my arms, I saw it as a contemporary symbol of deliverance. The Ten Commandments were just such a symbol to the people of the Exodus. It gave them courage to continue their journey and reach the Promised Land. In more recent times, the Ghost Dance vision had come in answer to the despair of another group. Likewise, the return of the buffalo, the uniting of diverse peoples around the Sacred Tree, could lay the foundation for a new world. Here in the Canyon of Porvenir, the Canyon of the Future—in the season of Passover, the season of springtime—I had seen how it could be so.

When I reached the canyon bottom, Doug was standing on the trail in his purple rainbow blanket, his white shirt wrapped around his head like a turban. I thought of Moses and laughed. Moses and White Buffalo Woman: prophet and prophetess, their homelands separated by an ocean as this canyon was separated by a creek. Doug had scaled the south side of the canyon, I the north. And the colors of our blankets had reflected our separate journeys. Mine had been fiery, out in the sun, while Doug's had been cool, in the violet shade of the forest.

Back down at the creek, Doug and I shared with each other the full stories of our journeys. That night, in an open field near the mouth of the canyon, we stood beneath the full moon. By the time it reached the center of the sky, it was surrounded by a full-circle rainbow. I imagined that rainbow as people of all colors united around a vision that at last appeared whole. I imagined the moon as White Buffalo Woman reflecting her wisdom in a time of darkness. Then I remembered the words of an old song from the Ghost Dance, called "The Millennium":

> The whole world is coming.
> A nation is coming. A nation is coming.
> The crow has brought the message to the tribe.
>
> Over the whole Earth they are coming.
> The buffalo are coming! The buffalo are coming!
> The eagle has brought the message to the tribe.

THE HEART OF THE EAGLE

In the summer of 1982, El Maestro and his apprentices returned to Xochimoki. They were on their way north to participate in a Lakota Sundance. The rigorous preparations required for this dance included frequent ritual cleansings. So at El Maestro's request, Gail and I had prepared a purification lodge, to be ready for the group when they arrived.

As the *kalpulli*'s rickety old school bus barely pulled itself up our dirt driveway, I thought about how the determination of its passengers made up for its mechanical weaknesses. Like birds in flight, these men were fully focused on the purpose of their journey. Nothing could hold them back.

That evening outside the lodge, as the rocks were heating in the fire, El Maestro shared a remarkable experience the group had had while driving through the Chihuahuan desert just two days before. He said it was late afternoon when he saw an eagle flying high above the bus. Immediately he told Poli, the apprentice who was driving, to pull over and stop. Everyone got out and looked up. The eagle stayed directly above the bus, hovering silently in small circles. Suddenly, though, the eagle caught a draft of air and began to glide across the desert toward the setting sun.

"Get back in the bus!" El Maestro urged, and they drove across the barren, roadless landscape following the eagle as best they could. Finally they reached a place where the eagle was circling again, and El Maestro signaled Poli to stop as before.

Once everyone was out of the bus, the eagle began to descend. It came soaring down directly toward the bus, as if the Great Spirit had shot an arrow to the Earth. It flew straight to El Maestro and landed on his right arm, its claws gripping into his flesh.

"All of us were amazed, unable to speak," El Maestro said. "The presence of this bird was so clear, so strong, so full of trust. When it looked into my eyes, I felt like I was nothing and everything at the same time.

"The eagle told me that it was offering its life to us, and that we should not doubt it," El Maestro went on. "It said that it wished to give itself in sacrifice and that I was the one who had to take it. What could I do but obey? I took its life right there in my hands, praying all the while."

El Maestro explained that at the moment the spirit of the eagle left its body, the entire desert began to glow brilliantly as if it were on fire. The sudden change was clearly apparent to everyone.

"That's when we saw that we were standing in the middle of a large field of peyote," El Maestro said. "Not until that moment did the sacred cactus make itself visible to us. With the sacrifice of the eagle, the medicine appeared."

El Maestro knew that the peyote was also a gift from the Great Spirit, so he instructed everyone to gather the medicine and place it in a burlap bag. Not even El Maestro had seen peyote buttons as big as the ones they gathered in the desert that afternoon.

"The Huichols say that the human being, the eagle, the peyote, and the sun are all one essence," El Maestro explained. "Because of our experience in the desert, I now understand this in a way that before I could only imagine."

By the time El Maestro had finished relating all the details of his story, the rocks were ready. Everyone prepared to enter the purification lodge for the *inipi* ceremony—or, as he preferred to call it, the *temazkal*.

From Alaska to Tierra del Fuego, almost all native peoples have some version of the purification lodge. During this first one with El Maestro, I came to more deeply appreciate the ceremony's universality. He drew from traditions of both north and south. At times he prayed in Lakota, at other times in Nahuatl, English, or Spanish.

During the second round of the temazkal, El Maestro spoke of the eagle again. He said that after he had sacrificed it, he was guided to remove its heart. Then, almost in the same breath, he explained that he was now holding something precious in his hand. He told us he had cut it into pieces and was going to pass it around the circle. We were each to take a piece, and once everyone had received the sacrament, we were to eat it.

A wave of anxiety sweeps through me as I sense that the sacrament is being passed in my direction. Though it is too dark to see anything, I know that the heart of the eagle is coming toward me and that I, like all the others, am expected to partake of it. I struggle to come to terms with this. How can I reconcile such an act with my own devoutly vegetarian lifestyle? How can I justifiably eat the heart of another animal?

When the sacrament arrives in my hand and I take a piece of it, the internal debate ceases. I know that I have to do it. I have to honor the spirit of the eagle that has so willingly given its life.

The small, fleshy section of the heart that I hold is soft on the surface yet firm within. Just to hold it makes me feel humble. Silently I pray that I will be worthy of its medicine. Once everyone has received a piece, El Maestro invokes the eagle's spirit. He tells us to eat while he chants.

Slowly I take my first bite, not sure what the heart will taste like or how I will handle it. I am surprised to discover that although it has a strange and bitter flavor, it is not at all unbearable or repugnant. I eat slowly, trying to fully appreciate what I have received. Once I have completely swallowed my section of the eagle's heart, I feel greatly relieved. The eagle is at last within me, and I can sense its spiritual nourishment coursing through my body.

In the third round of the lodge, the rocks that are brought in are extremely red. The heat seems to double—even triple—and El Maestro's voice peaks in fervor and passion. The heat pushes us to our limits. Our bodies hunch over toward the ground as we pray for redemption and relief.

By the fourth and last round, I begin to notice waves of pulsating energy moving up the back of my neck and into my head. In my mind's eye, I see a variety of colorful, geometric patterns that are continually changing and transforming. My awareness is greatly heightened, and I am pervaded by a sense of well-being. These inner visions and feelings remind me of my journeys with the sacred mushrooms.

I suddenly realize that El Maestro has cleverly tricked us by creating a splendid living metaphor. The spiritual food he has given us is not literally the eagle's heart, but rather the sliced segments of a peyote button. Yet in believing that I was really eating the heart of the eagle, I have approached my first experience with the peyote from a place of profound reverence. I have ingested the plant imagining that I was taking into me the very essence of the Great Spirit.

Later, outside the lodge, El Maestro explained that he had only given me a very small amount of peyote because he wanted me to be introduced gently to its spirit. "Now that you are initiated to its use," he said, "you will soon be ready to embark on a journey of much greater dimensions."

So saying, El Maestro handed me four medium-sized peyote buttons. "Take these," he said, "and guard them as the sacred food they are until such time that you know you yourself have ripened and are ready to harvest your visions of power. All the details of where, when, how, and with whom will be revealed shortly. Just remember the source of this medicine as it was shared with you in my story this evening. In that is contained the seed of all that you will receive."

While I felt El Maestro's unqualified support for my quest, still I knew that his gift carried special responsibilities. With our most recent exchange, I was determined to make use of the peyote in the most meaningful way I could.

I thought back to the things El Maestro had shared during his first visit to Taos in the spring. He had spoken of Taos as a unique cultural crossroads, the place where the Pueblo and Plains Indians met and mixed. Taos was surely a contemporary center for indigenous America, as well, just as Tenochtitlan and Palenque had been in more ancient times. But New Mexico also had its ancient center of cultural crossing—a place now far more remote than Taos that had once been the vital nexus of the entire Anasazi civilization. That place was Chaco Canyon, in the northwestern corner of the state, and it was there that I knew I had to make my next medicine journey. As the jungle-enshrouded temples of Palenque had provided me with the perfect environment for my first quest with the sacred mushrooms, so the desert-baked stone walls and kivas of Chaco Canyon would provide me with the ideal setting for my first quest with the sacred cactus.

As summer turned to autumn and the aspens in the mountains took on golden hues, the other details of my medicine journey also fell into place. There was no need to figure anything out. Patience allowed each puzzle piece to become apparent. And so, in the early days of October, I drove west from Taos with a friend named Daniel to share in a voyage of vision.

I had first visited Chaco Canyon almost exactly a year before. Like my first visit to Palenque, my stay had been all too brief—just long enough to leave an indelible impression of the site's magnificence and to fill me with a yearning to return.

No ancient site north of the Mexican border compared to Chaco in its vastness of dimension or intricacy of design. Its stonework was by far the finest, and its ancient use as a major ceremonial center was by far the most obvious. Some structural complexes at Chaco actually seemed to contain more kivas than dwelling spaces. I was sure that, like Palenque, it had once been a great mystery school, hosting pilgrims from many far-reaching communities.

My own sense of Chaco was partially confirmed by archaeological evidence. At one time, a network of more than four hundred kilometers of ancient roads had reached out from the canyon, like rays of light from the sun. Many excavated objects of ritual art seemed to indicate the likelihood of trade contact with far-flung bioregions of North America.

Especially notable was the evidence of contact with the pre-Columbian civilizations to the south. The skeletons of tropical parrots found in Chaco's ruins left no doubt that its inhabitants had had contact with the lands of México, most likely trading turquoise for feathers. Likewise, ceramic flutes and ocarinas had been uncovered alongside the eagle-bone whistles more typically used by North American tribes. This suggested the possibility of influence from cultures like the Tolteks, where the making of such wind instruments of clay was more common. Most striking to me were the T-shaped windows and doorways placed in perfect visual alignment. Only at Palenque had I previously seen this distinctive architectural feature.

Though Chaco was apparently not the original name of the site, El Maestro had a theory that the word reflected linguistic and cultural links to México. *Chac* is a Mayan word for the deity of rain, while *co* is a Nahuatl word meaning "place." Following this logic, Chaco would translate to "Place of the Rain," perhaps being a place to which some Maya migrated following a presumed drought in the late ninth century A.D. The

Hopi meanwhile speak of some of their clans who migrated north into the Four Corners region from a place they refer to as Palatkwapi, the "Red City of the South." Some Hopi claim that Palatkwapi is Palenque. Since the Hopi are among the descendants of the people who built Chaco, it could well be that there is a direct cultural link between Palenque and Chaco Canyon.

Most academics reject the idea that travel over thousands of miles was achieved by ancient Americans. Yet most indigenous sources I have consulted over the years have affirmed that such far-reaching travel did indeed occur in ancient times. There are also stories of sacred objects and codices that escaped destruction by Spanish invaders by being carried north to the remote canyonlands and mesas of the Hopi and Pueblo peoples. Some scholars have even suggested that certain native Southwestern masked characters and ceremonials were actually transplanted into these cultures from Mesoamerica at a much earlier time.

To the degree that these theories might be true, they helped explain to me why Mesoamerican spiritual leaders like El Maestro were so eager to reestablish contact with native people to the north. After nearly five centuries of rigid repression by the church, the sociopolitical climate in Méxiko was finally allowing indigenous people some space to express their ancient spiritual heritage—and to regain some of that lost heritage from their brethren to the north.

Certainly native people on both sides of the artificial border had much to share to empower each other. As Chaco represented an important historical precedent for such sharing and as peyote itself had played a vital role in bridging native cultures from south to north, I knew that my vision quest at Chaco would illuminate related issues. As I had learned at Palenque, the boundary line between conventional and alternate realities was no more real than the imaginary line between Mexico and the United States.

In the great kiva of Chaco Canyon known as Casa Rinconada, I sat facing Daniel. We sat on the opposing steps of the two T-shaped doorways that gave access to the kiva's vast interior. This was the central ceremonial space of the Anasazi civilization.

Daniel and I meditated on the archetypal principle of the Sacred Twins. In our left hands we each held ears of blue corn to signify the gift of life. In our right hands we held gourd rattles to signify our roles as co-creators in the dance of eternal growth. Our arms were crossed over our chests in the form of an X, and our bodies were wrapped in the same kind of Mexikan blankets that Doug and I had worn on my previous medicine journey exactly six months earlier.

The night was silent and the air cold as we sat beneath a roof of stars. Directly above the kiva, the moon shone brightly, just past full. To the south behind me, the constellations of Orion and its polar companions, Sirius and the Pleiades, moved slowly across the horizon. When I felt that I had entered into communion with the stones of Chaco, I stood and circled the inner perimeter of the kiva. Soon I passed in front of Daniel, and together we exited through the northern doorway.

Still in our meditative state, we walked to the north side of the narrow canyon—to Pueblo Bonito, the well-preserved remains of what was once the largest apartment complex in North America. One thousand years ago, the D-shaped design of this dwelling place rose to a height of five stories and contained at least eight hundred rooms, twenty-five kivas, and an estimated population of more than twelve hundred people.

As we quietly walked through the multicolored stone rooms of Pueblo Bonito, I sensed the Ancient Ones watching us. I could almost hear their footsteps and their breathing. The silence reverberated with their presence. The darkness pulsated with their shadows. The makers of this magnificent maze were everywhere. Yet in a few more hours, they would vanish into the walls while a flood of unknowing tourists passed through this secretly inhabited pre-Columbian metropolis.

With the first signs of approaching dawn, Daniel and I returned to the great kiva under a still-starry sky. We went to its center and prayed. Then I removed the *kopal* from my pouch. I placed it on a bed of twigs in my abalone shell. Simultaneously, Daniel and I each ignited the *kopal* with a match and watched the smoke rise.

I placed our medicine into separate gourd cups, which I afterward passed through the smoke. Then slowly we ate. When we were finished, we returned to the doorways, sitting opposite each other as before. This time I could feel an invisible council of Ancient Ones sitting to either side of me on the narrow stone ledges. They encircled the kiva all the way around to the other doorway.

Gradually the stars begin to disappear, giving way to the ever-changing colors of the predawn sky. As the last star dissolves into a deep expanse of cobalt blue, I start to notice tiny sparks of white light moving toward my third eye, as if through a funnel. Yet when I close my eyes, I see a huge, dark cavern with millions of black bats flying out of it. I know that these two impressions must represent the opening of the superconscious and subconscious realms, the awakening of both my outer and inner vision. The bats are telling me it is time to emerge from the underworld of the kiva, while the sparks of light foreshadow the sunrise.

I circle out of the kiva, followed by Daniel. Dawn is about to break on the eastern horizon. We dip our hands into a bowl of yellow cornmeal. Holding it out, we offer it to the directions, greeting our Creator as we greet the new day. In a momentary flash, the rays of the sun reach out to touch us and light up the kiva like a great golden ring.

All of a sudden, Daniel rushes down the hillside and violently regurgitates his medicine. It seems an odd counterpoint to the tranquil beauty of the dawn. When he returns, he is upset, discouraged that because he has vomited he might not experience the peyote's visionary effect. He asks me how I am feeling, and I tell him I feel neither nauseous nor especially "altered."

Ninety minutes later I still feel no dramatic changes from the peyote. We decide to hike up an ancient path to the top of the northern cliffs overlooking the canyon.

Reaching the old settlement of Kin Kletso at the base of the cliffs, we encounter my friend Matias on his way down to Pueblo Bonito. Matias first heard about my plans for a Chaco pilgrimage back in Taos and asked if he could join us. I declined, explaining that I was completing a ceremonial focus on the Sacred Twin archetype and that I had to go to Chaco with Daniel alone. Now, even though Matias is here, my focus remains the same. We quickly greet each other and continue on our separate ways.

Meanwhile, Daniel has gone on ahead. I suspect he is exploring Kin Kletso, although I don't see him anywhere. But as I approach a large stone wall, I notice the shadow of what appears to be a man looking toward the wall from the top of Kin Kletso's highest room. I turn, expecting to see Daniel, but there is no one.

When I turn to face the wall again, the shadow is still there. Suddenly I get a creepy feeling that it is watching me. I take a few steps backward toward the cliffs. I look once more at the highest room, reconfirming that there is no one to be seen. I glance back at the wall one last time. This time the shadow moves, as if slowly turning to face the cliffs. I nervously look toward the high room, and there is Daniel with a big smile on his face.

I sigh with relief as he walks toward me, realizing that it must have been his shadow all along. But when I look at the wall again, the same shadow is there, frozen in profile. Obviously it *can't* be Daniel, so what on Earth is it? ... There is only one explanation: the medicine has finally begun to take effect. I am entering a nonordinary reality, a reality in which many things are simply unexplainable in rational terms.

I hear a call from above and look up to see an enormous eagle swooping over our heads.

"Let's go," Daniel says, his eyes afire. He begins to climb over the large boulders piled between us and the cliff. I hurry after him.

"Are you feeling it?" he asks.

"Yes," I answer.

"So am I," he says, "really strong."

Reaching the coffee-colored cliff face, we find ourselves at the edge of a wide, vertical fissure. The base of the fissure leads to an ancient stepped path that was used by the Anasazi to get to the top of the canyon. We ascend rapidly, feeling the rush of energy brought on by the medicine.

Arriving at the top of the cliff, we stop to take a breather. I am still obsessed with the shadow. I wonder if it could have been a spirit ally such as Mescalito, the nonphysical emanation of the peyote. Or perhaps it was Kauyumari, the part-deer/part-man culture hero and trickster of the Huichols who is associated with the peyote pilgrimage. Or perhaps it was my shadow, isolated from my consciousness to the point where it took on a life of its own.

Daniel and I continue walking, at last feeling the warmth of the sun penetrating our night-chilled bodies. Wearing rope sandals and dressed in white cotton clothes with a blanket folded over my shoulder, I feel like an archaic desert pilgrim. The surrounding world of succulents, cactus, and sensuous sandstone vibrates with light and color.

Where the trail comes closest to the edge of the cliff, we stop to sit down. I fix my eyes on an enormous gap across the canyon—the opening to the lands of the south. I can almost see a great, processional line of feathered Ancient Ones entering this canyon for the first time: people of the parrot clan, pilgrims from another holy land.

As my gaze holds steady on the gap, my third eye takes on the task of concentration, and my physical vision diffuses over a much wider area. I relax my eyes completely, scanning the vast terrain without focusing. As I do so, a new kind of perception takes hold. I begin to see corridors of light that crisscross the canyon floor below and beyond me. I see them with tremendous clarity, yet more than just physically—I perceive them with my entire being.

I have read of ley lines before, the invisible currents of Earth energy that are woven like an intricate web around and through the planet. They link one point of power to another, forming natural magnetic fields that affect everything from geological evolution and plant growth to animal migration patterns and the seasonal cycles of weather. It is said that these lines have even determined the development of early civilizations, particularly with respect to the placement of shrines, temples, and other sacred structures.

I realize that the corridors of light are a visual indication of the presence of such ley lines. A major one enters Chaco Canyon through the gap in its southern wall, while many veins spring out from it. I can easily see how rocks, plants, and trees are everywere clustered along these light corridors—and even how Chaco's ancient, human-made structures were built to take best advantage of their powerful energies.

I can also see that Chaco Canyon's main road cuts through numerous ley lines. Amazingly, though, the leafy plants that grow alongside them are reaching toward each other on either side of the road, extending their growth to reconnect the light corridors. In this I see the unrelenting determination of nature to heal itself when the natural order is broken. I know that it can eventually overpower anything that stands in its way.

Suddenly I hear another high-pitched call. I look up as an eagle soars over and glides across the canyon.

"Come on," says Daniel. "We've got to keep moving."

After walking a short distance, I feel the urge to return to the edge of the precipice. We agree to meet later at the top of the cliff directly above Pueblo Bonito.

I go to a vantage point atop the northern rim from where I can see Pueblo Bonito a short distance to the east. Seating myself in a comfortable position, I close my eyes. Now the peyote comes into full play. Multicolored, geometric patterns unfold in mandalic sequences, like flowers opening to reveal still more precious flowers within.

As I drift deeper into this vision of cosmic order, I become aware of a curious buzzing sound, like the drone of insects. The sound enhances my unfolding vision. Two-dimensional geometries suddenly transform into three-dimensional expressions of sacred architecture. Buddhist stupas become Mayan pyramids, become mosques, become temples, become cathedrals—all appearing as quadrupled projections within mandalic wheels.

As the wheels turn, the cathedrals become mountains. The mountains change into valleys and the valleys into underwater canyons. The canyons change into kivas, and the kivas descend into the Earth. Through these visions, I see that kivas and other expressions of sacred architecture are as much a part of nature as a spiderweb or a beehive are.

The endless stream of inner mandalic images stops flowing as I open my eyes. Yet the world outside now seems just as much a mandalic reflection of organic unity as the world within. Thus the flow continues, and so does the curious, buzzing drone.

I realize that the sound is coming from Pueblo Bonito far below. It is a musical drone, created by human hands. Looking down, I can make out the figure of Matias sitting at the bottom of the largest kiva, playing an East Indian tamboura. From my vantage point, he looks not much bigger than an ant. Still, I can see that he is plucking the strings of his instrument. The natural acoustics of the canyon project its rich resonance all the way up to me.

Unknowingly, Matias has gifted me with the very sound I have most needed: a sound of universal harmony. And it has come precisely when I am ready for it. I thank him by playing my flute, and he looks up to see me. We wave to each other and I move on.

I follow the ridge of the canyon wall as it curves back to the north and then wraps around to the south and east. It brings me to the overlook directly above Pueblo Bonito, where large holes in the sandstone have been scooped out by pockets of collecting rainwater. At the very edge of the cliff there is a hole just large enough for me to sit in. From inside it, I can look straight down to Pueblo Bonito far feet below, yet feel completely sheltered and protected.

Here in this vision pit, I have the certain sense that the Earth is within me and that I am within it; we are interpenetrating each other. It feels like sexual intercourse through every cell of my being. The whole world is my beloved, sharing with me in the ecstasy of the Divine Presence.

In this ecstatic state, I begin to sing to the rhythmic accompaniment of my gourd rattle. My voice rises and falls on uninterrupted waves of energy. My singing is effortless. The energy sustains me completely, carrying me deep into new worlds, each with its own special patterns of sound. As the worlds change, the words change. I recognize them as environments of language, each one as unique as the different races of humanity, as diverse as the various ecosystems of the planet.

I feel as if I now understand the root impulses that bring about specific expressions of sound, image, and movement. I can see that there is a reason, a natural order, to the organic matching of certain languages, musical styles, dances, ecosystems, and architectural forms. Yet it is also clear to me that there is no genuine line of demarcation between these varied expressions. From one language to another, one skin color to another, one environment to another, there is a gradual shading of changes. I see them as one might see the diffuse and interpenetrating colors of a rainbow.

As my outer song transforms in melody and words, these realizations give way to a single voice inside my head. I hear it as the voice of the Ancient Ones:

"We are totally alive. We always have been and always will be. The rest of the world may be oblivious to our existence, but we are here, vibrating as a spiritual force and perceptible to all with open hearts.

"Now is the time to put forth the vision of love, harmony, and beauty such as we have created here through our steady dedication. Now is the time to reinforce the vibrations of balance in your world such as we have manifested in these structures. In this way, you will gradually transform the collective consciousness, bringing humanity into alignment with its highest purpose.

"Empower the positive and hold your vision strong. There is no need to feed the fears of destruction and disaster. Reaffirm the eternal harmony of creation and live it now. Live it in every moment. This is the great work."

As the voice disappears and I conclude my chant, I hear the whoosh of wings overhead: an eagle descends like lightning from the high cliff toward the canyon floor. I immediately stand, shouting, "HO!" and another voice shouts in response. Daniel stands behind me, wearing an ecstatic smile.

"Are you ready to fly?" I ask. He looks at me questioningly. "Come on," I say, "I'll race you to the top of these rocks."

At the peak of our energy, we leap and run over the smooth sandstone landscape that rises gradually toward the remains of Pueblo Alto. From this highest northern point of Chaco, we are rewarded with the day's most spectacular view. I throw off the last of my clothes and climb atop some steps that form a small pyramid. Here, naked and with arms outstretched, I salute the Four Directions, the Earth, and the sun, and give thanks to the Great Spirit at the center.

Daniel and I decide to conclude our medicine journey back at the great kiva where it began. Just as we arrive, Matias also arrives. Now I realize—and at last accept—that he has become a part of our journey. I invite him to join us for the final ceremony.

Entering the kiva, we make offerings to the ancestral keepers. We circle sunwise once together around the empty chamber. The second time around, we seat ourselves so that we are evenly spaced one from another and begin to meditate.

In my own meditation, I see how I have tried to control a situation in which a friend wanted to participate—a situation that was actually beyond my control. In retrospect, I recognize that the presence of my friend has been a blessing. In gratitude, I realize that I must always be ready to shift and adapt, for in rigid resistance I might miss my greatest opportunities.

As we conclude our silent meditations, Matias begins to play a beautiful improvisation on his bamboo flute. As he does so, I close my eyes and journey deep into the heart of the planet through a tunnel-like kiva that has no bottom. I am amazed to discover that the deeper I go, the brighter the light is—until finally it is so brilliant I can go no farther. I ascend from the inner world back to the surface and the night. But the white light still fills the kiva. What's more, it shines outward from the depths like a great beam lighting up the night sky.

I open my eyes, grateful again to Matias for inspiring me with his music, which, he explains, was a *raga* for the Earth. I reach into my bag for the green corn I have saved to use for our concluding ceremony. I wonder how I can divide it, thinking there are only two ears. Much to my surprise, I discover that in fact there are three. I laugh delightedly, realizing that this is an affirmation of our change from a twosome to a threesome. I see now that the T-shaped doorways of the kiva not only represent the Sacred Twins, but the unity of duality, the holy trinity, the two coming into oneness.

I circle the kiva and offer an ear to each of my brothers before returning to my spot. Then together we eat the raw, green corn, honoring it as spiritual food. Never has corn tasted so delicious, and never has it meant so much to me.

I think, too, of the Huichols—of how they honor a holy trinity formed by the corn, the deer, and the peyote. The corn and the deer sustain them physically, and the peyote sustains them spiritually. Yet so strong is the association between them that when the Huichols are on their pilgrimage to gather the peyote, they actually "hunt" the sacred cactus with miniature bows and arrows. Thus they refer to the peyote as the "blue deer."

Today we began our journey by taking into ourselves the blue deer, and we have concluded it by taking into us the green corn. Like the colors of the sky and the Earth, blue and green, we have unified them through our bodies and made them one.

I invite my brothers into the center of the kiva for the last act. We each take a handful of yellow cornmeal and turn to face the east to make an offering of gratitude and a prayer for the balance of life. As we raise our hands to the east, the eagle that has appeared to us throughout the day appears once more in the sky, precisely at the point toward which we reach, and then disappears behind us.

We turn to face the south. Again we offer the cornmeal in gratitude and prayer. To the west and the north as well we turn, honoring each of these directions. Now we turn to the center to offer our prayers to the Earth, and lastly up toward the sun, which is hidden behind dark clouds. Yet as we reach out, the clouds part, forming an opening through which a brilliant beam of light illuminates the kiva.

Looking into the sun, I see the eagle one last time. I stare at its flashing eyes, its golden heart. From my own heart bursts a cord of light that connects me to the heart of the eagle. Like the corn, the deer, and the peyote, we also are a trinity—of man, eagle, and sun. And these six powers are all one.

CHAPTER 10

THE GATES OF HUIMAIVU

With the conclusion of the Moon of the Changing Season began the Moon of Falling Leaves. It grew to fullness, and then a letter arrived from El Maestro. In it he wrote that he wanted me to return to México as soon as possible, but no later than the next new moon in mid-November. He was inviting me to join him and the other apprentices on a pilgrimage to certain ceremonial centers in the southern part of the country.

In his letter, El Maestro went on to say that he was at last ready to introduce us to the most guarded and ancient source of his knowledge, so that each one of us would be independently empowered to receive knowledge from it. He said he had foreseen that his apprentices would soon be going in different directions, and he needed to do this before that happened. He added that it was especially important for me to connect with this mysterious source, explaining that it would provide me with a missing link for everything I had learned. The following evening, El Maestro came to me in a dream.

I see his hand—the hand of my teacher. He is pointing south, and he says, "Behold!" I look to the south and see the jaguar and the feathered serpent. El Maestro says, "These two are you in balance."

I see his other hand. He points north, and he says, "Behold!" I look to

204 «

the north and see the buffalo and the eagle. My teacher says, "These two are you in balance."

Now I see both of El Maestro's hands. He is spinning them around me, making a wheel of smoke. His voice says, "Behold!" and I turn to look. In each direction stands one of the animals I have just seen: the jaguar in the west, the snake in the south, the buffalo in the north, and the eagle in the east. El Maestro says, "These four are you in balance. You stand at the center of their wheel."

He lifts the smoke with his hands. Standing beside each of the four sacred animals is a human and a friend: Lucinda by the jaguar, Jorge by the snake, Doug by the buffalo, and Daniel by the eagle. "Behold!" says El Maestro. "These four are your mirrors. With each you have journeyed, and with each you have seen. They have helped to guide you to the four sacred animals of your dream."

Again he spins his hands, this time making four roads of smoke. They go from the center where I stand to each of the Four Directions. They rise from the ground and reach into the sky. "Behold!" says El Maestro. "And behold again! On each of these roads you have climbed, each time climbing higher until you reached the top." As he says this, I turn to the east. I see myself naked with arms outstretched, standing beside the eagle.

"Behold!" El Maestro says again, louder than before. I look to the ground where his hands are growing out of the Earth. In each hand he holds a sacred medicine plant—the mushroom in his left hand, the peyote in his right. Then he says, "These two are you in balance."

Now the smoke swirls around me. I can see nothing but smoke; I hear nothing but El Maestro's voice. "Behold!" he shouts. "Behold that which you do not yet see. Four times you have climbed. Now you shall descend. Four times with another, now without a friend. Three times with the medicine plants, now without their aid. Two times into canyons, now one last time is the journey so made."

All is silence—dead silence. The smoke swirls more wildly than before. I can't even tell if my feet are touching the ground. I am terribly frightened.

"Where?" I cry out. "Where is the canyon?"

"Behold!" El Maestro answers. "You must seek your revelation in the Canyon of Copper. You must seek it with the human beings. Discover your humanity, for it is you who stand in the center of the wheel. It is you who make the four powers one. It is you who make the world whole."

"But I've never heard of this canyon," I protest.

"Go to the Canyon of Copper," El Maestro reiterates. "A place awaits you there where you must find your humanity. Without it, the source of my knowledge will shatter you to pieces."

With these final words, the smoke swirls away, leaving me standing alone in a black void.

The next day, nothing seemed as real as the dream. It hung on my soul, weighing down all activity and effort. I couldn't shake it. I realized I would have to answer its call very soon, because in less than two weeks I was expected at Kalpulli Koatlan. Yet I still had no idea of where to find the mysterious canyon.

Fortunately, I didn't have to wait long for an answer. That night in town, I ran into a Czechoslovakian friend named Yirka, who had just returned from an extended trip to México. On his way back to Taos, he had taken the train through a vast and wild landscape in the state of Chihuahua known as Barranca del Cobre, the Canyon of Copper. He told me it was a spectacular region covering an area ten times that of the Grand Canyon. He said it was also home to one of the most traditional surviving indigenous cultures in North America—the Raramuri, more commonly known as the Tarahumara.

I was relieved to have this information, but it also left me worried. In so vast a terrain, how would I know where to go? El Maestro had said there was a specific place.

On Yirka's suggestion, I decided to take the train to a town called Creel, which was in the center of Raramuri country and the beginning point for most expeditions into the canyon. And though my time was limited, at least the Canyon of Copper was close to the main route from Taos to Mexico City. With luck, I would accomplish my mission and still reach the *kalpulli* in time.

I arrived in Creel before dawn after an all-night train ride from the capital of Chihuahua. A strong wind blew flakes of snow the size of golf balls against the train's dusty windows, making it almost impossible to see anything outside. I threw my backpack over my shoulders and apprehensively headed toward the exit door.

When I stepped out, all my senses confirmed that I was ill prepared for the weather. Never had I imagined I would be caught in a blizzard in México. I had brought only lightweight clothes and no hat or gloves. Within minutes, I was shivering uncontrollably in the middle of the town's deserted plaza, completely alone.

I marveled at the madness that had brought me here. Perhaps I had gone too far with my faith in dreams. It would be at least a couple of hours before any shop would open, and there was no one around to ask for information. Only an occasional homeless dog scurried down the dirt streets. I felt like one of them as I walked to some nearby buildings for temporary shelter from the storm.

Though I knew I could find a hotel, I wanted to get out of Creel as soon as possible. The town was at the very top of the canyon, and I was hopeful that down below it would be warmer. So I waited out the last cold hours of darkness until morning.

As the sky began to brighten, it became apparent that the weather and the darkness were not the only factors contributing to Creel's desolate atmosphere. The town felt like a place forgotten, a place lingering a century behind, trapped in the unfulfilled promises of the industrial revolution. It stagnated in a gray cloud. It reeked of poverty. From its dispirited colors and forms, I could see that it had been long separated from nature by a brutal history of miners and missionaries, alcohol and guns.

By eight o'clock, some shops were opening and some people at last were walking the muddy, snow-covered streets. Still, I could get no clear information about transport into the canyon. Finally an old, creaking bus spurting filthy exhaust pulled up beside the train depot. I rushed over to ask the driver where he was going.

"Batopilas," he said.

I asked him if it was at the bottom of the canyon, and he nodded affirmatively. That was all I needed to know.

A short distance out of Creel, the snow stopped falling and the sun broke through the slate-blue clouds. Glistening white powder blanketed the resting Earth, and the boughs of pine trees drooped from the heavy weight of sparkling icicles. Sand-castle-like rock formations added drama to this winter wonderland, thrusting themselves erratically between the trees. Slowly the sun radiated through the glass window of the bus, relieving my chill and freeing me to appreciate the beautiful legacy of the storm I had so recently damned.

An hour or so later, the unpaved road began to descend into the canyon, treating me to my first far-reaching views of this wildly uneven land. It was not as colorful as the Grand Canyon, but it was without question of greater dimensions. Somewhere down there, I thought hopefully, was the fulfillment of my dream.

The bus pulled over by a small stone house, where we stopped for food. The five other passengers—four men and a woman, all mestizo—seemed a bit mistrusting of me, but probably no more than I was of them. No doubt they were wondering why this oddly dressed gringo had come to such a remote and rugged part of their country.

The bus continued down, down, down. The farther we descended, the more pitiful the road became. Frequently the bus slowed for ruts and bumps, and sometimes its engine stopped altogether. In such cases, the driver and his assistant would jump out and fiddle with the engine, and amazingly we'd be off and running again. In any case, the ride was exhausting; even more so because I had hardly slept on the train. All night I had been forced to listen to blaring ranchero music, which I had long since grown to dislike. Continuing our descent, we passed the almost deserted villages of Cusarare and Basihuare, which the Raramuri had abandoned for their winter homes in the warmer depths of the canyon.

Then at last came the inevitable: a flat tire. Frustrated as I was, everyone else seemed unfazed. Within an hour, we were on our way again. Still, I was worried that with one more flat and no more spares, we could be seriously stranded.

With this in mind, I offered to run in front of the bus, throwing the biggest and sharpest rocks off to the sides. This shocked my mestizo companions, but for the next couple of hours that is exactly what I did, and the activity helped me to purge a great deal of accumulated negativity. In running, I also began to feel a genuine connection to the place, as well as to the Raramuri, whose name actually means "Foot Runners."

Two hours later, the driver and passengers no longer regarded me with the same distance. I had won them over. I wasn't just a faceless gringo anymore; now everyone was curious to know more about me and why I had come.

When I explained that it was my intention to hike and explore the canyon, the other passengers warned me about the dangers of going into the canyon alone. "It's still full of wild Indians," said one man bedecked in cowboy boots and hat. "They'll shoot you with arrows and eat you," said another, his hand resting on the pistol that hung in the holster to his side.

It was obvious to me that these people didn't like the Raramuri. Although their own skins were brown, they had been indoctrinated with the values of the white man from across the sea. I didn't dare explain to them that I actually *wanted* to make contact with the indigenous people.

Finally we reached the bottom of the canyon, where it was warm and green, with an abundance of subtropical vegetation. The bus plowed for hours along a narrow road beside a rushing river. As the day neared its end, we came around a bend where the mouth of a dramatically steep side canyon came into view.

Something about this canyon pulled at me like a magnet. Impulsively I asked the driver to stop, explaining that I wanted to get off. He laughed and told me I was crazy. The others protested vehemently, again warning me of the danger. Under the circumstances, it was difficult not to doubt my instincts, but I insisted on getting off the bus. Still the driver refused to stop. Like it or not, I was bound for Batopilas.

A while later, I asked if anyone knew the name of the side canyon we had just passed. The woman answered, telling me it was called Huimaivu. Just hearing the strangely familiar name clinched my decision: one way or another, I had to go back there.

After a fourteen-hour trip, we pulled into Batopilas at last. It was almost midnight in the old mining town. Occasionally the bus headlights illuminated palm and banana trees. I was amazed to think that not long ago I had been standing in a freezing blizzard. I checked into the only hotel and collapsed on a lumpy mattress.

The following morning, I discovered that the bus would not be returning to Creel for another day. Even if I waited, I still had no reason to believe that the driver would let me out at Huimaivu. Given my time constraints, I decided the best alternative was to start walking back to the canyon.

After a few hours of walking, I saw an open-bed pickup full of locals approaching. I put out my thumb and was invited to climb on in back. I was struck by how much faster this truck was able to cover the same ground that yesterday had seemed so endless. But well before reaching Huimaivu, the driver pulled over and parked in front of a small *ranchera*. Everybody got out, all apparently headed to nearby homes and settlements.

From there I began walking again, this time accompanied by a teenage boy headed in the same direction. He was not Raramuri, but he knew much of their language, which he enthusiastically began to teach me. "*Vakoche* is the river we walk beside," he said. "*Vawiki* is the flowing water. *Kawiki* is the mountains all around us, and *tutuguri* is the sun above."

"What about Huimaivu?" I asked.

"Huimaivu means 'the Place of the Black Earth,'" he responded. The name fit; I remembered that my dream had left me in total blackness.

Finally we came to where my new friend had to follow a different road. I asked him how much farther it was to Huimaivu. He told me that less than a kilometer ahead I would find a place to cross the river and that I must follow the trail along the other side until I came to the mouth of Huimaivu Canyon.

"*Nateteraba* [thank you]," I said.

He answered with, "*Kivara,*" a Raramuri expression meaning both hello and good-bye.

I walked the last kilometer on the road and descended to the banks of the river. But the river was wide and quite deep in places. It was hard for me to pick out the shallowest crossing. Since it was already getting dark, I decided to sleep by the shore and tackle the river in the morning. I laid my sleeping bag out across a bed of smooth, round rocks and climbed in.

I was awakened by delicate bird songs in the predawn light. Just as I lifted my head, I noticed that a few hundred feet upstream, a Raramuri man in a white cotton shirt and loincloth was crossing the river. I watched his entire passage carefully, taking note of every twist and turn.

As soon as he had disappeared on the other side of the river, I rolled up my sleeping bag and gathered all my gear. I didn't bother to dress because I would need to carry everything above my head to keep it dry. Walking upstream to the place where I first saw the Raramuri man, I entered the cold river as naked as the day I was born. Carefully I balanced myself as I crossed, doing my best to keep a steady footing on the uneven stones. Occasionally this was made very difficult by gushes of fast-moving water, but somehow I managed to reach the other side without falling.

Once on the trail, I felt quite content. It was a beautiful, sunny day, and all my attention was free to appreciate and absorb the spectacular beauty of this rugged land. I had already surmounted the biggest hurdles of my journey—or so I thought.

After a few miles of hiking, I spotted a Raramuri man headed down the trail in the opposite direction. He, like the other man, was dressed in a white cotton shirt and a loincloth. His legs were spindly yet muscular, and his naked feet seemed to grip the ground with the fleet security of a mountain goat. He wore a bright red bandana around his head, as well as a woven fiber strap that helped to support the burlap sack of corn he had tied to his back. When the intense black pupils of his eyes suddenly met mine, he seemed slightly startled.

"*Kivara,*" I said to him.

The man's expressionless gaze turned quickly to a smile. "*Kivara,*" he answered. Then he said in Spanish, "What are you doing here?"

For simplicity's sake, I explained that I was a student of indigenous music and that I had come to learn more about the music of the Raramuri. He seemed unsure if he should trust me, but when I pulled a native Mexikan flute from my pack and began to play, it was obvious that the ice had been broken.

I spent more than an hour with this man, sitting and talking beside the trail. We seemed to have an easy rapport, and we discussed a wide range of subjects pertaining to life in our respective countries.

Finally he asked me, "Where do you go from here?" I told him I was hoping to hike all the way into Huimaivu Canyon but that I was uncertain about how to continue.

"Just cross the bridge and follow the trail," he said. "If you want, when you get there you can stay in my home."

"Really?" I asked.

"Yes, yes. I live in Huimaivu. You are welcome there. I must go to a village across the river, but I will be back by evening."

"How will I know which house is yours?"

"My name is Valente Palma. You are welcome in my home."

With that, my new friend stood and shook my hand, then turned to go. "*Nateteraba,*" I said.

"*Kivara!*" he called out, already well down the trail.

And so, with renewed confidence, I continued along the winding path. It was almost noon by the time I reached the mouth of Huimaivu Canyon. Looking into it, I could see that there were two massive, black stone sentinels guarding the final entrance. The crack between them appeared to be so narrow as to be impassable. I imagined them as the two huge, dark doors of a secret castle, pulled open just enough to allow a sliver of light to shine through. I dubbed them the "Gates of Huimaivu."

But the gates were up ahead, and first I had to deal with the facts of the moment. The crossing bridge was in serious disrepair. Its metal cables were frayed. More serious still, many wooden planks were missing, in some places leaving gaping holes almost a yard across. If I should fail to negotiate one of these, I would fall fifty feet straight down into rushing rapids and boulders.

I decided to search for an alternate route along the mouth of the canyon; however, I soon became discouraged. There was obviously no trail, and the slopes were extremely steep. I could just as easily slip and fall off the cliff as I could from the dilapidated bridge. So I chose the bridge.

I cinch up my waist and shoulder straps as tightly as possible to reduce the rocking motion of my heavy pack. I am hoping that the shoulder bag hanging from my left side and the staff I clench in my right hand will not throw me off balance at a critical moment. Regardless, I know I have to cross. I take a deep breath and focus all my attention on getting safely to the other side. I exhale and begin walking.

Upon reaching the first big gap, I pause and leap across to the next available plank, half holding onto the cables so that I can catch myself if I fall. Having successfully passed the first gap, I observe that the next couple come easier. Even so, I am shaking like a leaf by the time I reach the other side.

After sitting for a few minutes to regain my composure, I get up to look for the trail. Much to my chagrin, I can find no trail. Worse still, the slopes of the canyon's mouth are even steeper here, so scrambling across them is out of the question. My only alternative is to go back across the bridge.

The fact that I am quite nervous and upset makes my return crossing far more shaky, but somehow I make it on automatic pilot. Back on the other side, I consider the possibility of retracing my steps and forgetting my quest into the canyon. On the other hand, since I have already crossed the skeleton bridge twice, the thought of scrambling over loose rocks and dry brush and pulling myself across sheer rock walls no longer seems inconceivable.

When I look once more at the rock-spire Gates of Huimaivu, I know I have to go on. Deep down I have a sense that I must be utterly mad. Yet even deeper is the overriding conviction that somehow I must reach the Gates of Huimaivu. Trail or no trail, I *must* enter the hidden valley.

Slowly I begin to edge my way into the mouth of the canyon, moving on all fours whenever necessary and always leaning my body into the cliff. I wish now that I wasn't carrying so much, but I know I have to deal with things as they are, not as they might have been.

At one point, my left foot slides out from under me and knocks free some loose rocks, which bounce and fall to the churning waters below. Fortunately, the bush I grab onto holds firm, and I pull myself back up. From there on, there are no more trees or bushes, only thorny cactuses. I cannot afford to lose my concentration again for even a second.

Throughout this ordeal, whenever I reach a place where I can pause safely, I turn and look ahead toward the Gates of Huimaivu. I project my consciousness forward and see myself already there. The gates command my devotion to my quest and strengthen my resolve to succeed. They empower me to be courageous, to surmount all obstacles.

Finally, miraculously, I reach the other side of the sheer cliff and step onto more level ground. I have picked up many scratches, but these are a small price to pay for having made it across. My joyous shout of thankfulness echoes across the canyon. Now, though there is still no trail, at least I can walk.

After a while, even the trail appears. It leads me easily and directly to the Gates of Huimaivu. Between them I stand and breathe in the Earth through my feet. Then I cross through the gates and enter the valley.

The valley of Huimaivu was enormous, lush, and green, surrounded by high canyon walls on all sides. The trail followed the inner slopes of one of these walls, slowly descending in switchbacks until it reached the valley floor.

From here I could see more clearly that I was indeed within the embrace of a Native American paradise. Many varieties of fruit and palm trees grew along the river and its tributaries, and fields of corn and vegetables dotted the hilly landscape. In the distance I saw stone structures that I thought must be the homes of the Raramuri. And in some spots I could even make out tiny, moving figures clad in brightly colored clothes.

Excited as I was by the magnificent beauty of Huimaivu, I was cautious about entering, for I did not want to disturb its idyllic tranquillity in any way. I knew that its people were not expecting me. Somehow, I must arrive without being invasive. I slowed my pace and quieted my steps, doing all I could to be more sensitive to my surroundings.

As I got closer, I was able to tell more about the structure of the Raramuri dwellings. They were unlike anything I had ever seen before. Each one consisted of two enormous boulders, each easily weighing many tons. They were propped up against one another in such a way that they formed a sheltered, triangular space beneath. Then much smaller rocks were built up in walls about two to three feet high. These encircled the boulders and also defined a roofless area for each enclosure. Within these enclosures the Raramuri lived. How, I wondered, did these supposedly "primitive" people ever move boulders of such massive dimensions? I got the definite feeling that the boulders had been positioned this way for a very long time.

Soon I reached a fork in the trail that led in three directions. Instinctively I took the middle fork, which led me directly to one of the boulder houses. Outside, two young girls were playing with their baby sister. They seemed curious but unconcerned as I approached.

"Excuse me," I said, "I'm looking for the home of Valente Palma."

"This is his home," the oldest girl said. "He's my father."

Once more I was amazed at the synchronistic quality of my pilgrimage. Without any conscious idea of where my feet were carrying me, I had walked right up to the home of the one person I knew in the entire valley. I explained to the girls that I had met their father on the trail a few hours earlier, and I told them of his kind invitation.

"You can stay right there and wait till my mother comes back," the oldest girl said. "She's working in the fields now."

I decided this would be best, as I was still worried about disturbing the privacy of the people of Huimaivu. I thanked the girls and laid my pack down against a large rock just beyond the unroofed section of their enclosure. Then I climbed atop the rock to sit and wait.

Puffy white clouds passed across a deep blue sky. Gradually the warm sun crossed the valley and descended toward the western walls of the canyon. Still I waited. At long last, the mother came. She was dressed in the typical manner of Raramuri women, in a white cotton blouse and a red skirt with flowered print. On her head she wore a blue cloth with ear flaps.

The mother was not so ready to trust me, and our communication was rather difficult because she spoke very little Spanish. I wasn't even sure she understood that I had met her husband on the trail. Our brief exchange left me feeling awkward and uncertain whether I was welcome. I decided to wait on the rock a while longer, hoping Valente would be back soon. Meanwhile, the mother and her daughters went about their business within the enclosure, oblivious of my presence.

After the sun had set, the air quickly grew cold. I saw the women making a fire in the interior section of their home. I pulled from my pack the little warm clothing that I had. I wondered where I was going to spend the night. I had also run out of food, and I was getting hungry. I realized that I had set myself up for an undesired experience of deprivation. Even worse, I felt like my presence was imposing on others. I wasn't even sure why I was here. I started to feel very foolish and sorry for myself.

Then, to my surprise, the older daughter came over and invited me inside for something to eat. The mother was much more friendly now, as she offered me some freshly made tortillas and coffee. The family also passed around a gourdful of roasted cornmeal called *piñole*. They took handfuls of it and placed it in their mouths a little at a time, swishing it around with a bit of water before swallowing. I tried it as well and found it very flavorful.

After eating, the older daughter told me that her mother said I was welcome to sleep in the outdoors part of their enclosure. I thanked them for their generosity and went to get my pack. From where I lay down in my sleeping bag, Huimaivu Canyon looked like a big, black bowl beneath an infinity of floating stars. Feeling warm and secure there, I fell into a restful sleep.

The next day began just as gloriously as the previous one. All of nature seemed to be celebrating the return of the sun. I went back to my rock to sit and wait, expecting Valente to come back soon. But he didn't. After waiting the whole morning, there was still no sign of him. Even his wife appeared to be concerned.

I decided not to wait any longer for Valente to introduce me to the people of Huimaivu. Besides, by now many of them had already noticed me sitting on my rock. I had seen them staring at me from various homes and hillsides. And so, in the afternoon, I began to wander the valley trails.

My sojourn was quite beautiful, but nothing happened. I met no one. Again I started to wonder why I had come. At last, by the banks of a wooded stream, I was greeted by a young Raramuri man named Gregorio. "I've been watching you sitting on the rock," he said.

After we had talked for a while, Gregorio invited me to visit his family on the hill. He turned out to be Valente's cousin. All his close relatives—parents, brothers, sisters, nieces, nephews, wife, and children—lived with him in a clustered grouping of homes on the hill. All were extremely friendly and curious to know everything about me. They graciously shared with me their coffee, tortillas, and *piñole*.

Toward evening I told Gregorio I was going back to Valente's to see if he had arrived yet. "Don't bother," Gregorio said. "Valente probably won't be back for days. Besides, you're welcome to stay with us."

I thanked him but explained that I at least had to go back to retrieve my things.

Sure enough, Valente had still not come home. His wife's mood was heavy. I couldn't be certain, but to my eyes she had the sad and bitter expression of a woman whose unfaithful husband had left her hanging again. Under the circumstances, I decided it best to accept Gregorio's offer. I said good-bye to the Palma family and returned to Gregorio's.

After nightfall, I was treated to a concert of Raramuri music by Gregorio, his father, and brothers. They played repetitive, trancelike music on reed flute, balsa-wood rattles, hoop drums covered with goatskins, and a kind of mouth bow called a *chaparakay*. Gregorio also played a homemade violin, an instrument that, although of European origin, the Raramuri had quickly adapted to their musical repertoire. Following a few hours of this, the men's eyes began to close, and they soon faded off into the Dreamtime.

I crawled into my sleeping bag, where I lay awake reviewing the events of the past few days. I felt that I had been extremely fortunate in most respects. Yet what did I have to show for it? There had been no dramatic revelations here, nothing to compare to my visions at Paricutin, Palenque, Porvenir, or Chaco. Maybe I should ask my Raramuri hosts if they could guide me through a ceremony with *ciguri,* their word for the sacred peyote cactus.

But no, it was not proper to request such a sacred thing. And even if my hosts were to offer it, El Maestro had made it clear in the dream that I was not to use any medicine plants on this journey. Finally, when I calculated how much time I had left, I began to worry that I might not be able to accomplish my mission and make it back to Kalpulli Koatlan by the new moon.

In the morning I asked Gregorio if there was another way out of the canyon. He said yes, that there was a trail out the other side that led to the town of Rio Urique, where the bus passed on its way back to Creel from Batopilas.

"But why do you want to leave so soon?" he asked. "Please stay with us longer."

"You are very kind, Gregorio," I said, "but I must be in Mexico City within a few days. Last night I realized that I have to leave today if I am to make it in time."

"Then I will go with you," he said. "The trail is very difficult to follow. I will take you to Rio Urique."

Within the hour, Gregorio and I set out on the trail together as the members of his family called out to please come back soon. I was touched by the warmth and generosity of these people whom most of the rest of the world would call "backward," even "savage." To the contrary, if human kindness was a factor in civilization, then these people were some of the most civilized I had ever met.

Our hike lasted the better part of the day. As we slowly ascended from three thousand to eight thousand feet, we went through a wide variety of terrain and vegetation. Gregorio refused to let me carry my own pack, yet he outpaced me with ease. Both of us drank only water and ate only *piñole*. I discovered that this was the power food of the Raramuri, the food that sustained them on their long-distance treks through the canyon. This was their simple source of strength.

As we neared the high plateau, we reached a wooden shack, the summer home of Gregorio's family. He opened it and took me inside. Stuffed above the roof beams was a large store of dried corn of many varieties. Gregorio pulled down some white ears and some yellow ears and handed them to me. "These are for you to take home and plant," he said. Then from a hook on the wall, he removed two long, hanging strands of small white objects that made a rattling sound. "This is for your music," he said.

When I asked what they were, he said, "They are the dried cocoons that we collect from the trees after the moths have left them. We fill them with little pebbles and sew them together on strips of cotton, then wear them around our bodies when we dance." Gregorio demonstrated, hanging a strand diagonally across his torso as he bounced up and down.

When we left the shack, Gregorio told me that he had gone as far as he could. From here the trail was easy, he said. He pointed the way and said it was only another couple of hours to Rio Urique. Then he handed me my pack.

I thanked my new friend profusely for everything and bade him good-bye. By midafternoon, I had reached Rio Urique. Though my energy level was still fairly high, my feet were killing me and my stomach was growling after two days of eating only pinole and tortillas.

Where the trail reached the road, I recognized the little house that served as the bus stop for this remote village. I remembered that the driver had gotten some food here, so I reasoned that with luck I, too, might be able to buy a meal.

Once at the house, I knocked on the door. At first it seemed that nobody was home, but about five minutes later, an attractive young woman finally answered.

"I hope I'm not disturbing you," I said.

"No, no, please come in," she responded. "What can I do for you?"

First I asked her when the next bus to Creel would be passing through, and she said in about three hours. Then I asked her if there was anything to eat.

Initially the young woman hesitated, but then she said, "Yes, please sit down." She guided me into a small room with a wooden table and a few chairs, where I finally removed my pack and sat down. There I waited for what seemed like an eternity.

In fact, it was about an hour and a half later when my hostess returned. She placed a plate of food on the table and told me to enjoy my meal. When she saw the shocked expression on my face, she said, "I'm sorry it took so long. Please forgive me, but I didn't have any food in the house. So I went outside and killed one of our chickens, because I could see that you were very hungry."

"Oh, thank you very much, Señorita," I said, trying to conceal my horror.

I sat alone, staring at the plate of food. I realized that I should not be surprised, since in my fervor to eat I had forgotten to ask what was available. Now I had to deal with the reality that was before me, both literally and figuratively.

The life of the chicken now on my plate had been sacrificed specifically for me; it was too late to change that. Even if I didn't eat the chicken, that still wouldn't bring it back to life. Besides, I couldn't send the chicken back. The woman of this house, in her genuine concern for my well-being, had just taken ninety minutes of her time to prepare this meal. To refuse it would be completely disrespectful to both her and the chicken. And anyway, I was famished. Thus did my many years as a strict vegetarian come to an end.

As I rode on the bus out of the inner canyon toward Creel that night, a part of me felt very content with my experiences in the land of the Raramuri. I had survived a challenging and perilous journey, met and shared with a truly wonderful people, and learned some valuable things about myself and human nature. On the other hand, I could not escape the nagging feeling that I had failed. Whatever it was that I had come here for, I was certain that I had not found it.

CHAPTER 11

THE DREAM OF DISMEMBERMENT

On the appointed eve of the November new moon, weary from the thousand-plus miles I had just traveled on buses and trains, I arrived at my home away from home: Kalpulli Koatlan. It was good to be back in the embracing arms of old friends and fellow apprentices. It was especially good to see El Maestro and to walk with him again in the foothills of the Mountain of the Serpent.

In the first days of our reunion, I was bursting with unanswered questions. Still, I said nothing to El Maestro about the Canyon of Copper, nor of my dream. El Maestro showed no sign that he knew anything about it, either. Without his validation, I began to wonder if the dream had been a ploy of my imagination—and whether my journey had been a mistaken detour.

All these concerns soon faded, however, as preparations for our group pilgrimage quickly gathered momentum. The last of El Maestro's apprentices were arriving from the Four Directions. Within a few days, a group of approximately twelve had gathered, and we began our caravan toward the Yukatan.

I had been looking forward to this pilgrimage ever since I had first met El Maestro. He had promised that someday he would take me across México to visit the ancient pyramids and temples—and that someday he would unravel for me their artfully encoded wisdom. Now, it seemed, that promise was about to be fulfilled.

Given El Maestro's Nahuatl ancestry, it was not surprising that our first destination in the lands of the Maya was the Toltek-influenced ceremonial center of Chichén Itzá. Here, almost two years earlier, I had witnessed the serpentine body of shadow and light descending the Pyramid of Kukulkan. Now, with El Maestro, I was to see that the balance of shadow and light was the preeminent teaching that the Toltek-Maya had written into the stones.

Almost every ancient Mesoamerican ceremonial center has what is known as a *tlaxtli*, or ball court. The court at Chichén Itzá is the largest anywhere, with a length of 272 feet. Yet because of its remarkable acoustics, it is possible to stand in the temple at one end and clearly hear the words of another person spoken softly in the temple at the other end. The builders of this *tlaxtli* obviously understood how to use natural law to maximum advantage.

And that was exactly El Maestro's point. He rejected entirely the accepted notion that the famous Mesoamerican ball game (from which both soccer and basketball are said to have evolved) was a sport of cruelty that ended with the beheading of one of the team captains. To the contrary, he said, the game was a cosmic drama in which the ball represented the stars and planets in motion. The players were akin to the deities of these celestial bodies. Their victories and losses, beheadings and subsequent regenerations—as represented in the bas-reliefs—were symbolic rather than literal. They reflected the cosmic cycles of the days, seasons, years, and great ages of time. They explained the comings and goings of the moon, the sun, the planets, and the stars. And they did this in a way that was both entertaining and understandable.

If the ball game had been a sport, El Maestro said, it was more a sport of prophecy. Through the way the players moved and the game progressed, astronomer-priests were able to interpret and predict future events and conditions.

Most striking, though, was El Maestro's point that even without human Players, the *tlaxtli* served its primary function as an astronomical observatory. This function was inherent in its architectural design, just as the Pyramid of Kukulkan was designed to serve as a precise marker of the equinoxes.

El Maestro explained that the stone rings at both ends of the court were not designed as "hoops," as in a basketball court; rather, they were meant to catch beams of light from the sun and moon on certain dates and to project them in a precise manner onto the bas-relief symbols carved on the walls below. Similarly, the rings could also cast very distinct and specific shadows onto the carvings on certain dates. Thus were shadow and light used by the ancients to mark the important passages of time.

To the east of the *tlaxtli*, El Maestro pointed out how many temples and platforms contained carved representations of eagles and jaguars—symbols of light and shadow in balance. Then, as we continued walking eastward across the enormous plaza, I had the familiar feeling of my consciousness expanding outward in all directions.

"El Maestro," I began, "in all the time I've been visiting the ancient places of Méxiko, I've always noticed that somehow the landscape feels more expansive wherever there are pyramids and temples. The arc of the sky seems broader. Even my own mind feels stretched far beyond the limits of my physical body. Yet I've never been able to explain it."

El Maestro's response was one of the simplest and most profound things he ever said to me. "Modern people make buildings to enclose space," he said. "Our ancestors designed their buildings to open space."

As I looked around, I had the sudden recognition of how true this was. Every angle of every structure contributed to my sense of expansion. The architecture allowed me to be outside in such a way that I felt embraced by the vastness of the universe.

At last we neared the northern side of the Pyramid of Kukulkan. Elaborating further on how Chichén Itzá was designed as a great calendar in stone, El Maestro spoke of the ninety-one steps that led up each of the four sides of the pyramid.

"This structure has a total of 364 steps," he said. "They are united by a marker atop the pyramid that yields the number 365, the same as the number of days in a year. The stones of the pyramid have also been cut and laid in such a way that each side has exactly fifty-two upward-facing rectangles. These rectangles mark the fifty-two-year cycle that is the basis of our ancient calendar. So you can see that in a sense the Pyramid of Kukulkan is really a giant astronomical computer."

Finally our eastward walk led us up the steps of a now roofless building known as the Temple of the Warriors. At the back of this temple was a very large stone slab supported by twenty standing figures, each about two feet tall.

"Why twenty?" asked one of the apprentices.

"Because each sacred month has a total of twenty days," responded El Maestro. "By now it should be clear that virtually everything you see here has calendric meaning."

"Even the statue of the Chak Mool at the entrance to this temple?" asked another apprentice.

"Absolutely," answered El Maestro. "If you look carefully at this reclining stone figure, you will see that he is holding a sort of plate in his lap. The archaeologists tell us that this is where the savage priests of this city placed the bloody heads of their decapitated victims. They say this even though they have no evidence to prove it and in spite of the evidence to the contrary. For when you closely examine the plate of the Chak Mool, you will see that it is extremely shallow, no deeper than half an inch at best. Had the Maya wanted it to hold a human head, they would surely have made it much deeper.

"The plate of the Chak Mool is actually an astronomical mirror," continued El Maestro. "At one time it was kept filled with a solution of liquid mercury so that it could reflect the stars of the night sky. When certain stars or constellations were seen shining in this mirror, it was known without doubt that an important date had been reached. The Chak Mool helped the Maya to more accurately follow their ceremonial calendar.

El Maestro went on to say that he had brought us here so we could appreciate the true design functions of Chichén Itzá from an indigenous point of view. He said he wanted us to see the ridiculousness of some of the "expert" explanations regularly given to thousands of tourists who come here.

"Most of what these tourists are told about Chichén Itzá is in some way related to the theme of human sacrifice," he said, "like the story of the bloody heads that the priests supposedly left in the lap of the Chak Mool, or the sacrificed victims whose bloodstained corpses were thrown down the steps of the Pyramid of Kukulkan, or the sacrificial ball game.

"Again, I ask you to look very carefully at the architecture of Chichén Itzá and tell me if any of this really makes sense. If the pyramid had been made with the intent of throwing dead bodies down its steps, wouldn't its angle have been much steeper? Count for yourselves the number of steps on the pyramid, then try throwing something down them and see where it lands. See which theory of usage makes sense. If you take the time, you will inevitably be drawn to the same conclusion I have come to: that Chichén Itzá was not built by a race of barbarians."

El Maestro helped me to appreciate Chichén Itzá in a much more profound way. I was happy to see that so much of the knowledge of the Maya was still intact in the form of stone. But this did not mitigate the sorrow I felt over the needless destruction of their less durable knowledge. For it was near Chichén Itzá that the sixteenth-century Spanish bishop Diego de Landa, in his Christian fervor to eradicate the works of the "devil worshipers," purposefully incinerated a mountain of Mayan books—thousands and thousands of irreplacable codices. It was a destruction as tragic as the intentional burning of the Library of Alexandria, which had contained the collected wisdom of much of the ancient world east of the Atlantic Ocean.

Yet among the Maya, such tragedy was no surprise. It had already been foretold by the jaguar priest and prophet Chilam Balam, in the years just before the Spanish arrived:

> Eat, eat, while thou hast bread;
> Drink, drink, while thou hast water;
> For on that day, dust possesses the Earth.
> On that day, a blight is on the face
>   of the Earth.
> On that day, a cloud rises.
> On that day, a mountain rises.
> On that day, a strong man seizes the land.
> On that day, things fall to ruin.
> On that day, the tender leaf is destroyed.
> On that day, the dying eyes are closed.
> On that day, three signs are on the tree.
> On that day, three generations hang there.
> On that day, the battle flag is raised,
> And the people are scattered afar
>   in the forests.

Our path away from Chichén Itzá led us to many other ancient Mayan centers: from the Chak-faced temples and ochre-colored arches of Labna to the monumental Pyramid of the Magician at Uxmal; across the gently rolling hills of the Puuk and the pancake-flat plains of the Yukatan to the rich tropical rain forests of Lakandonia, there to be immersed once more in the eternal mysteries of Palenque. But this time we came to know her beautiful sister as well—the exquisite and far more reclusive Yaxchilan, sleeping in serenity by the secluded shores of the undulating Usamacinta River.

Once the Nile of the Maya, the Usamacinta River was still a vital artery in this jungle paradise. Still the river fed and watered its sweet, hidden jewel of Yaxchilan, whose name means "Place of the Sacred Tree." Forgotten for centuries to all but the Lakandon Maya, its overgrown temples still stretched for miles on a teardrop-shaped peninsula around which the river flowed. Only its highest pyramid, the House of Hachakyum, afforded a view above the explosion of green that embraced it. Only this pyramid offered the chance to glimpse a pair of squawking scarlet macaws in flight, their brilliant red, blue, and yellow feathers flashing between endless stretches of forest and sky.

Yet in the race to develop its last frontiers, the Mexican government, with multinational corporate support, was now planning a massive hydroelectric development that would dam the Usamacinta and flood much of the surrounding rain forest, including the Mayan treasures of Piedras Negras and Yaxchilan. Millennia of cultural evolution, eons of expanding biological diversity—so much could be lost in what amounted to no more than the flash of wings.

Hadn't there already been destruction terrible enough that in fear the people were scattered afar in the forests? I pondered. Wasn't it yet tragic enough that Bishop de Landa had burned the sacred books of the Maya? Was this tragedy only to be surmounted by even greater tragedy: the burning of the living library of the forests? These forests were the final refuge of the Hach Winik, the "Real People," and the very source of their knowledge—a knowledge so great that not even the holy writings of the Mayan civilization could compare in their breadth or depth. Why this needless destruction? Why these cruel endings? Were these the only preludes that humanity, in its vast and brilliant imagination, could create before entering again into the cycle of rebirth?

On our way back north from the lands of the Maya, we drove into the Gulf Coast oil-boom city of Villahermosa. Its modern buildings and busy traffic seemed oddly out of place after our immersion into the primal and ancient realms of Mesoamerica. I wondered why El Maestro had instructed Akatl, who was driving, to take us into the city's chaotic center when we could just as easily have driven around it. But when we pulled up beside a high wall surrounding a densely wooded park, I knew he had brought us here for an important reason.

El Maestro asked us all to get out of our vehicles and to take nothing except what we were wearing. Then he led us to the park entrance. There, one by one, the guard let us through. A large sign announced that we were entering Parque-Museo La Venta. Once within, the urban noise faded, replaced by the sounds of buzzing cicadas and singing birds. Large-leafed plants and trees shaded the paved walkways. Remarkably, despite the park's manicured nature, the untamed presence of the jungle remained.

Even more remarkable, though, were the many massive stone carvings in gray basalt that seemed to magically emerge from the lush foliage along the park's winding paths. Their symbols and characters were unlike any I had seen before. Whatever culture had carved them, I was certain it was one I had not yet encountered.

At last El Maestro broke the mystified silence. "Not far from Villahermosa, along the swampy, coastal lowlands to the west, are the remains of the oldest pyramid in México. It is made of earth and is conically shaped, looking somewhat like a small volcano. Today the site of this pyramid, known as La Venta, stands in the middle of a large field of oil refineries. It is poorly kept and receives little, if any, respect. But at one time, La Venta was the vibrant center of a great civilization. Flourishing almost three thousand years ago, it was home to the ones who today are remembered as the Olmeks.

"The Olmeks built on a monumental scale. Over time, their megalithic sculptures sank into the swamps. In the early part of this century, these same sculptures began to be rediscovered by archaeologists, who had to dredge them up. As the oil industry started to move into the area, it became obvious that the sculptures would have to be moved if they were going to be preserved. This outdoor museum was established as the new home for the Olmeks' memory in stone."

Farther along the trail, we passed a series of enormous spherical, carved Olmek heads, many of them considerably taller than a full-grown man. Elsewhere were carvings of Olmek mothers with their babies in their arms, an image that I had rarely seen depicted before in Mesoamerican monumental art. Jaguar men seated in unusual poses were another recurring theme. I had the definite sense that these Olmek stone creations were far older than any I had previously seen from other cultures.

Finally the path led us through an opening of the forest grove to a gigantic, rectangular hunk of stone. El Maestro instructed us to sit on the ground in front of the monolith. Carved into its center was a short, stout man who appeared to be emerging from a cave—a cave that was also the mouth of a jaguar. He was leaning forward in the jaguar pose, and on his head he wore a conical crown with flaming wings on either side.

Most strikingly, something about this Olmek jaguar man reminded me of El Maestro—in spite of the fact that his facial features were barely discernible. Where before there had been eyes, a nose, and a mouth, now there were only hints of these, and all his features were covered by bluish-green lichens. The resulting effect of his dulled gaze and expression was disturbingly eerie.

Once more El Maestro broke the silence. "The one you see here is my *nagual*," he said, "the still, yet ever-changing reflection of myself existing in an intangible dimension of time and space. You are now sitting before the very source of my knowledge, just as I have come to sit here year after year—always to renew my connection, always to remember. It is here that I learn what can no longer be learned from other people, not even from the living elders of our race. It is here that I recall what no longer can be learned from all our ancient codices that were burned long ago. It is here that I retrieve the treasure of our nation. It is here that I come to see the past fully present, to dissolve the illusory barriers of perception and enter into eternal knowing.

"Never fall victim to the belief that what has been forgotten has been lost," El Maestro went on. "The energy of what was once known exists forever, and this monolith is a gateway to that knowledge. As it has been for me, so may it be for you.

"Over these past few years, I have given you the keys. Today I bring you to the door. Now I will leave you for a while, and the one who is my *nagual* will speak to you. If you hear nothing, do not worry, for what you receive in these moments may first need to be absorbed by your soul." With that, El Maestro left us.

A hush falls over the forest as the sun goes behind the clouds. In the shadows, I stare into the eroded face of the emerging jaguar man, and then I close my eyes. All I can see is the bluish-green color of the stone-clinging lichen, as if my lids are not a shield but a magnifier of the outside world. I melt into the color of the lichen. I melt into it with all of my mind. I am aware of nothing but the blue-green color, and then a whispered voice:

> Within her womb, I am gathering jade,
> Precious stones of life everlasting.
> Dwelling for ages in the depths of her womb,
> I taste the latent seed of eternity
> That forever inseminates the world.
> My cord wraps around me.
> I feel it; I hold it;
> I know all its secrets from beginning to end.
> When I emerge from her womb,
> The cord is in my hand,
> The jade is in my heart;
> My heart is a House of Jade.

Suddenly I am aware of talking around me. I open my eyes and see that El Maestro has returned.

I was perplexed. I was sure he had left us only a moment ago. Yet the nearly faded light indicated that at least an hour had gone by, if not two.

"Before we leave here," said El Maestro, "I want to speak of the makers of these books in stone, the ones that are known as the Olmek, the ones we call 'Olin Mekatl.' This is their full name in the Nahuatl language, and it is from this name that the abbreviated term Olmek is derived. But in their full name is revealed the essence of who these people are, a knowledge of which the Mexika were well aware.

El Maestro went on to explain that the Olin Mekatl were the mother culture of the Americas, the first great civilization in this part of the world. They were the first mathematicians and keepers of history. Their name, he said, literally means "movement of the measuring cord," for the *mekatl* was a cord used by them to record events from the past and calculate into the future. By tying knots at different lengths along the *mekatl*, they were able to measure both time and space. Thus, the Olin Mekatl established the sophisticated mathematical, calendrical, and architectural systems upon which later American civilizations were based.

"The man who is carved into this monolith is emerging from the mouth of a jaguar," El Maestro said. "This can be said with certainty, because along the rim of the mouth directly over the man's crown is the X glyph that the Olin Mekatl used for the jaguar. As you already know, the jaguar is the symbol of memory, which for the Olin Mekatl was very important. So the cord you see gripped firmly in the hands of the emerging man is in reality the *mekatl*. Through it he carries into the world the memory of all that has come before him.

"But the cord also leads to the future. So it is that on the left side of this monolith, the cord finally ends in the hands of a person who is not Olin Mekatl at all, but Maya. It is the Maya who inherited the mathematical genius of the Olin Mekatl and who later bequeathed it to the rest of Mesoamerica.

"As for the Olin Mekatl," El Maestro said, "they disappeared. Where they went is not known. It is one of the many mysteries that still surrounds them. Their origins remain a mystery as well, at least officially. But I tell you that they were not of my skin color, not of my race. They were of a race that has almost disappeared from the Earth. They were akin to the short, black-skinned people who still live on certain islands in the Indian Ocean. They came from a land far across our western sea, a land that sank beneath the waves much as did Atlantis in later times. They were refugees who arrived in America carrying the wisdom of their mother civilization. And throughout their history, they paid special tribute to the mother in all things, as can be seen in the stones that fill this park."

With El Maestro's final words, the last rays of the setting sun receded from the forest. Everyone stood; it was time to leave.

En route back to Central Mexico from the jungles of Chiapas and Tabasco, we had the opportunity to explore yet another ancient realm of Mesoamerica: that of the Zapotek and Mixtek civilizations of Oaxaca. Like the Tolteks and the Maya, these cultures had also created large and impressive ceremonial centers, complete with pyramids, ball courts, and detailed bas-relief carvings that elaborated on their sophisticated cosmologies. The first of these sites we visited was Mitla.

Originally known as Miktlan, its name literally translates as the "Place of the Dead"—in other words, the underworld. Why it was given such a name is usually explained by the fact that there are a number of tombs beneath the temples of the site. However, El Maestro was quick to remind us that always throughout Mesoamerica, death was also referred to as a transitional state from a previous limited existence into a new and more expanded reality. To speak of death was also necessarily to speak of rebirth. In the case of Miktlan, this transformational function was served through its unique architectural features.

The walls of the temples of Miktlan, both interior and exterior, were covered with a wide variety of intricate, geometric patterns formed by mosaics of cut stone. Indeed, geometric patterns were the only designs on these temples. There were no representations of humans, animals, plants, or spirits to be seen. Yet the geometric designs were utterly compelling in and of themselves.

Staring at panel after panel of these stone geometries, I was struck by the tremendous feeling of motion they generated within my mind and body. It came as no surprise when El Maestro explained that the patterns were all stylized representations of Ketzalkoatl, the sacred serpent power that governs the movement of all things. By meditating on these patterns for extended periods, he said, it was possible to shift into alternate realities. El Maestro also acknowledged the belief of some locals that Miktlan was designed and built by none other than Ce Akatl Topiltzin Ketzalkoatl.

From Miktlan, the road toward Oaxaca led us to a small town known as El Tule. There, in the courtyard of the town's main church, grew a giant *ahúehuete*, an ancient variety of cypress tree. It was of such enormous proportions—reaching 150 feet into the sky with a trunk of equivalent diameter—that it actually dwarfed the church. El Maestro led us into the courtyard, where we read a sign that said the tree dated back to the time of Christ. He insisted, however, that the El Tule Tree actually dated back almost six thousand years, making it the oldest known tree in the world.

As we walked around the El Tule Tree I realized that it was literally a world unto itself, sheltering many forms of insects and birds within the embrace of its broad trunk and mighty branches. According to Zapotek legend as told to us by El Maestro, the first man and woman emerged together from the body of this tree. Another local belief was that Ketzalkoatl was buried there. Thus mythically spanning the link from birth to death, this primordial tree became for me the living symbol of the Sacred Tree of Life.

The following morning we arose very early in order to make it to Oaxaca's most renowned ceremonial center, Monte Alban, by sunrise. The pyramids and temples of Monte Alban stretched across a huge, flattened mesa in the very middle of the Valley of Oaxaca, affording a spectacular view of the mountains in all directions. It was like a city in the sky, obviously an ideal place from which to observe the heavens.

El Maestro explained that Monte Alban was extremely ancient. Its history spanned all the known high civilizations that had passed through this valley, from the Olin Mekatl to the Mixtek. So it really was like a big history book made out of stone. And as this book made clear, the Zapotec, like the Maya, had inherited much of their knowledge from the Olin Mekatl.

Crossing north to the opposite end of the site, we came upon a tomb that El Maestro referred to as the Tomb of the Two Ketazlkoatls.

"What do you mean by that?" I asked.

"By studying the carvings and the glyphs here," he answered, "I can tell that the man who is buried in this tomb lived two full lifetimes as an ordained embodiment of Ketzalkoatl. He chose to return into a second incarnation at Monte Alban in order to aid in the completion of certain pyramids whose construction he had been guiding. I know this is an alien concept to the modern mind, but in ancient Mesoamerica, such practices were quite common. Spiritual leaders would sometimes reincarnate four or five times in a row at one ceremonial center in order to complete a project they had begun."

By early afternoon, we had returned to our hotel in the city of Oaxaca. All of us were exhausted after many days of ceaseless hiking, climbing, and driving—often with little food, water, or sleep. As apprentices, it was part of our training to willingly endure these challenges and be stronger for them. But finally El Maestro had seen fit to give us a break, for which we were most grateful. Around two in the afternoon, I collapsed on the bed of my hotel room and spent the next five hours in horizontal bliss.

When I awoke, I got dressed and went to the lobby to find the others, who were also just rousing from our much-needed break. Rested at last, we all started to realize how hungry we were, and so off we went to the festive central plaza of Oaxaca in search of a restaurant. While walking, I noticed that I felt disoriented, as though walking in a dream.

As we crossed the plaza past the bandstand, balloon sellers, and cotton candy vendors, suddenly my eyes became riveted on a beautiful, dark-haired young woman. She was coming toward me with a wide grin on her face, just on the edge of laughter. It was a smile I knew well. I rushed toward her and took her into my arms.

Never did I imagine I might see Kate on this journey. It had been months since our last time together, when I had driven with her from Taos to the Arizona-Mexico border. On the way, we had pulled over to the side of the road, climbed a mountain, and made love in the middle of a circle of saguaro cactus. The next day, she was off on her adventure south of the border, and I had no idea when we would see each other again.

Kate joined us for a dinner of several courses, during which we caught up on stories of our travels. I greatly admired her courage as a woman for daring to travel alone in a country noted for its machismo. No doubt her strength and clarity had worked to her advantage. Her experiences had been positive and rich. Even from a few short months ago, I could see the evidences of a wonderful awakening in her.

Following dinner, Kate informed me that she had already rented a hotel room down the street from ours. But given the opportunity to spend the night together, we decided her room could bear being empty, and she came back with me instead. After so much "doing without" on so many levels, the afternoon and evening came as a blessed renewal into the realms of the senses. Deeper into the night, as I slept with Kate on our narrow bed, I entered into a strange and lucid dream.

I am standing in the dimly lit waiting room of an old restaurant. A few of the other apprentices are with me, and we are talking in whispered tones about the mysteries of the Maya civilization. The yellow flame of a candle flickers on the ledge of the wall, illuminating the room just enough to see that everything else is in shades of red or black.

Suddenly I feel that I am being watched. I turn to look. Sitting on a stool is a short, stout, dark-skinned man. He wears no shirt, only black pants. His hair is black as well. He has piercing, bloodshot eyes with deep black pupils. He is staring directly at me—or more accurately, *through* me. My first impression is that he is a Mayan *brujo*, or sorcerer, but I soon realize that he is El Maestro . . . yet different from El Maestro.

Most notably, the man has no arms—they appear to have been cut off. Thick red blood drips from the awful stumps attached to his shoulders. Still, he sits motionless, giving no indication of pain. His macabre presence repulses and terrifies me, yet at the same time I am in awe of him.

Slowly and methodically, the bizarre, armless man begins to speak— in an entirely unfamiliar and sonically disturbing language. The words send waves of nausea through my body. I want to pull away from him but can't. My eyes are locked into his. Transfixed, I watch as his face starts to melt from the center out. It is melting into a formless, bluish-green glow. The sight of this fills me simultaneously with horror and ecstasy. Combined with the nausea, I feel that I am physically losing hold of myself. I am overwhelmed, no longer in control of anything.

Very slowly I begin to fall sideways to my left. Now the floor below me is gone. All around me is a void. Into this nothingness I fall, and as I pass what before was the horizontal plane of the floor, the molecules of my body disintegrate, shattering me into a trillion fragments of matterless energy.

I am gone. I begin and end nowhere. I am everything and nothing. All is empty space—a black void except for the distant light of endless stars, a silent universe except for the whispered voices of all the ancestors I have ever known or been. They are my memory, teaching me what I have forgotten in a space where time does not exist. They are the stars, the lights that still shine when all else has disappeared.

Yet through the eternity of these ancient whispers comes the clear and present sweet-toned voice of a woman. I recognize it as Kate's. "Be careful," she says. "You may not see the sun again."

The message jolts my consciousness like an alarm, awakening me to the sudden recognition that my dream is over. I am no longer in my body. I can see it lying motionless on the bed next to Kate's, with my left arm around her. But I cannot feel her, the bed, or any part of my physical self.

At this moment, I know why I heard Kate's voice. I have to make a choice: to live or to die. And there is no question: I want to live, to continue the journey of my soul through the body lying on the bed. With all the force of my will, I push my consciousness back into my body. With all the focus I can muster, I concentrate my being from the infinite to the specific, moving through a resistant pressure of almost unbearable density and weight. Ever so slowly, I gradually reenter the temple of my soul, until at last I am home again.

I open my eyes and turn over in bed, my heart beating fast as I rush to fill my lungs with air. At the same moment, Kate awakens and nervously says, "What's wrong?" I ask her if she remembers saying anything to me. She says no. Lying on my back, profoundly thankful to be alive, I begin to tell her my story.

The following morning I started thinking about all the circumstances that had set me up for my out-of-body journey. The disruption of my normal biorhythms had certainly played a role. My reimmersion into the life, death, and rebirth mythologies of Ketzalkoatl had no doubt caused a preoccupation with this theme. Still, there had to be more to it.

After breakfast, I asked El Maestro if he could find some space in our busy group schedule for the two of us to talk. He suggested we go across the street to the plaza and talk right away. There, on a bench beneath the calming shade of a large-leaved tree, I proceeded to recount my experiences of the night before. "Why did this happen to me, and what does it all mean?" I asked.

"First of all," he said, "you must find an appropriate way to honor your girlfriend, Kate, for she has given you a tremendous gift. Were it not for her presence beside you, you probably would never have returned. Although neither of you knew it consciously, a part of your spirit knew you were in danger. Unknowingly, you called on Kate and drew her in like a magnet to meet you in Oaxaca. While she slept beside you, in her own dream she remained unaware that her spirit was simultaneously tracking your journey. It was her love for you that called you back. Otherwise, you would have continued drifting beyond the point of no return."

"But what about you?" I asked. "What was the role that you played in my dream?" Even as I spoke, I knew the answer without being told. The face of the brujo in my dream was the very face of the man carved in stone from La Venta, the one El Maestro had said was his *nagual*. I had melted into that jade color in the center of his face, through the mask of form into the unfathomable dimensions of eternal life. I had cracked through the stone of fixed reality to the place where there are no limitations. As El Maestro had predicted, his *nagual* had planted seeds of change that were not to fully flower until many days later.

"Like the other apprentices," said El Maestro, "your subconscious received the impression of my *nagual* at La Venta. In your case, this impression was translated through the realm of dreaming. Your perception of that translation as terrifying was a choice that you, and only you, made. You chose to take an evolutionary step in your being through a cathartic process, and you almost didn't survive it.

"I tried to warn you of the potential danger you were moving toward. I knew that you were not quite prepared to encounter my *nagual*, but there was no other time it could happen. So I came to you in the dream to reveal the hidden patterns of your life journey, that you might understand the larger picture and see what was missing. I came to point you to the Canyon of Copper because that place had a teaching to give you—a teaching that was essential to your being strong enough to endure what has followed."

"You mean that you knew about my dream all along?" I asked. "You knew about my trip to the Canyon of Copper?"

El Maestro nodded yes.

I told him I couldn't believe it, that all this time I thought I had made a ridiculous mistake. I asked him why he hadn't said anything.

"It was not for me to say," responded El Maestro. "All you needed to do was ask, and I would have been happy to discuss it."

I sighed, realizing how foolish I'd been. "Well, then I suppose you also know that I failed to find the revelation in the Canyon of Copper."

"To the contrary," said El Maestro. "In my own dreaming, I saw you on your journey, and you did remarkably well. You received exactly what I sent you there to receive. The only problem is that you never realized it."

I said I had no idea what he was talking about.

"But your spirit knows, Jim. Your heart knows. Your body knows. Only your mind does not understand the great gift you claimed for yourself. You went to the Canyon of Copper to discover your humanity, to claim your own life as sacred. There may be four sacred animals that empower you, but it is the way in which they make you human that is most important. There may be four sacred directions to your journey, but unless you can truly find yourself standing in the center, they are of no value.

"The day you found your way into Huimaivu was the day you claimed your life. You gathered all of yourself into your center, and you held that focus without any distraction because of your great love for who you are in this incarnation. On that day, you discovered the power of will within yourself to surmount the insurmountable, to survive against all odds. You discovered the power that has forever enabled our ancestors to open a clear path of life, not only for themselves but so that we, their children's children, might also live. On that day, you entered the lineage of your ancestry as a true human being.

"Still, your mind did not see it. You were certain there was something more. And so you created for yourself the perfect reflection of what you were not recognizing. You created it by calling my *nagual* into your dream as a man without limbs. He became a mirror for you of all your residual psychological separation between inner self and outer experience. His limbs, the extensions of his physical being, were cut off from his body, like an initiate's journey to the Four Directions in which he or she cannot find their connection to the core of self-awareness. This was to show you what happens when we do not integrate the many extensions and expressions of our complex and wondrous selves into one whole being. Because, finally, your journeys are part of you, your animal guides are part of you, your teachers and friends are all parts of you, as much as your arms and legs are. They are contained within your consciousness, not something separate 'over there.'

"At last the reflection of my *nagual* became so overwhelming for your mind that you had no alternative but to surrender to it and thus play out the implications of your dream vision. You fell to your side. You shattered into a million pieces, just as you could have done had you fallen off the cliffs of Huimaivu. But whereas before you'd found all the necessary focus to physically pull yourself through an arduous test, mentally you still hadn't grasped its significance. And so you fell through the gap of your understanding into an immeasurable abyss.

"This time even your self-love was not enough to rescue you. You needed the love of another, and fortunately she was there. She could see in the realm where you remained blind. Yet in the larger view, even her presence was the result of your own self-love.

"So did she become your vehicle for calling yourself back. She was like your *mekatl*, the rope by which you found your way out of the cave, the umbilical cord by which you were given a vital link to life from out of the womb of your past history and into the bright light of your rebirth. And this combined with the strength of your will enabled you to pass through the gates of form and reenter your body. It was because you had met the challenge of your prior test. You had passed through the Gates of Huimaivu to enter the sacred valley.

"In the safety of that valley is a place where human beings still care for each other and share the fruits of their love. They share not only with their own families and their own communities; they even share with strangers. This you saw, and this you experienced in the days that you lived among the Raramuri. This, too, was part of your discovery of what it means to be human. It is a part of our humanity that is increasingly being lost, but it must be regained if we are going to survive.

"We human beings are here to help each other, to support each other, to love each other. We cannot be fully human if we are isolated and alone. But to share our love, always we must first love ourselves. It may sound simple, but to live by this principle is at times not easy. Just the same, if we forget to care for our own being, then how can we ever hope to assist others? Only when we come from our own living center can we give our greatest gift to the world."

WHERE THE ANCESTORS SING

Later that same morning, El Maestro informed us that our pilgrimage was coming to an end. It was time to return to Koatepetl. Unbeknownst to us until now, El Maestro had called a winter solstice council of native representatives from the Four Directions to meet atop the Mountain of the Serpent.

"Together all of us are going to seek a clarity of vision," he explained, "to bring forth those things our ancestors prophesied would be reborn in these times. Centuries ago we were told by the great Kuauhtemok to bury our pyramids, our precious writings and objects of power. We were told to carry on our ceremonies and teachings, but only in places where we would not be visible to our oppressors. We did this, understanding that one day the signs of change would again be upon us.

Now those signs are here, and it is no longer appropriate for us to practice our sacred ceremonies in secret. Like the sun preparing to turn its course away from the long days of shadow, we must prepare ourselves to emerge from obscurity and once again shine the light of ancient wisdom on all the world."

El Maestro explained that a Lakota-style Sundance would soon be performed in México for the first time since the European invasion. He also said pyramids would be built again in México. In the coming year, in fact, the stone foundation would be laid for the first pyramid to be built in nearly five hundred years. With these things, he added, there would be a resurgence of sharing between the native peoples of north and south.

"That which was forcibly stopped in America shall begin anew," he asserted. "That which was lost shall be reclaimed. That which was hidden shall be made visible. The legacy of our ancestors shall be born again in us—we of many races who are finding our way back to a nativeness of spirit. The Earth is our teacher, just as it has been for indigenous peoples of all times."

Thus we returned to Koatepetl. But upon our return, we encountered a most unsettling sight. At the top of this sacred historical mountain, someone had planted an enormous Christian cross. Wasting no time on emotional discharge, El Maestro immediately asked a few of us to hike up the mountain with him to investigate.

What we found confirmed our worst imaginings. During the time we had been traveling in southern México, a twenty-five-foot crucifix of raw steel had been crudely embedded and bolted into the very stones at the center of our ceremonial circle. Now, at the exact spot where we had customarily offered our prayers, stood the prominent and indelible symbol of five centuries of spiritual violations against native people. Even the steel girder itself conjured images of the Western world's technological assault against the natural world.

"We must not let ourselves be dissuaded by the insensitivity of those who have committed this act of ignorance," El Maestro said in a serene voice.

I was amazed by his calm response. After all, this was his altar, his sanctuary. Still, the rest of us were shocked and enraged. Some angrily protested while others stood sulking or muttered bitter words. One of the new apprentices from the north wanted to know who could be responsible for such a heinous crime.

"There is no doubt in my mind that this has been done by the local church," said El Maestro. "The church knows quite well of our beliefs and practices, and they are far from approving. It has always been their intention to root us out of Koatlan."

As El Maestro spoke, I recalled stories told to me by Tekpatl, Poli, and others of how they were frequently harassed during their dance practices by stone-throwing locals who accused them of devil worship. And this against a historical backdrop of far more severe attacks committed in the name of God. Surely a serious response was long overdue.

But when I raised the point to El Maestro, his words clearly stressed a nonconfrontational approach. "The church is far more powerful in this country than you might realize, Jim. In some ways they are more powerful than even the government or the military. There is no point in trying to fight them directly. We will only exhaust ourselves in a hopeless effort. Our victory must come because we remain spiritually strong—because we continue to follow our path in spite of everything they do."

With that, El Maestro removed a pipe from his beaded leather bag. He carefully placed the two parts together and filled the bowl with tobacco. Then, holding a flame to the sacred herb, he began to puff until waves of smoke were curling down the stem from his mouth.

Now cupping the bowl in one hand as he pointed the mouthpiece skyward with the other, El Maestro began to pray. All of us gathered around him, many of us crying. For virtually at our feet the cold steel was bolted into the rock. And, inescapably, between us and the sun stood the sign of the oppressors, visibly subverting every prayerful motion of the Sacred Pipe. In a most bizarre irony, it now appeared more as if El Maestro was praying to an inanimate Christian cross than to the living manifestations of the Creator.

I reflected on our Mexika New Year's ceremony here, when El Maestro had spoken of Koatepetl as the birthplace of Huitzilopochtli, the archetype of the spiritual warrior. It seemed fitting now that all of us, each in our own way, were feeling that warrior energy atop the sacred mountain.

I knew that El Maestro was feeling it, too, for he had been deeply wounded by his people's oppression. The difference was that he was able to express it with supreme clarity of intent. On this occasion, he did it by praying with his pipe. As he did so, I realized that he was not stifling his warrior energy but acting on it.

El Maestro had taught us that a spiritual warrior takes only *effective* action. In the short run, reacting with violence and anger might *feel* most effective, but in the long run it only compounds the unwanted reality. Though I knew this, I was still not at peace. I wanted drama. I wanted challenge and confrontation. As much as I respected El Maestro for his way, I still had to find a way that worked for *me*—a way that accepted my emotions and used them as fuel to act from a place of clarity.

And so on that day atop the Mountain of the Serpent, before a giant metal cross, I made an inner resolution. I committed myself to a lifetime of active prayer. I vowed to express this prayer through writing, speaking, singing, and all other forms of communication by which I might take a stand in defense of spiritual and cultural freedom.

After all, the issue was far greater than an isolated incident atop Koatepetl; the issue was global. In the name of Christianity, Islam, and other religions prone to fear-based fundamentalism, countless millions of people had been murdered and countless traditions destroyed on every continent. Even in modern times, I knew, the attack on indigenous peoples continued, as missions "pacified" the natives before corporate and government interests came in to rape and plunder the land. Meanwhile, ceremonies ceased, languages died, and the wisdom of millennia was forgotten.

By the end of the day, we were down the mountain again at the *kalpulli*. There, El Maestro filled the others in and elaborated on his reasons for nonconfrontation.

"The people have many ears in Koatlan," he said. "Since the church is determined to keep alive the myth that our culture and religion are dead, the fact that we are planning to hold a Sundance or to build a pyramid would be perceived as a tremendous threat. The church would like to create a holy war for control of the mountain, but we are not going to oblige them by striking back. We will simply go forward as originally planned.

"Tomorrow morning we will ascend Koatepetl," El Maestro announced calmly. "In two more days, it will be winter solstice. We will prepare ourselves in the purification lodge by day and with prayer circles by night. We will council about the future of our people—of all people—and together we will explore how to manifest the kind of world we want to pass on to future generations."

Then, to our surprise, he added, "The cross that is now atop the mountain will be included in our ceremonies. The teachings that relate to the cross hold profound meaning within the native tradition. By understanding these teachings, we will learn how to transform this travesty. Thus it is my hope and prayer that we will all gain insight into how to meet the far greater transformational requirements of our present planetary crisis."

The following night atop Koatepetl, during a prayer circle in the tipi, I had a vision.

I am entering a deep, human-made tunnel illuminated only by a small circle of light that is always ahead of me. From that light, I can see that an intricately layered cobblestone floor stretches the entire length of the passageway.

After walking in the tunnel for some time, I come upon a naturally painted carving in the middle of the floor. It is a rainbow-colored Naui Olin, the symbol of Four Movement. It is raised in low relief upon a smooth circular surface and defined by the cobblestones around it.

Continuing farther still, I finally approach what appears to be the end of the tunnel. It is marked by a rectangular room illuminated by a small skylight. As my eyes adjust to the light, I see on the wall at the tunnel's end a marvelous carving of a circular solar face. It resembles the face on the famous Mexika calendar stone, the Kuauhxicalli, but its features are more Olin Mekatl. Most notably, the face is surrounded by sixteen arrows grouped in sets of four—four arrows to each of the Four Directions.

The prayer circle in the tipi continued all through the night, accompanied by the steady beat of a water drum and gourd rattles. Occasionally it was punctuated by the passing of a large bowl of cooked peyote buttons with broth. No doubt this medicine had helped to spark my vision of the ancient tunnel. But time, place, and sound had also contributed to it.

My journey through the tunnel seemed to go on for hours. At times I felt certain that I was within the body of the sacred mountain. Then at last we sensed the slow arrival of light outside the tipi. The beat of the percussion wound down to a stop, and all of us left the lodge. Outside a gentle fire was being tended by others who had not taken part in the all-night ceremony. We were happy for this warmth, because the temperature of the predawn air was quite cool. A thick fog hung amidst the trees on the forested mountain.

For a long time we sat around the fire in silence, each absorbing the precious visions of the night. When finally someone spoke, the words came in an oddly forceful and abrupt way.

"I would like to know who authorized El Maestro to conduct the medicine ceremony we've just had," said a heavy-set Indian man with long, black hair. "Where I come from, only a *real* medicine man is allowed to conduct such ceremonies. I know all you people think it's great to share culture, but frankly, white folks don't belong inside a peyote meeting."

While most of us were shocked at these words, El Maestro remained calm and unflappable. "Before I respond to your comments," he said politely, "may I ask who invited you to be here?"

"Nobody invited me, man," the intruder said. "I don't need to be invited. I was sent by some of the Lakota elders to check you out. They caught wind that you're planning a Sundance down here, and that's just not cool. What's more, this imitation Peyote Church meeting is a disgrace. As far as I'm concerned, you're stealing ceremonies. There's a lot of bad medicine coming down on this mountain."

"If you think there's bad medicine here," retorted El Maestro, "then maybe you ought to consider the true history of what you so confidently condemn. The Peyote Church was begun by a Kiowa man named Quanah Parker at the end of the last century, following a number of visits he had made to the Huicholes here in México. It was the Huicholes who taught Parker about the ceremonial use of peyote, and from that he developed the rituals he brought back north.

"In order not to have trouble with the white authorities in the United States," El Maestro went on, "Parker adapted the rituals to include Christian doctrine. So before you accuse us of imitating a sacred rite, just be aware that the ceremony we've done tonight is probably closer to the original tradition of our Native American ancestors than any other peyote meeting you've attended.

"And as far as stealing ceremonies, it's hard to steal something that belongs to you. Because as you now understand, the peyote ritual originated in this part of the continent. Yes, we're borrowing, too, by using the tipi and the water drum. But that's exactly why we're gathered here: to honor and celebrate the great tradition of sharing and cultural exchange among our native peoples—a tradition, I might remind you, that includes sharing with those who do not have the same color skin as ourselves."

The Indian man appeared visibly shaken by El Maestro's powerful response. Even so, he tried his best to act as though he had been unmoved. "Hey, man, it's the white people who fucked us over in the first place, so don't try to impress me with your smooth talk."

At that point, one of the non-Indian apprentices suddenly stood up. "Listen, I don't think it's wise for you to speak to El Maestro with such lack of respect. He happens to be the elder in this circle, so for somebody who claims to be defending the traditions, your words are way out of line."

"Don't give me that shit, you white 'wannabe'. It just so happens that I *am* a shaman, so I have no need to kiss the feet of your so-called El Maestro—or listen to you, for that matter. I can say anything I want."

"Fine," said El Maestro. "You've said enough. I'm going to ask you to leave now. Everyone else here has chosen to participate in creating and maintaining a sacred space. If you can't abide by that, then it's best you depart from our circle. But before you go, there's one last piece of information I'd like to share with you: In the native way, it's not considered appropriate to call oneself a shaman. Only the people of your community can refer to you in that way, never yourself. Even our shamans in their eighties and nineties don't call themselves shamans—unless, of course, they're really not shamans at all."

On those words, our unidentified and unwelcome guest glared angrily at El Maestro and spoke one last time. "OK, Mr. Maestro, you've got your wish; I'm out of here. But just remember, I'll be making my report. You haven't seen the last of me."

After the man was gone, I turned to El Maestro and quietly asked, "Who do you think the Lakota people are who sent him to spy on us?"

"I don't know, and he may not be telling the truth," answered El Maestro. "But even if he is, it doesn't surprise me. There are a lot of Indian people out there who don't approve of sharing our traditions with non-Indians. Aside from that, there is a lot of division and jealousy within our own community. Some people are very protective and mistrustful. We can't blame them for that; we've all had an extremely difficult time the last few hundred years. But more division will get us nowhere. Our pain can only be healed when we come together as one."

For the rest of the morning, we all slept in our tents, giving our souls a chance to settle from the power of the night and the drama of the dawn. But by high noon, we were once again gathered in a group, this time around the steel cross at the top of the mountain. As El Maestro had promised, he intended to use this cross to help illustrate his teachings.

"Today we are going to examine the history of the cross as a spiritual concept in both Western and indigenous American tradition," he said. "There are similarities and differences, all of which are important to our understanding."

El Maestro explained that the most basic truth shared by cultures honoring the cross is that their perception of the world is strongly determined by the number four: four elements, four seasons, four directions. For this reason, when the Europeans came to America, the native people recognized the symbol, and it was easy for them to embrace it.

But it soon became clear, he said, that there were two important differences in the interpretation of this sacred symbol. First of all, for Europeans the cross represented the holy spirit, while for the native people it represented the physical world.

"The circle, not the cross, is our symbol of spirit," said El Maestro, "because the circle is infinite; it contains everything. Through the circle all things come into sacred relationship with each other. The circle and the cross work together, creating a harmonious balance. They remind us that spiritual reality finds its expression through the physical. These two things can never be separate. But what has happened to the circle in the Western world? For the most part, it has disappeared."

El Maestro said the second main difference has to do with the intersecting lines that form the two crosses. In the Native American cross, both lines are of equal length. But in the Christian cross, the vertical line is much longer than the horizontal line.

"The implications of this difference are profound," he said. "What this means is that while native cultures emphasize equality of relationship, Western society emphasizes vertical, or hierarchical, relationships: men over women, rich over poor, masters over slaves, people over plants and animals, and ultimately European people over the other races of the world.

"Because the Christian cross is taller than it is wide, it tends to promote the idea that spirit must be sought above," he went on. "It suggests that God is in the sky. The Native American cross tells us something very different. Embraced by the circle and with bars of equal length meeting in the center, it says that spirit can be found equally in all directions—above, below, and all around—and equally in all life-forms. We humans are not here to be *over* each other, but to be *with* each other and all creation. We share a spiritual equality with all things."

Finally, El Maestro explained how the symbol of the cross had influenced European and Native American interactions on a grand scale. He spoke of how four great indigenous civilizations of the Americas—the Mexika, the Inca, the Maya, and the Pueblo—had been invaded, each in turn, from east, west, north, and south by the conquering Spaniards.

"Thus were we in the form of our own culturally organized cross laid out upon the cross of Europe and crucified," said El Maestro. "Thus was their cross forcibly driven everywhere into our lands, just as it is right here. Like a sword with its point thrust into the very body of the Earth, so was the cross of Europe felt, bleeding our land of its precious life.

"Adding insult to injury, we became the accused perpetrators of the savagery of human sacrifice. Our sacred books and carvings, which everywhere told the story of our lord Ketzalkoatl, were encountered by the perplexed Europeans. They spoke of the one who gave of his heart that we all might learn, who sacrificed himself that we all might live. And these commemorative symbolic teachings of the life of Ketzalkoatl were utterly misinterpreted.

"When our own spiritual practices were outlawed and silenced, how could we prove otherwise? The active evidence of our spiritual ways faded into the mists of history as we were condemned before the world.

"But consider how it might have been had the scenario brought a race of invaders to Europe, rather than the other way around: Christianity is outlawed. The churches are forcibly emptied of their worshipers. Along come the historians and later the archaeologists. What do they see? A pathetic man in tremendous pain, nailed upon a cross and bleeding to a slow and miserable death. "How cruel! How barbaric!" they would say. "Surely the people of these countries must be a savage race, that they would practice such an inhuman ritual and honor it upon their central altar. Oh, how many tens of thousands must have suffered at the bloody hands of their priests! It's a good thing that we conquered them and put an end to their savage ways.

"Outlandish as my story might seem," El Maestro went on, "it is exactly what happened here in México. Just as European art glorified the life and death of their Christ, so did Mesoamerican art glorify the life and death of our Ketzalkoatl. And so when it came time for the conquerors to examine what remained following the devastation they brought upon us, the art told a story that on the surface appeared obvious. The new history books were written, and we were made to bear the cross of blame for the worst abuses against humanity.

"I do not mean to say that we were perfect, nor to suggest that the Europeans were all wrong," El Maestro hastened to add. "In any case, we cannot change the past, but we can try to understand it more honestly. Through that there is hope for redemption. By owning our true history, we can free ourselves to make the best choices in the present. In the same way, we cannot erase or remove this cross from our sight. But we can attempt to understand it, for it has been placed here with good reason."

Looking around, I could see that I was not the only one who was surprised by this statement.

"As many of you already know, this mountaintop is a crossroads," El Maestro said. "It is here that one of the greatest migrations in American history was initiated to the Four Directions. The symbolic power of that event is contained forever within this mountain. So it is the mountain that has manifested this very cross. Now its history continues to unfold, drawing to it those who are called to play out the symbolic journey of the cross— even the Christians who were compelled to place here their own version of the cross. We are all part of that great journey. We have come from the Four Directions, and we will return to the Four Directions. And through our interactions—our crossings—we will grow from what we have learned of each other."

Finally El Maestro spoke of the origin myths of the Mexika and the Inca: of their historical interactions and, specifically, of the fact that by the late fourteenth century they were meeting to forge a hemispheric spiritual movement called the Union of the Eagle and the Condor. This, he said, was to be the embodiment of the teachings of Ketzalkoatl and the Incan prophet Viracocha. Its flag had the symbol of a red eagle for North America and a blue condor for South America. The two birds had their necks intertwined and their heads facing each other, forming a perfectly balanced, four-directional cross.

"Today we await the return of the true Ketzalkoatl and the true Viracocha," he said. "We invite them as redemptive forces into our lives, so that we can fulfill our mission of hemispheric unity. The Union of the Eagle and the Condor is not dead; it has only taken a long nap. In fact, our gathering here is part of its reawakening."

Approaching the eve of the winter solstice, our gathering on the mountain swelled by the hour, with new arrivals from across México and beyond. That night, the longest of the year, we sat outside around a council fire as El Maestro revealed the details of his planned activities for a cultural renaissance. He spoke of the next summer solstice six months away as the time when the foundations of a new pyramid would be laid at an as-yet-unspecified site in central México. Each of us was invited to bring a large stone from whatever place we called home, to contribute to the pyramid's international foundation.

El Maestro also reiterated his intention to hold a Sundance around the same summer solstice time. By now a group of Lakotas had arrived, and we had talked with them about our early morning encounter. None of them was certain who our angry stranger had been, but they did not seem surprised by his presence.

"There's a lot of infighting back home," said a young Lakota woman. "In many ways we've become our own worst enemy, and it hurts my heart to see this. So much energy is wasted in needless battles. Instead, it ought to be directed toward our real problems, like corporate and government greed, alcoholism, drugs, and general apathy. Whatever we can do to regain our spiritual strength is valuable—including support for one another as natives and forging greater unity with others of like mind and spirit. That's why I support this Sundance in México. In my heart I feel it's a good thing."

Our sharing that evening left us all feeling inspired. Moreover, the contacts I made that night would determine my future path for years to come. It was then that I first met the members of Huehuekoyotl, or "Old Coyote," a group of traveling performers who had recently established a land base on the outskirts of Tepoztlan. I was attracted by their indigenous-based but highly eclectic and creative style. They also embodied a refreshingly spontaneous and playful passion for "life as art." I happily accepted their invitation to attend a New Year's Eve ceremony at the site of their new community.

On that night, I also got reacquainted with a young Mexika man named Mazatl, who happened to be an excellent musician. I had first met him atop Koateptl almost two years before, and the two of us had since then independently become fascinated with the relatively unknown pre-Columbian instruments of the Mexika and the Maya.

Mazatl told me that he and his sister's boyfriend, Gerardo, were planning an ascent of Popokatepetl within the next few days and asked me if I would like to join them. I realized this was not only a chance to deepen my friendship with Mazatl but to finally reach the top of the mountain that called me like no other.

A few days later, I found myself back at Tlamakas, once again on the saddle between the two great volcanoes. At five in the morning my friends and I were awake and ready to climb. Fortunately, this time I was better prepared. I had already had a full day to adjust to the 12,000-foot altitude, I had plenty of warm clothes, and my stomach was empty, which I had been told would reduce the tendency toward headaches. On this day, I had decided, I would eat only spirulina tablets (Mexika algae) and a bit of chocolate—good, traditional Mesoamerican energy foods.

Together with Mazatl and Gerardo, I began walking rapidly to counteract the severe chill of the predawn air. Stars shimmered brightly through the rarefied atmosphere, soon giving way to the approaching light. Before long, Popokatepetl was beckoning us in its morning majesty, bathed in the golden hues of a glorious sunrise. In all directions, the day was spectacularly clear. It looked like we had an excellent chance of making the summit.

But one unanticipated factor placed our quest in jeopardy. As I ascended, passing my previously attained height of 15,500 feet, I began to drift into a world of visions. And wonderful visions they were—as wonderful as any I had experienced on the medicine plants. No doubt my "food fast," combined with the altitude, was conspiring to produce this effect. Another possible cause, I thought, might be that the slopes of Popokatepetl were known as the home of Xochipilli, the Lord of Ecstasy.

Spiraling energy patterns akin to those found on pre-Columbian pottery swirl all around me. I am overcome with joy and laughter, like the frolicking dancers of Tlalokan so colorfully depicted in the painted murals of Teotihuakan. Why should I struggle with this climb? I ask myself. Why even bother to move my legs? After all, am I not already soaring up the mountain, caressed by the wings of angels?

Gradually but steadily, I lose my motivation to continue the climb. I am happier just to lie by a rock and experience this inner bliss. Only the continual prodding of Mazatl and Gerardo keep me moving, reminding me of our goal to reach the top. But with increasing frequency I am compelled to pause, and often I just collapse in a prone position and close my eyes.

At last, though, thanks to my friends' determination, we climb to within a few hundred feet of the crater rim. Still there is no snow on the side we've chosen to ascend. Whereas a snowpack would have helped our grip, with every step our feet slide back almost as far on the loose, volcanic scree. At 17,000-plus feet, my mind can no longer comprehend why I should put my body through such an arduous challenge.

Suddenly a gigantic whirlwind rises out of the crater and begins whipping down the slope with tremendous force. We drop to the ground to avoid being thrown off balance and sent tumbling. The whirlwind moves toward us only part way, as if to let us know it is guarding the crater and we should go no farther.

Witnessing this, we decide to turn back. We would be fools to dare the mighty wind. Yet from this lofty place, I feel certain we have reached a goal of another sort. Something about this very spot is perfect, even though it isn't the summit. Something about this very spot fills me with an almost palpable sense of Lord Ketzalkoatl.

I begin to pray, remembering how the teachings of Ketzalkoatl were disseminated from this very mountain. I pray that once again these teachings might be awakened from within the Heart of the Mountain, to find their way back into the heart of humanity.

As I pray, an eagle soars directly above us. Successively it is joined by others, until finally there are five eagles weaving a pattern overhead—a pattern of four moving directions circling around an eternal center. Our winged brethren seem like emissaries of Scorpio (the astrological sign whose symbols are the snake, the eagle, and the volcano) and also like sacred messengers of Ketzalkoatl's affirming presence.

The soaring eagles follow us all the way down the mountain. When we reach Tlamakas at last, a single white cloud floats above the still-hidden crater of Popokatepetl—in the precise form of a feather.

From the heights of Topiltzin, Ketzalkoatl's historical test of faith, I made my way by taxi and bus toward the reputed town of his birth. Mazatl and Gerardo, meanwhile, returned to Mexico City in order to attend to family matters.

In Tepoztlan, I met up with one of the members of Huehuekoyotl, who drove me out to the site of their budding community. Nestled among the lushly forested cliffs that extended east from the center of town, the place immediately enchanted me with its exotic beauty. It was also quite close to the very site where Ketzalkoatl was said to have been born.

On the eve of the new year, the entire community of Huehuekoyotl gathered to participate in a post-sunset *temazkal*. I loved the idea of bringing in the new year this way—purging old patterns that no longer felt healthy while focusing strong spiritual energy on the beginning of a new cycle.

The *temazkal* was a long ceremony, since there were many of us—and all performers at that. But it was well worth the experience. We shared the excitement of knowing we were on the edge of far more than just a new year.

After the *temazkal*, we enjoyed a feast in the largest of the houses. Then came the home movies of the troupe's eclectic theatrical events across México, followed by an explosion of live music-making with instruments of almost every imaginable cultural origin.

Around midnight, with the party still in full swing, one of the men invited me into the kitchen. Standing by a large pot on the stove, he asked me if I would like to partake of some special tea.

"What kind?" I asked.

"Peyote," he replied.

I looked inside the pot. Here and there, small peyote buttons floated about in a clear greenish-yellow broth. Never before had I taken medicine plants outside of a strictly ceremonial context. Yet it seemed to me that our whole evening had been a ceremony. I had the sense that I was primed for a vision of major import. Maybe the peyote tea would help to trigger it.

Then I remembered that I had already eaten. Surely I couldn't take medicine plants on a full stomach. So I decided on what seemed a logical compromise. "OK," I told my brother, "I would like some tea, but only the broth. I don't want to eat any buttons."

I thanked him as he poured me a cup, then went outside to pray as I slowly drank the tea. Later I went inside again to join the others for the big moment of the evening.

It's about 12:30 a.m. The musical frenzy has already peaked, and most of the celebrants have either begun to drift into the Dreamtime or to more purposefully seek their places of sleep. On the other hand, I am just starting to experience a surge of energy.

Much to my surprise, the effect of the peyote tea is quite strong, in spite of the fact that I drank only the broth. Not wanting to be confined inside, I excuse myself and step out into the tropical night air. Here I feel more at ease; I want only to be in nature.

Soon I am called by the verdant foothills of the cliffs behind me. Every detail of their exotic foliage is clearly discernible by the light of the nearly full moon. The many leafy plants and cactuses emanate their life force with full vibratory intensity. They seem to be dancing around me, writhing and spiraling like a sea of dragons.

In the midst of this primal dance, I am unable to contain my passionate love for Earth and its pulsing life. *"Serpiente, serpiente, serpiente!"* I chant over and over. My voice swells with rich overtones. As I repeat the word, the whole world turns reptilian. Leaves look like scales, flowers like tongues. Greens and violets and fiery oranges course around me in rivers of color and enter the open veins of my being.

I turn to face the moon, which floats over bizarrely shaped mesas beyond the valley to the east. I see what appear to be giant amoebas and other enormous, single-celled creatures covering the mesas and filling the valleys and sky. They are glowing iridescent and constantly changing.

Before long, they have completely transformed, appearing as primitive, undersea life-forms. Now these, too, evolve, until an entire underwater world of fantastic fish and outrageous oceanic invertebrates are swimming through the valley before me.

The scene transforms one last time, as the fish turn into spaceships. Appearing more as vehicles of light than machines of metal, the ships take off and circle to land again—all in a luminous, primordial choreography.

At last my attention is pulled by a glowing red light a short distance below. I descend the cliffside to discover that it is the still-burning embers from the *temazkal* fire. Sitting beside them is a Huehuekoyotl woman named Ina.

"I thought I was the only one awake," she says.

"Not at all," I respond. "Even if I was asleep, you'd still have lots of company. The whole valley is alive."

"Yes, I suppose you're right," says Ina, her voice revealing a sense of sorrow and alienation.

As we talk, I discover that Ina is an avid political activist, working mainly on environmental issues, economic injustices, and the rights of indigenous peoples. But in spite of her activism, she seems to have little hope for the future, taking a rather cynical view of life in general. It seems strange that I am drawn into this conversation with her so immediately following my blissful visions of nature. Yet somehow I feel compelled to keep talking with her.

Ina begins asking me about my personal background and my reasons for being in México. When I mention El Maestro, she flares up like the embers of the fire.

"Don't you know El Maestro is an agent of the Mexican government? He's been steadily infiltrating the native movement here for years, learning everything about the activities of other leaders and then reporting to his superiors. You've got to be more careful about who you work with, Jim; otherwise you're liable to hurt the very people you want to help."

"How can you say that?" I respond. "I've known El Maestro for three years now. Whatever his faults, he's not insincere. He's devoted his whole life to the indigenous movement, especially to México. Besides, I've also witnessed his amazing spiritual abilities, and I can't imagine a government agent having a working knowledge of such things."

"But they do," Ina disagrees. "That's exactly the point. The government isn't stupid. They work with insiders. They fool us by playing through the ones we least expect. And," she adds ominously, "El Maestro is not the only agent you've had close associations with."

I begin to feel increasingly irritated by Ina's rising wave of paranoia. "*Now* who are you talking about?" I quip.

"I'm talking about Rarihokwats," she says.

"Rarihokwats! That's absurd!"

"No, it's true. Even the man you say sent you to México is a big-time government agent, working in the most insidious and clever ways to hurt indigenous people."

"That's ridiculous," I say. "You'll never make me believe any of this. You don't even know the men you're accusing."

"Fine," Ina responds. "Go ahead and continue working with our enemies. Go ahead and hurt those you claim to love. Just don't say I didn't warn you."

I leave without answering; I am too upset. I can hardly believe I have let Ina draw me into her negativity—especially while under the magnifying influence of peyote. I feel filthy and disgusting. I have wasted precious time when I could have been having glorious visions.

I walk into the valley, away from Huehuekoyotl, away from Ina. By the rotting stump of an ancient tree, I begin to pray. I feel myself in a tremendous crisis, as though at a breaking point, ready to explode. I pray to be freed from all judgment and negativity. I pray to be a vehicle for the truth, whatever it might be. In this place of Ketzalkoatl's birth, this place that has imbued me with the ecstasy of serpent power, I pray with all my heart to be shown how I might serve the return of the feathered serpent.

Hardly a moment has passed when I hear a voice singing from the cliffs high above. It has the quality of a spirit voice rising from out of the past. One by one, other voices join it until the sound is like a magnificent chorus of ancient melodies. Now I hear drums beating, gradually followed by rattles, flutes, and conch-shell trumpets. Before long, the entire cliff face beyond Huehuekoyotl is resounding with music. Tears roll down my face. I am in a state of indescribable joy. I know my prayer is being answered.

I am hearing the Ancient Ones, whose music has been sleeping for almost five centuries. I am hearing the sounds of the Mexika and the Maya, the Toltek, and the Olin Mekatl. Though the Ancient Ones have been dormant, they are not dead; they are alive and awakening. Here, at long last, I am *remembering* them. And here, on this blessed night, I am being empowered to bring their forgotten music back into the world.

All my life I have been a musician, yet somehow I have never fully recognized its potential as a force for healing. Tonight I realize that a big change is upon me. Tonight I know that with music, the universal language that transcends ideologies, I will help to transform a world divided by hate into a world united in love. With music I will create harmony on an Earth that is sorely out of balance. Through the music of the Ancient Ones, I will find a way to do these things far more effectively than I have ever known.

Thus did I see clearly now the path of my life opening before me. The Four Directions of my diverse experiences and journeys were about to fuse into a central purpose that embraced them all. Like a feathered serpent, they were woven together. Thus would I devote myself to the return of the Ghost Dance and the fulfillment of Black Elk's vision. Thus would I open myself to the return of Kokopelli, the humpbacked flute player, that his song might again be heard echoing across the land. Thus would I give myself to the return of the "Indian Magnificence" and the balancing of opposites embodied in the Sacred Twins. Thus would I commit myself to the spiritual oneness of all peoples, that in their diverse colors they might once again unite in love around the Great Flowering Tree.

CHAPTER 13

FLOWER OF THE ANCIENT ONES

From Tepoztlan I returned to Mexico City to share the news of my vision with Mazatl. I told him that I felt we were destined to make music together, to combine our talents in reviving the ancient heritage of his country through sound. He said that he, too, had held such feelings, particularly since our ascent of Popokatepetl.

More than a year passed before Mazatl and I took the necessary steps to bring our musical duo into being. We chose the name Xochimoki, the same name that I had previously given to the Growhole. Our coming together embodied similar dreams of uniting north and south, and of giving contemporary expression to those ancient roots of greatest creative and spiritual value.

By summer solstice of 1984, Mazatl and I had begun our work together. We embarked on a journey throughout México to visit the ancient temples and pyramids and to receive their memories in the form of sound. We also traveled through jungles and other places of abundant nature to be inspired by the music of birds, monkeys, insects, and other living presences. Steadily our collection of indigenous instruments grew, as did our knowledge of the surviving original musical traditions of México that were hidden in remote communities of mountaintop and valley, coastline and forest.

All the while, we were keenly aware that our work was part of a re-enactment of history and the fulfillment of prophecy. Like others who had journeyed to the Four Directions from the same mountain where we had met, we now were beginning a mythical journey as two brothers devoted to the same dream. Linking cultures in creative celebration, our destiny as bridge-builders would eventually take us throughout the Americas and beyond.

Also as a direct result of my vision at Huehuekoyotl, I soon brought my studies with El Maestro, Rarihokwats, and many other teachers to a close. It was not that Ina's words had caused me to doubt or mistrust them. Nor did I no longer respect or honor them. I knew they were not government agents as she suspected.

To the contrary, these men were the victims of a government-instigated plot to discredit them and prevent them from doing their extremely important work on behalf of indigenous people. I had witnessed that plot unfold from Massachusetts to México, from Akwesasne to Santa Fe, led by a self-proclaimed native spiritual leader who was actually a pawn of the forces out to destroy the native way of life. The trail he left spawned much disharmony and confusion. Ina had been one of those caught in his clever spell of deceit.

Where Ina had perceived clearly was in recognizing how insiders are indeed used by the government to break up political movements. And where those movements have spiritual dimensions, the government is likely to enlist individuals who have familiarity working in those dimensions as well. Though I did not enjoy dealing with these dark issues during my visionary night journey at Huehuekoyotl, in retrospect I came to appreciate Ina's contribution to my experience. For as El Maestro had taught me, there is a balance of light and shadow. Both are necessary. By my facing the darkest depths, the cathartic trigger was provided for my ultimate vision at Huehuekoyotl, which carried me into the dawn.

Most importantly, through the sum of my experiences on that New Year's eve, I realized that it was time for me to move on. A new phase of my life was beginning—a phase in which it was no longer appropriate for me to be primarily a student or apprentice. I had to take the teachings I had received and apply them, to put them to the test and to live them in the most useful and relevant way I could. Otherwise, I knew, I would ultimately fail both my teachers and myself.

And so, with the conclusion of one great personal journey of discovery, a new one immediately began. Such is the way of things, and such was my destiny. With my roots at last firmly planted in each of the Four Directions, I was like a young tree ready for a spurt of new growth. Soon I would leaf and flower. Before long I would bear wonderful fruit. Eventually singing birds would find shelter in my branches. And thus would I find my place in the living community of the Earth.

PRONUNCIATION

∧∧∧∧∧∧∧∧∧∧∧∧∧∧∧∧

G U I D E

Mayan Words

akox: ah-'kosh

huipiles: wee-'pee-lays

Hunahpu: hoo-nah-'poo

ixim: ee-'sheem

Kukulkan: koo-kool-'kahn

Maximón: mah-shee-'mohn

Oâm Ja: oahm 'ha

Panajachel: pah-nah-hah-'chel

Pop Wuj: Pop 'woo

Xbalanke: eesh-ba-'lan-kay

yaxche: ya-'shay

Yumil Ka'ax: yoo-'meel kah'ahsh

Nahuatl Words

Words ending in tl are very common in the Nahuatl language. The "l" is only half pronounced, almost like a click.

Ce Akatl: say-'ah-kaht(l)

Cihuatan: see-wah-'tahn

cihuatl: 'see-waht(l)

Huehuetenango: way-way-tay-'nan-goh

huehuetl: 'way-wayt(l)

Huitzilopochtli: weet-seel-oh-'posh-tlee

Itzachilatlan: eet-sah-chee-'lah-tlahn

Iztakkuautli: ees-tahk-kwah-'oo-tlee

Ketzalkoatl: 'kay-tsahl-'koh-aht(l)

Kikiztli: kee-'kees-tlee

Kuauhxikalli: kwah-oo-shee-'kah-lee

México: 'meh-shee-koh

Michhuahkan: meesh-oo-ah-'kan

Mixkoatl: meesh-'koh-at(l)

Naui Olin: now-ee oh-'leen

Nepohualtzintzin: nay-poh-wahl-'tseen-tseen

teahui: tay-'ah-wee

Tenochtitlan: tay-nosh-'tee-tlahn

Teotihuakan: tay-oh-tee-wah-'kahn

Teotl: 'tay-oht(l)

Tezkatlipoka: tez-kah-tlee-'poh-kah

tlaxtli: 'tlash-tlee

Topiltzin: toh-'peel-tseen

Xochikalko: so-chee-'kahl-koh

yolliztli: yohl-'lees-tlee

Other Words

bodhisattva: boh-dee-'saht-vah (Sanskrit)

Powhatan: 'pow-tan

Rarihokwats: lah-lee-'hok-wahtz

RECOMMENDED
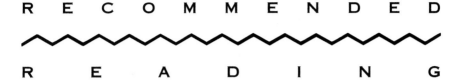
READING

Armas, Margarita Nolasco. *Seris, Yaquis, y Tarahumaras*. México, D.F.: Museo Nacional de Antropologia, 1968.

Artaud, Antonin. *The Peyote Dance*. Translated from the French by Helen Weaver. New York: Farrar, 1976.

Balin, Peter. *The Flight of Feathered Serpent*. Venice, CA: Wisdom Garden Books, 1978.

Bensinger, Charles. *Chaco Journey*. Santa Fe, NM: Timewindow Publications, 1988.

Berrin, Kathleen. *Art of the Huichol Indians*. New York: Harry N. Abrams, Inc., 1978.

Bierhorst, John. *A Cry from the Earth: Music of the North American Indians*. New York: Four Winds Press, 1979.

———. *Four Masterworks of American Indian Literature*. New York: Farrar, Straus, and Giroux, 1974. Includes the story of Ketzalkoatl.

Brown, Dee. *Bury My Heart At Wounded Knee*. New York: Bantam Books, 1972.

Brown, Joseph Epes. *The Sacred Pipe: Black Elk's Account of the Seven Rites of the Oglala Sioux*. Baltimore, MD: Penguin Books, 1972. Includes teachings about White Buffalo Woman.

Chávez, Adrián I. *Pop Wuj*. México, D.F.: Ediciones de la Chata, 1979.

Coe, Michael, Dean Snow, and Elizabeth Benson. *Atlas of Ancient America*. New York: Facts on File, Inc., 1986.

Copeland, Marion W. "Ohiyesa and Elaine—The Eastmans in New England." *The Country Side* magazine, Winter 1981-82.

Eastman, Charles. *Indian Boyhood*. Lincoln, NE: University of Nebraska Press, 1991.

———. *The Soul of the Indian*. Lincoln, NE: University of Nebraska Press, 1980.

Erdoes, Richard. *Lame Deer, Seeker of Visions: The Life of a Sioux Medicine Man*. New York: Simon & Schuster, 1972. Includes teachings about White Buffalo Woman.

Fontana, Bernard, Edmond Faubert, and Barney Burns. *The Other Southwest: Indian Arts and Crafts of Northwestern New Mexico*. Phoenix, AZ: The Heard Museum, 1977.

Hertzberg, Hazel W. *The Great Tree and the Longhouse: The Culture of the Iroquois.* New York: The MacMillan Co., 1966.

Hofmann, Albert, and Richard Evans Schultes. *Plants of the Gods: Origins of Hallucinogenic Use.* New York: Alfred van der Marck Editions, 1979.

Karttunen, Frances. *An Analytical Dictionary of Nahuatl.* Austin, TX: University of Texas Press, 1983.

Katchongva, Dan. *Hopi: A Message for All People.* Rooseveltown, NY: Akwesasne Notes, 1975.

_____. *From the Beginning of Life to the Day of Purification.* Translated from Danaqyumptewa. Los Angeles: Land and Life, Inc., 1977.

Kelly, Joyce. *The Complete Visitor's Guide to Mesoamerican Ruins.* Norman, OK: University of Oklahoma Press, 1982.

Léon-Portilla, Miguel. *Native Mesoamerican Spirituality.* New York: Paulist Press, 1980.

LePlongeon, Augustus. *Sacred Mysteries Among the Mayas and Quiches.* Minneapolis, MN: Wizards Bookshelf, 1973.

Lhuillier, Alberto Ruz: *The Civilization of the Ancient Maya.* México, D.F.: Instituto Nacional de Antropologia e Historia, 1980.

Littman, Mark. *Skywatchers of Ancient Mexico.* Salt Lake City, UT: Hansen Planetarium, 1982.

McLuhan, T. C. *Touch the Earth.* New York: Pocket Books, 1972. Includes quotes from Black Elk, Ohiyesa, Chief Seattle, Sitting Bull, and Smohalla.

Marti, Samuel, and Gertrude Prokosch Kurath. *Dances of Anahuac.* Chicago: Aldine Publishing Co., 1964.

Mayo, Anna. "You Wore a Tulip." *Village Voice* (May 13, 1986). An article about the aftereffects of the Three Mile Island nuclear accident.

Mooney, James. *The Ghost Dance Religion and Wounded Knee.* New York: Dover Publications, Inc., 1973.

Nicholson, Irene. *Mexican and Central American Mythology.* New York: Hamlyn Publishing Group, 1967.

Niehardt, John. *Black Elk Speaks.* New York: Pocket Books, 1972.

_____. *When the Tree Flowered.* New York: Pocket Books, 1973.

Ordoño, Cesar Macazaga. *Diccionario de la Lengua Nahuatl.* México, D.F.: Editorial Innovación, s. a., 1979.

Roys, Ralph L. *The Book of Chilam Balam of Chumayel.* Norman, OK: University of Oklahoma Press, 1967.

Shearer, Tony. *Beneath the Moon and Under the Sun.* Albuquerque, NM: Sun Publishing Co., 1975.

Steucek, Guy L., David A. Zegers, William Field, and Elizabeth H. Field. "Iodine-131 in Thyroids of the Meadow Vole in the Vicinity of the Three Mile Island Nuclear Generating Plant." *Health Physics,* 41 (August 1981).

Tarbet, Tom. *The Essence of the Hopi Prophecy.* Los Angeles: Land and Life, Inc., n.d.

Tompkins, Peter. *Mysteries of the Mexican Pyramids.* New York: Harper & Row Publishers, 1976.

Vestal, Stanley. *Sitting Bull: Champion of the Sioux.* Norman, OK: University of Oklahoma Press, 1969.

Wallace, Paul A. *The White Roots of Peace.* Saranac Lake, NY: Center for Adirondack Studies, 1981.

Wasserman, Harvey. "Harrisburg Vapors—Three Mile Island's Legacy." *Valley Advocate* (March 26, 1980).

Wasson, R. Gordon. *The Wondrous Mushroom: Mycolatry in Mesoamerica.* New York: McGraw-Hill Book Co., 1980.

Waters, Frank. *Book of the Hopi.* New York: The Viking Press, 1963.

———. *Masked Gods.* New York: Ballantine, 1970.

———. *Mexico Mystique.* Chicago: The Swallow Press, Inc., 1975.

Ywahoo, Dhyani. *Voices of our Ancestors: Cherokee Teachings from the Wisdom Fire.* Boston: Shambhala, 1987.

R E C O M M E N D E D

L I S T E N I N G

Recordings with Ancient Instruments and Songs of Mesoamerica

Instituto Nacional de Antropologia e Historia. *Música Indigena de México*. México, D.F.: I.N.A.H., 1981.

Instituto Nacional Indigenista. *Encuentros de Música Tradicional Indigena: Los Mayas Peninsulares*. México, D.F.: FONAPAS—I.N.I., 1980.

Los Folkloristas. *Raiz Viva*. Discos Pueblo—P. General Anaya No. 52-2A, México 21, D.F.

Los Folkloristas. *México*. Discos Pueblo.

Mendelssohn, Lilian. *Pre-Columbian Instruments*. Folkways Records, 701 Seventh Ave., New York City, 1972.

Perez, Luis. *En El Ombligo de la Luna*. México, D.F., 1981.

Tribu. *MASEHUAL: el hombre de este sol*. Cademac, Sur 113B número 2148, colonia Juventino Rosas, México 08700, D.F., 1990.

Williams, Ani, and Mazatl Galindo. *Song of the Jaguar*. Earthsong Productions, P.O. Box 780, Sedona, AZ 86336, 1989.

Williams, Ani, and Mazatl Galindo. *Children of the Sun*. Earthsong Productions, 1991.

Xochimoki. *New Music/Ancient Sources*. Eartheart, P.O. Box 1443, Venice, CA 90294, 1984.

Xochimoki. *Quetzal: Music from the Heart of Maya*. Eartheart, 1986.

Zepeda, Antonio. *Templo Mayor*. Olinkan, Colina de las Ventiscas 72, Boulevares, Edo. de México, C.P. 53140, México, 1982.

Zepeda, Antonio. *La Region el Misterio*. Olinkan, 1986.

Zepeda, Antonio. *Retorno a Aztlan*. Olinkan, 1989.

Recordings with Songs, Chants, and Texts of Native North America

Berenholtz, Jim. *Turquoise Waters: Songs from the Spirit World*. Eartheart, 1986. Includes some of the chants mentioned in *Journey to the Four Directions*.

Bierhorst, John. *A Cry from the Earth: Music of the North American Indians*. Folkways Records, New York City, 1979.

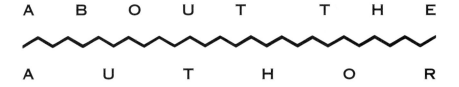
Jim Berenholtz is a multifaceted artist who has been training with native cultures in the ancient wisdom of the Earth for more than twenty years. As cofounder of the musical duo Xochimoki, he is a leader in the revitalization of pre-Columbian musical traditions, particularly those of Mesoamerica. His performances have taken him all over the world, from peace conferences in Egypt and Costa Rica to the Earth Summit in Rio de Janeiro, Brazil. While at home, he tours as an artist in the schools under the auspices of the Los Angeles Music Center.

Jim is the composer of *Buffalo Nation,* a full-length opera about the Ghost Dance and Wounded Knee, as well as numerous other works for musical theater. He has created scores for many ballets and films, including the science fiction feature *Lords of the Deep.* His musically eclectic audio recordings are known for their evocative mystical qualities. As a vocalist, instrumentalist, and dancer, he has taught and performed at the Los Angeles Theatre Center and La Mama E.T.C. in New York City.

Jim is widely known for his important work as a ceremonial artist, helping to create multicultural ritual gatherings of indigenous peoples from Machu Picchu to Malibu. In 1987 he served as the international coordinator for the Sacred Sites Festival associated with Harmonic Convergence. As a teacher of ceremonial arts, he has appeared at the Findhorn Foundation in Scotland, the Fondacion de Soleil in Switzerland, the Lama Foundation in New Mexico, and Kalani Honua in Hawaii.

Journey to the Four Directions is Jim's first book. The casein-on-paper mandala paintings included in it are indicative of his vibrant style as a visionary artist. His paintings have been exhibited in galleries throughout New Mexico, where he lived during most of the 1980s. He presently lives in Southern California with his nine-foot Burmese python, Tlahuizkalpantekuhtli.